Lecture Notes in Artificial Intelligence   11105

Subseries of Lecture Notes in Computer Science

More information about this series at http://www.springer.com/series/1244

Fabrizio Riguzzi · Elena Bellodi
Riccardo Zese (Eds.)

Inductive Logic Programming

28th International Conference, ILP 2018
Ferrara, Italy, September 2–4, 2018
Proceedings

 Springer

Editors
Fabrizio Riguzzi (iD)
University of Ferrara
Ferrara
Italy

Riccardo Zese (iD)
University of Ferrara
Ferrara
Italy

Elena Bellodi (iD)
University of Ferrara
Ferrara
Italy

ISSN 0302-9743   ISSN 1611-3349   (electronic)
Lecture Notes in Artificial Intelligence
ISBN 978-3-319-99959-3   ISBN 978-3-319-99960-9   (eBook)
https://doi.org/10.1007/978-3-319-99960-9

Library of Congress Control Number: 2018937377

LNCS Sublibrary: SL7 – Artificial Intelligence

This Springer imprint is published by the registered company Springer Nature Switzerland AG
The registered company address is: Gewerbestrasse 11, 6330 Cham, Switzerland

Preface

This volume contains the regular papers of the 28th International Conference on Inductive Logic Programming (ILP 2018) held in Ferrara, Italy, during September 2–4, 2018.

Inductive Logic Programming (ILP) is a subfield of machine learning, which relies on logic programming as a uniform representation language for expressing examples, background knowledge, and hypotheses. Due to its strong representation formalism, based on first-order logic, ILP provides an excellent means for multi-relational learning and data mining. The ILP conference series, which started in 1991, is the premier international forum for learning from structured or semi-structured relational data. Originally focusing on the induction of logic programs, it has expanded its research horizon significantly over the years and welcomes contributions on all aspects of learning in logic, multi-relational data mining, statistical relational learning, graph and tree mining, learning in other (non-propositional) logic-based knowledge representation frameworks, exploring intersections to statistical learning, and other probabilistic approaches.

The conference will be co-located with two events:

- ACAI 2018: Advanced Course on AI, a summer school on Statistical Relational Artificial Intelligence, August 27–31, 2018
- PLP 2018: 5th Workshop on Probabilistic Logic Programming, September 1, 2018

This year we changed the submission model, trying to encourage participation, simplify the publication process, and attract high quality submissions. Two different tracks were organized, defining five kinds of submissions:

1. The journal track, whose accepted papers were published in the *Machine Learning Journal's* special issue on Inductive Logic Programming – ILP 2017 and 2018, accepting both new submissions and the best papers from ILP 2017.
2. The conference track, allowing four types of submissions:

   a. Long papers describing original mature work, containing appropriate experimental evaluation and/or representing a self-contained theoretical contribution.
   b. Short papers describing original work in progress, presenting preliminary results, brief accounts of original ideas, and other relevant work of potentially high scientific interest that does not yet qualify for the long paper category. Accepted papers appear in CEUR proceedings.
   c. Works in progress papers describing ideas and proposals that the author(s) would like to present at the conference.
   d. Papers relevant to the conference topics and recently published or accepted for publication by a first-class conference or journal.

The conference had two proceedings: the present LNAI proceedings for accepted long papers (submission category a), and the CEUR proceedings for up-and-coming papers (submission category a, describing promising but less mature works) and short papers (submission category b). Submissions from categories c and d were presented at the conference but not included in any proceedings.

There were 24 submissions in total for categories a and b: 18 long papers and 6 short papers. We accepted 14 long papers split into 10 regular papers, published in these proceedings, and 4 up-and-coming papers, published in the CEUR proceedings. We accepted 4 out of the 6 short papers and they appear in the CEUR proceedings. All papers received 2.83 reviews on average by members of the Program Committee. Each accepted paper was presented at ILP 2018.

Submissions covering a wide range of topics are included in these proceedings, spacing from learning theories and rules to connections with deep learning, from the exploitation of knowledge graphs to applications of ILP to diagnostic systems to minimize the maintenance cost and downtime of equipment.

We had the pleasure of welcoming three invited speakers at ILP 2018:

- William Cohen, Professor at Carnegie Mellon University, USA:
  "Using Deep Learning Platforms to Perform Inference over Large Knowledge Bases"
- Marco Gori, Professor at the University of Siena, Italy:
  "Learning and Inference with Constraints"
- Maximilian Nickel, Research Scientist at Facebook AI Research:
  "Hierarchical Representation Learning on Relational Data"

Three prizes were awarded:

- Best paper (supported by Springer);
- Best student paper among regular papers (supported by the *Machine Learning Journal*);
- Best student paper among up-and-coming papers (supported by the *Machine Learning Journal*).

The winners were announced during the conference and published on the conference website at http://ilp2018.unife.it/.

We would like to really thank all the people who contributed to the success of ILP 2018: the members of the Organizing Committee, the members of the Program Committee, the additional reviewers that have been solicited, and the sponsors.

July 2018

Fabrizio Riguzzi
Elena Bellodi
Riccardo Zese

Organization

Conference Chair

Fabrizio Riguzzi University of Ferrara, Italy

Program Chairs

Elena Bellodi University of Ferrara, Italy
Riccardo Zese University of Ferrara, Italy

Sponsorship Chair

Marco Lippi University of Modena and Reggio Emilia, Italy

Program Committee

Dalal Alrajeh Imperial College London, UK
Annalisa Appice University Aldo Moro of Bari, Italy
Alexander Artikis NCSR "Demokritos," Greece
Hendrik Blockeel Katholieke Universiteit Leuven, Belgium
Agnès Braud University of Strasbourg, France
Krysia Broda Imperial College London, UK
Rui Camacho University of Porto, Portugal
James Cussens University of York, UK
Jesse Davis Katholieke Universiteit Leuven, Belgium
Inês Dutra Universidade do Porto, Portugal
Saso Dzeroski Jozef Stefan Institute, Slovenia
Nicola Fanizzi Università degli Studi di Bari, Italy
Stefano Ferilli Università degli Studi di Bari, Italy
Cèsar Ferri Universitat Politècnica de València, Spain
Nuno A. Fonseca EMBL-EBI, UK
Tamas Horvath University of Bonn and Fraunhofer IAIS, Germany
Katsumi Inoue National Institute of Informatics, Japan
Nobuhiro Inuzuka Nagoya Institute of Technology, Japan
Kristian Kersting TU Dortmund University, Germany
Angelika Kimmig Cardiff University, UK
Ross King University of Manchester, UK
Nicolas Lachiche University of Strasbourg, France
Francesca Lisi Università degli Studi di Bari, Italy
Donato Malerba Università degli Studi di Bari, Italy
Stephen Muggleton Imperial College London, UK
Sriraam Natarajan University of Texas at Dallas, USA

Aline Paes	Universidade Federal Fluminense, Brazil
Jan Ramon	Inria, France
Céline Rouveirol	University of Paris 13, France
Alessandra Russo	Imperial College London, UK
Vítor Santos Costa	Universidade do Porto, Portugal
Ashwin Srinivasan	Birla Institute of Technology and Science, India
Alireza Tamaddoni-Nezhad	Imperial College London, UK
Tomoyuki Uchida	Hiroshima City University, Japan
Christel Vrain	University of Orléans, France
Stefan Wrobel	University of Bonn and Fraunhofer IAIS, Germany
Gerson Zaverucha	Federal University of Rio de Janeiro, Brazil

Additional Reviewers

Nikos Katzouris	NCSR "Demokritos," Greece
Gautam Kunapuli	University of Texas at Dallas, USA
Andrea Pazienza	Università degli Studi di Bari, Italy
Chiaki Sakama	Wakayama University, Japan

Sponsors

We gratefully thank all the organizations and institutions that supported this event:

– Gold sponsors

  • Siemens

– Silver sponsors

  • Springer
  • *Machine Learning Journal*, Springer
  • INdAM-GNCS
  • Centro Software
  • Association for Logic Programming

– Bronze sponsors

  • Italian Association for Artificial Intelligence
  • Delta Commerce
  • UniTec
  • Open1

– University and Research Departments, and Italian Institutions

  • Department of Mathematics and Informatics, University of Ferrara
  • Department of Engineering, University of Ferrara
  • Comune di Ferrara (Ferrara municipality)

Contents

Derivation Reduction of Metarules in Meta-interpretive Learning 1
Andrew Cropper and Sophie Tourret

Large-Scale Assessment of Deep Relational Machines 22
Tirtharaj Dash, Ashwin Srinivasan, Lovekesh Vig,
Oghenejokpeme I. Orhobor, and Ross D. King

How Much Can Experimental Cost Be Reduced in Active Learning
of Agent Strategies? 38
Céline Hocquette and Stephen Muggleton

Diagnostics of Trains with Semantic Diagnostics Rules 54
Evgeny Kharlamov, Ognjen Savković, Martin Ringsquandl,
Guohui Xiao, Gulnar Mehdi, Elem Güzel Kalayc, Werner Nutt,
Mikhail Roshchin, Ian Horrocks, and Thomas Runkler

The Game of Bridge: A Challenge for ILP 72
Swann Legras, Céline Rouveirol, and Véronique Ventos

Sampling-Based SAT/ASP Multi-model Optimization as a Framework
for Probabilistic Inference 88
Matthias Nickles

Explaining Black-Box Classifiers with ILP – Empowering LIME
with Aleph to Approximate Non-linear Decisions with Relational Rules 105
Johannes Rabold, Michael Siebers, and Ute Schmid

Learning Dynamics with Synchronous, Asynchronous and General
Semantics 118
Tony Ribeiro, Maxime Folschette, Morgan Magnin, Olivier Roux,
and Katsumi Inoue

Was the Year 2000 a Leap Year? Step-Wise Narrowing Theories
with Metagol 141
Michael Siebers and Ute Schmid

Targeted End-to-End Knowledge Graph Decomposition 157
Blaž Škrlj, Jan Kralj, and Nada Lavrač

Correction to: How Much Can Experimental Cost Be Reduced in Active
Learning of Agent Strategies? E1
Céline Hocquette and Stephen Muggleton

Author Index 173

Derivation Reduction of Metarules in Meta-interpretive Learning

Andrew Cropper[1(✉)] and Sophie Tourret[2]

[1] University of Oxford, Oxford, UK
andrew.cropper@cs.ox.ac.uk
[2] Max Planck Institute for Informatics, Saarbrücken, Germany
stourret@mpi-inf.mpg.de

Abstract. Meta-interpretive learning (MIL) is a form of inductive logic programming. MIL uses second-order Horn clauses, called metarules, as a form of declarative bias. Metarules define the structures of learnable programs and thus the hypothesis space. Deciding which metarules to use is a trade-off between efficiency and expressivity. The hypothesis space increases given more metarules, so we wish to use fewer metarules, but if we use too few metarules then we lose expressivity. A recent paper used Progol's entailment reduction algorithm to identify irreducible, or minimal, sets of metarules. In some cases, as few as two metarules were shown to be sufficient to entail all hypotheses in an infinite language. Moreover, it was shown that compared to non-minimal sets, learning with minimal sets of metarules improves predictive accuracies and lowers learning times. In this paper, we show that entailment reduction can be too strong and can remove metarules necessary to make a hypothesis more specific. We describe a new reduction technique based on derivations. Specifically, we introduce the *derivation reduction* problem, the problem of finding a finite subset of a Horn theory from which the whole theory can be derived using SLD-resolution. We describe a derivation reduction algorithm which we use to reduce sets of metarules. We also theoretically study whether certain sets of metarules can be derivationally reduced to minimal finite subsets. Our experiments compare learning with entailment and derivation reduced sets of metarules. In general, using derivation reduced sets of metarules outperforms using entailment reduced sets of metarules, both in terms of predictive accuracies and learning times.

1 Introduction

Meta-interpretive learning (MIL) [4,6,25] is a form of inductive logic programming (ILP). MIL uses second-order Horn clauses, called *metarules*, as a form of declarative bias [28]. Metarules define the structure of learnable programs, which in turn defines the hypothesis space. For instance, to use MIL to learn the *grandparent/2* relation given the *parent/2* relation, the *chain* metarule would be suitable:

$$P(A, B) \leftarrow Q(A, C), R(C, B)$$

F. Riguzzi et al. (Eds.): ILP 2018, LNAI 11105, pp. 1–21, 2018.
https://doi.org/10.1007/978-3-319-99960-9_1

The letters P, Q, and R denote existentially quantified second-order variables (i.e. variables that can be bound to predicate symbols), and the letters A, B and C denote universally quantified first-order variables (i.e. variables that can bound to constant symbols). Given this metarule, the background *parent/2* relation, and examples of the *grandparent/2* relation, MIL uses a Prolog meta-interpreter to generate a proof of the examples by finding substitutions for the second-order variables. In this scenario, MIL could perform the substitutions {P/grandparent, Q/parent, R/parent} to induce the theory:

$$grandparent(A, B) \leftarrow parent(A, C), parent(C, B)$$

Many ILP systems, such as BLIP [7], Clint [29], DIALOGS [9], MOBAL [14], and MIL-HEX [13], use metarules[1] (or variants of them). Non-ILP program induction systems, such as ProPPR [32], SYNTH [1], and DILP [8], also use variants of metarules. However, despite their widespread use, there is little work determining which metarules to use for a given task. Instead, suitable metarules are typically assumed to be given as part of the background knowledge[2].

In MIL, deciding which metarules to use is a trade-off between efficiency and expressivity. The hypothesis space increases given more metarules (Theorem 3.3), so we wish to use fewer metarules. But if we use too few metarules then we lose expressivity. For instance, it is impossible to learn the *grandparent/2* relation using only monadic metarules. To address this issue, Cropper and Muggleton [3] used Progol's entailment-reduction algorithm [23] to identify irreducible, or minimal, sets of metarules. Their approach removed entailment redundant clauses from sets of metarules, where a clause C is entailment redundant in a clausal theory $T \cup \{C\}$ when $T \models C$. To illustrate this form of redundancy, consider the clausal theory:

$$C_1 = p(A, B) \leftarrow q(A, B)$$
$$C_2 = p(A, B) \leftarrow q(A, B), r(A)$$

The clause C_2 is entailment redundant because it is a logical consequences of C_1.

Cropper and Muggleton showed that, in some cases, as few as two metarules are sufficient to entail an infinite fragment of second-order dyadic datalog. Moreover, they showed that learning with minimal sets of metarules improves predictive accuracies and reduces learning times compared to non-minimal sets. However, entailment reduction is not always the most appropriate form of reduction. To illustrate this point, suppose you want to learn the *father/2* relation given the background relations *parent/2*, *male/1*, and *female/1*. Then a suitable hypothesis would be:

$$father(A, B) \leftarrow parent(A, B), male(A)$$

---

[1] Metarules are also called *program schemata* [9], *second-order schemata* [29], and *clause templates* [1].

[2] Assuming suitable background knowledge, especially syntactic bias, is a frequent criticism of ILP from other areas of machine learning.

To learn such a theory, one would need a metarule of the form $P(A, B) \leftarrow Q(A, B), R(A)$. Now suppose you have the metarules:

$$M_1 = P(A, B) \leftarrow Q(A, B)$$
$$M_2 = P(A, B) \leftarrow Q(A, B), R(A)$$

Running entailment reduction on these metarules would remove M_2 because it is a logical consequence of M_1. But it is impossible to learn the intended *father/2* theory given only M_1. As this example shows, entailment reduction can be too strong because it can remove metarules necessary to specialise a clause (where M_2 can be seen as a specialisation of M_1).

To address this issue, we describe a new form of reduction based on derivations. Let $\vdash$ represent derivability in SLD-resolution [15], then a Horn clause C is derivationally redundant in a Horn theory $T \cup \{C\}$ when $T \vdash C$. A Horn theory is derivationally irreducible if it contains no derivationally redundant clauses. To illustrate the difference between entailment reduction and derivation reduction, consider the metarules:

$$M_1 = P(A, B) \leftarrow Q(A, B)$$
$$M_2 = P(A, B) \leftarrow Q(A, B), R(A)$$
$$M_3 = P(A, B) \leftarrow Q(A, B), R(A, B)$$
$$M_4 = P(A, B) \leftarrow Q(A, B), R(A, B), S(A, B)$$

Running entailment reduction on these would leave the single metarule M_1 because it entails the rest of the theory. By contrast, performing derivation reduction would only remove M_4 because it can be derived by self-resolving M_3. The remaining metarules M_2 and M_3 are not derivationally redundant because there is no way to derive them from the other metarules.

1.1   Contributions

Our main contributions are:

- We introduce the derivation reduction problem, the problem of removing derivationally redundant clauses from a clausal theory, and show that the problem is undecidable in general (Sect. 3)
- We introduce a derivation reduction algorithm (Sect. 3)
- We run derivation and entailment reduction on finite sets of metarules to identify minimal sets (Sect. 4)
- We theoretically study whether sets of metarules can be derivationally reduced (Sect. 4)
- We experimentally compare learning with derivation and entailment reduced metarules, where the results show that using the former set results in higher predictive accuracies and lower learning times (Sect. 5).

2   Related Work

Meta-interpretive Learning. Although the study of metarules has implications for many ILP approaches [1, 7–9, 14, 29, 32], we are primarily motivated by MIL. MIL is a form of ILP based on a Prolog meta-interpreter. The key difference between a MIL learner and a standard Prolog meta-interpreter is that whereas a standard Prolog meta-interpreter attempts to prove a goal by repeatedly fetching first-order clauses whose heads unify with a given goal, a MIL learner additionally attempts to prove a goal by fetching second-order metarules, supplied as background knowledge, whose heads unify with the goal. The resulting meta-substitutions are saved and can be reused in later proofs. Following the proof of a set of goals, a logic program is formed by projecting the meta-substitutions onto their corresponding metarules, allowing for a form of ILP which supports predicate invention and learning recursive theories.

Metarules. Metarules were introduced in the Blip system [7]. Kietz and Wrobel [14] studied generality measures for metarules in the RDT system. A generality order is necessary because the RDT system searches the hypothesis space (which is defined by the metarules) in a top-down general-to-specific order. A key difference between RDT and MIL is that whereas RDT requires metarules of increasing complexity (e.g. rules with an increasing number of literals in the body), MIL derives more complex metarules through resolution. This point is important because the ability to derive more complex metarules through resolution allows us to start from smaller sets of primitive or core metarules. The focus of this paper is identifying such core sets.

Using metarules to build a logic program is similar to the use of refinement operators in ILP [26, 31] to build a definite clause literal-by-literal[3]. As with refinement operators, it seems reasonable to ask about completeness and irredundancy of a set of metarules, which we explore in this paper.

Logical Redundancy. Detecting and eliminating redundancy in a clausal theory is useful in many areas of computer science. In ILP, logically reducing a theory is useful to remove redundancy from a hypothesis space to improve learning performance [3, 10]. In general, simplifying or reducing a theory often makes a theory easier to understand and use, and may also have computational efficiency advantages.

Plotkin [27] introduced methods to decide whether a clause is subsumption redundant in a first-order clausal theory. The same problem, and slight variants, has been extensively studied in the propositional case [18, 19]. Removing redundant clauses has numerous applications, such as to improve the efficiency of SAT [12]. In contrast to these works, we focus on reducing theories formed of second-order Horn clauses, which to our knowledge has not yet been extensively explored. Another difference is that we study redundancy based on

---

[3] MIL uses example driven test-incorporation for finding consistent programs as opposed to the generate-and-test approach of clause refinement.

SLD-derivations. Langlois et al. [16] also considered derivations. They studied combinatorial problems for propositional Horn clauses. By contrast, we focus on derivationally reducing sets of second-order Horn clauses.

The work most relevant to this paper is by Cropper and Muggleton [3]. They used Progol's entailment-reduction algorithm [23] to identify irreducible, or minimal, sets of metarules. Their approach removed entailment redundant clauses from sets of metarules. They identified theories that are (1) entailment complete for certain fragments of second-order Horn logic, and (2) minimal or irreducible, in that no further reductions are possible. They demonstrated that in some cases as few as two clauses are sufficient to entail an infinite language. However, they only considered small and highly constrained fragments of metarules. In particular, they focused on metarules where each literal is dyadic and each term variable appears exactly twice (we call this fragment *exactly-two-connected*, see Definition 4.2). In this paper, we go beyond entailment reduction and introduce derivation reduction. We also consider more general fragments of metarules.

3   Logical Reduction

We now introduce the derivation reduction problem, the problem of removing derivationally redundant clauses from a clausal theory. Before introducing this problem, we describe preliminary notation and also describe *entailment reduction*, to which we compare our new approach.

3.1   Preliminaries

We assume familiarity with logic programming notation [21], but we restate some key terminology. A clause is a disjunction of literals. A clausal theory is a set of clauses. A Horn clause is a clause with at most one positive literal. A Horn theory is a set of Horn clauses. Most of the concepts introduced in this section can be defined for any resolution-based proof system, but, because MIL is based on a Prolog meta-interpreter, we focus on SLD-resolution [15]. To identify clauses derivable from a theory, we first define a function $R^n(T)$ of a Horn theory T as:

$$R^0(T) = T$$
$$R^n(T) = \{C | C_1 \in R^{n-1}(T), C_2 \in T, C \text{ is the binary resolvent of } C_1 \text{ and } C_2\}$$

We use this definition to define the SLD-closure of a Horn theory:

Definition 3.1 (SLD-closure). *The SLD-closure $R^*(T)$ of a Horn theory T is:* $\bigcup\limits_{n \in \mathcal{N}} R^n(T)$

We can now state our notion of derivability:

Definition 3.2 (Derivability). *A Horn clause C is derivable from the Horn theory T, written $T \vdash C$, if and only if $C \in R^*(T)$.*

We also introduce *k-derivability*:

Definition 3.3 (k-derivability). *Let k be a natural number. Then a Horn clause C is k-derivable from the Horn theory T, written $T \vdash_k C$, if and only if $C \in R^k(T)$.*

Some definitions and results in this section rely on Kowalski's *subsumption theorem* for SLD-resolution [15], which is based on SLD-deductions [15]:

Definition 3.4 (SLD-deduction). *Let T be a Horn theory and C be a Horn clause. Then there exists a SLD-deduction of C from T, written $T \vdash_d C$, if C is a tautology or if there exists a clause D such that $T \vdash D$ and D subsumes C.*

We denote a SLD-deduction restricted by k-derivability as $\vdash_{d_k}$. To illustrate the difference between $\vdash$ and $\vdash_d$, consider the clauses M_1 to M_4 defined in the introduction. We have $\{M_1\} \vdash_d \{M_2, M_3, M_4\}$ but $\{M_1\} \not\vdash \{M_2, M_3, M_4\}$. Kowalski's *subsumption theorem* shows the relationship between SLD-deductions and logical entailment:

Theorem 3.1 (SLD-subsumption theorem). *Let T be a Horn theory and C be a Horn Clause. Then $T \models C$ if and only if $T \vdash_d C$.*

A more general version of this theorem also applies to unconstrained resolution [26].

3.2   Entailment Reduction

Muggleton [23] provided two definitions for eliminating entailment redundant clauses from a clausal theory:

Definition 3.5 (Entailment redundant clause). *The clause C is entailment redundant in the clausal theory $T \cup \{C\}$ whenever $T \models C$.*

Definition 3.6 (Entailment reduced theory). *A clausal theory is entailment reduced if and only if it does not contain any redundant clauses.*

If C is entailment redundant in $T \cup \{C\}$ then T is entailment equivalent to $T \cup \{C\}$ because $T \models T \cup \{C\}$ and $T \cup \{C\} \models T$. Muggleton's definitions apply to clauses, but can easily be adapted to Horn clauses.

Because entailment between arbitrary Horn clauses is undecidable [22], determining whether a Horn clause is entailment redundant in a Horn theory is also undecidable[4]. Algorithm 1 finds a k-bounded entailment reduction (henceforth called an *E-reduction*) T' of a Horn theory T.

In Sect. 4, we use a Prolog implementation of Algorithm 1 to find E-reduced sets of metarules.

---

[4] Entailment reduction is decidable in the case of a function-free theory [23].

Algorithm 1. k-bounded entailment reduction

Input: a Horn theory T and a natural number k
Output: a k-bounded E-reduced theory T'
  $T' = T$
  while there is a clause C in T' such that $T' \setminus \{C\} \vdash_{d_k} C$ **do**
    $T' = T' \setminus \{C\}$
  end while

3.3 Derivation Reduction

We now describe a new form of reduction based on derivability. We first define *derivationally redundant* clauses:

Definition 3.7 (Derivationally redundant clause). *A Horn clause C is derivationally redundant in the Horn theory $T \cup \{C\}$ if and only if $T \vdash C$.*

We can now define *derivationally reduced* theories:

Definition 3.8 (Derivationally reduced theory). *A Horn theory is derivationally reduced if and only if it does not contain any derivationally redundant clauses.*

We now define the *derivation reduction problem*:

Definition 3.9 (Derivation reduction problem). *Given a Horn theory T, the derivation reduction problem is to find a finite theory $T' \subseteq T$ such that (1) $T' \vdash C$ for every Horn clause C in T, and (2) T' is derivationally reduced.*

Note that a solution to the derivation reduction problem must be a finite set. For convenience, we name the output of the derivation reduction problem:

Definition 3.10 (Derivation reduction). *Let T and T' be the input and output respectively from a derivation reduction problem. Then we call T' a derivation reduction (or D-reduction) of T.*

The following proposition outlines the connection between an E-reduction and a D-reduction:

Proposition 3.1 *Let T be a Horn theory, T_E be an E-reduction of T, and T_D be a D-reduction of T. Then $T_E \subseteq T_D$.*

Algorithm 2 finds a D-reduction T' of a Horn theory T. Note that a fragment can have multiple D-reductions. For instance, consider the theory T:

$$C_1 = P(A, B) \leftarrow Q(B, A)$$
$$C_2 = P(A, B) \leftarrow Q(A, C), R(C, B)$$
$$C_3 = P(A, B) \leftarrow Q(C, A), R(C, B)$$

One D-reduction of T is $\{C_1, C_2\}$ because you can resolve the first body literal of C_2 with C_1 to derive C_3 (with variable renaming). Another D-reduction of T is $\{C_1, C_3\}$ because you can likewise resolve the first body literal of C_3 with C_1 to derive C_2.

As with the entailment reduction problem, the derivation reduction problem is undecidable for Horn theories:

Theorem 3.2 (Horn decidability). *The derivation reduction problem for Horn theories is undecidable.*

Proof. Assume the opposite, that the problem is decidable, which implies that $T \vdash C$ is decidable. Since $T \vdash C$ is decidable and subsumption between Horn clauses is decidable [11], then finding a SLD-deduction is also decidable. Therefore, by the SLD-subsumption theorem, entailment between Horn clauses is decidable. However, entailment between Horn clauses is undecidable [30], so the assumption cannot hold. Therefore, the problem must be undecidable.

Algorithm 2. Derivation reduction

Input: a Horn theory T
Output: a D-reduced theory T'
   $T' = T$
   while there is a clause C in T' such that $T' \setminus \{C\} \vdash C$ **do**
       $T' = T' \setminus \{C\}$
   end while

In future work, described in Sect. 6, we want to study the decidability of the derivation problem for other forms of logic, such as datalog. To overcome the aforementioned undecidability issue, we use a k-bounded d-reduction algorithm (algorithm omitted for brevity). The k-bounded version is similar to Algorithm 2 but additionally takes as input a resolution depth bound k which is used to constrain the SLD-derivability check step. This k-bounded version has the worst-case time complexity:

Proposition 3.2 (k-bounded derivation reduction complexity). *Given a Horn theory T and a natural number k, k-bounded derivation reduction requires at most $O(|T|^k)$ resolutions.*

Sketch proof 1. In the worst case the algorithm searches the whole SLD-tree which has a maximum branching factor $|T|$ and a maximum depth k. Thus, the overall complexity is $O(|T|^k)$.

In Sect. 4, we use the k-bounded entailment and derivation reduction algorithms to logically reduce sets of metarules. From this point onwards, any reference to the entailment or derivation reduction algorithms refer to the k-bounded versions.

3.4   Language Class and Hypothesis Space

In Sect. 4 we logically reduce fragments of second-order datalog formed of metarules, where a fragment of a theory is a syntactically restricted subset of that theory [2]. We make explicit our notion of a metarule, which is a second-order Horn clause:

Definition 3.11 (Second-order Horn clause). *A second-order Horn clause is of the form:*

$$A_0 \leftarrow A_1, \ldots, A_m$$

where each A_i is a literal of the form $P(T_1, \ldots, T_n)$ where P is either a predicate symbol or a second-order variable that can be substituted by a predicate symbol, and each T_i is either a constant symbol or a first-order variable that can be substituted by a constant symbol.

We denote the language of second-order datalog as $\mathcal{H}$, which we further restrict. Our first restriction is on the syntactic form of clauses in $\mathcal{H}$:

Definition 3.12 (The fragment $\mathcal{H}_m^a$). *We denote as $\mathcal{H}_m^a$ the fragment of $\mathcal{H}$ where each literal has arity at most a and each clause has at most m literals in the body.*

Having defined this fragment we can characterise the size of the hypothesis space of a MIL learner given metarules restricted to this fragment. The following result generalises previous results [4, 20]:

Theorem 3.3 (Number of programs in $\mathcal{H}_m^a$). *Given p predicate symbols and k metarules (not necessarily distinct), the number of $\mathcal{H}_m^a$ programs expressible with at most n clauses is $O((p^{m+1}k)^n)$.*

Proof. The number of clauses which can be constructed from a $\mathcal{H}_m^a$ metarule given p predicate symbols is at most p^{m+1} because for a given metarule there are potentially $m+1$ predicate variables with p^{m+1} possible substitutions. Therefore the set of such clauses $S_{k,p,m}$ which can be formed from k distinct $\mathcal{H}_m^a$ metarules using p predicate symbols has cardinality at most kp^{m+1}. It follows that the number of programs which can be formed from a selection of n rules chosen from $S_{k,p,m}$ is at most $O((p^{m+1}k)^n)$.

Theorem 3.3 shows that the MIL hypothesis space increases given more metarules, which suggests that we should remove redundant metarules. The next section explores this idea.

4   Reduction of Metarules

We now logically reduce fragments of second-order datalog, where the fragments correspond to sets of metarules. The goal is to identify a finite minimal set of metarules from which a larger (possibly infinite) set can be derived. To reason about metarules using Prolog (i.e. when running the Prolog implementations of the reduction algorithms), we use a method called encapsulation [3] which transforms a second-order logic program to a first-order logic program. To aid readability of the results, we present non-encapsulated (i.e second-order) metarules.

We focus on fragments of second-order datalog useful to ILP. We follow standard ILP convention [3, 8, 26] and only consider fragments consisting of connected clauses:

Definition 4.1 (Connected clause). *A clause is connected if the literals in the clause cannot be partitioned into two sets such that the variables appearing in the literals of one set are disjoint from the variables appearing in the literals of the other set.*

We further restrict the fragments using syntactic restrictions on their clauses, namely on literal arity and clause body size (Definition 3.12). We denote the case that each literal has arity of exactly a as $=$. For instance, the fragment where each clause has at most two literals in the body and each literal has arity of exactly 3 is denoted as $\mathcal{H}_2^{3=}$. We consider two fragments: *exactly two-connected* and *two-connected*, both of which contain only connected clauses. Our goal is to first identify k-bounded E-reduction and D-reductions for these fragments using the reduction algorithms described in Sect. 3. To identify reductions for an infinite fragment, such as $\mathcal{H}_*^a$, we first run the reduction algorithms on the sub-fragment $\mathcal{H}_5^a$ using a resolution bound 10 (i.e. $k = 10$). Having found k-bounded reductions for the fragment $\mathcal{H}_5^a$, our goal is to then theoretically determine whether larger (preferably infinite) sets can be derived from these reductions.

4.1   Exactly-Two-Connected Fragment

We first consider an *exactly-two-connected* fragment, studied by Cropper and Muggleton [3]. The restriction is:

Definition 4.2 (Exactly-two-connected clause). *A clause is exactly-two-connected if each term variable appears exactly twice.*

We denote the exactly-two-connected fragment of $\mathcal{H}$ as $\mathcal{E}$. Figure 1(a) shows the results of applying the entailment and derivation reduction algorithms to $\mathcal{E}_5^{2=}$. Both algorithms return the same reduced set of two metarules in $\mathcal{E}_2^{2=}$. This result corroborates the result of Cropper and Muggleton [3]. Figure 1(b) shows the results of applying the entailment and derivation reduction algorithms to $\mathcal{E}_5^2$, a fragment not studied by Cropper and Muggleton. Again, both algorithms return the same reduced set of metarules in $\mathcal{E}_2^2$. We now show that $\mathcal{E}_\infty^2$ has the same D-reduction as $\mathcal{E}_2^2$:

Theorem 4.1 ($\mathcal{E}_\infty^2$ reducibility). *The fragment $\mathcal{E}_\infty^2$ has the same D-reduction as $\mathcal{E}_2^2$.*

Proof. See Appendix A for the proof.

$$\boxed{\begin{aligned} &P(A,B) \leftarrow Q(B,A) \\ &P(A,B) \leftarrow Q(A,C),R(C,B) \end{aligned}}$$

$$\boxed{\begin{aligned} &P(A) \leftarrow Q(A) \\ &P(A) \leftarrow Q(A,B),R(B) \\ &P(A,B) \leftarrow Q(B,A) \\ &P(A,B) \leftarrow Q(A),R(B) \\ &P(A,B) \leftarrow Q(A,C),R(C,B) \end{aligned}}$$

(a) Reductions of $\mathcal{E}_5^{2=}$

(b) Reductions of $\mathcal{E}_5^2$

Fig. 1. (a) and (b) show the results of applying the E-reduction and D-reduction algorithms to the corresponding fragments

An immediate consequence of Theorem 4.1 is the result:

Corollary 4.1. *The fragment $\mathcal{E}_\infty^2$ has the same E-reduction as $\mathcal{E}_2^2$.*

Proof. Follows from Theorem 4.1 and Proposition 3.1.

4.2   Two-Connected Fragment

A common constraint in ILP is to require that all the variables in a clause appear at least twice [24, 29]. We study a slight variant of this constraint which we call *two-connected*:

Definition 4.3 (Two-connected clause). *A clause is two-connected if each term variable appears in at least two literals*

We denote the two-connected fragment of $\mathcal{H}$ as $\mathcal{K}$. Figure 2 shows the results of applying the entailment and derivation reduction algorithms to $\mathcal{K}_5^{2=}$. Unlike the exactly two-connected fragment, the algorithms do not return the same reduced sets of metarules. Whereas the E-reduced set is in $\mathcal{K}_2^{2=}$, the D-reduced set is not in $\mathcal{K}_2^{2=}$. In fact, although the majority of clauses have been removed, the D-reduced set still contains a clause with five body literals. Figure 3 shows the results of applying the entailment and derivation reduction algorithms to $\mathcal{K}_5^2$. Again, whereas the E-reduced set is in $\mathcal{K}_2^2$, the D-reduced set is not in $\mathcal{K}_2^2$, and again contains a clause with five body literals. We now show that the D-reduction of $\mathcal{K}_5^2$ is not in $\mathcal{K}_2^2$:

Proposition 4.1 ($\mathcal{K}_5^2$ irreducibility). *There is no D-reduction of $\mathcal{K}_5^2$ in $\mathcal{K}_2^2$.*

Sketch proof 2. We use the clause $P_0(x_1, x_2) \leftarrow P_1(x_1, x_3), P_2(x_1, x_4),$ $P_3(x_2, x_3), P_4(x_2, x_4), P_5(x_3, x_4)$ as a counter example. We explore the different ways to derive this clause from strictly smaller clauses. We reach a contradiction each time. See Appendix B for the full proof.

We also show that $\mathcal{K}^2_\infty$ has no D-reduction:

Theorem 4.2 ($\mathcal{K}^2_\infty$ **irreducibility**). $\mathcal{K}^2_\infty$ *has no D-reduction.*

Sketch proof 3. We define a transformation that turns an irreducible clause, such as the counter example in Proposition 4.1, into a larger irreducible clause. See Appendix B for the full proof.

4.3   Discussion

We have used the entailment and derivation reduction algorithms to reduce four fragments of second-order datalog, corresponding to sets of metarules. Theorem 4.2 shows that certain fragments do not have finite reductions. This result has implications for the completeness of any ILP system which relies on metarules. In MIL, for instance, the result implies incompleteness when learning programs in the fragment $\mathcal{K}^2_\infty$.

E-reduction	D-reduction
$P(A,B) \leftarrow Q(B,A)$	$P(A,B) \leftarrow Q(B,A)$
	$P(A,B) \leftarrow Q(A,B),R(A,B)$
$P(A,B) \leftarrow Q(A,C),R(C,B)$	$P(A,B) \leftarrow Q(A,C),R(C,B)$
	$P(A,B) \leftarrow Q(A,B),R(A,C),S(C,D),T(C,D)$
	$P(A,B) \leftarrow Q(A,C),R(A,C),S(B,D),T(B,D)$
	$P(A,B) \leftarrow Q(A,C),R(A,D),S(B,C),T(B,D),U(C,D)$

Fig. 2. Reductions of $\mathcal{K}^{2=}_5$

E-reduction	D-reduction
$P(A) \leftarrow Q(A)$	$P(A) \leftarrow Q(A)$
	$P(A) \leftarrow Q(A),R(A)$
	$P(A) \leftarrow Q(B),R(A,B)$
$P(A) \leftarrow R(A,B),Q(A,B)$	$P(A) \leftarrow Q(A,B),R(A,B)$
$P(A,B) \leftarrow Q(B,A)$	$P(A,B) \leftarrow Q(B,A)$
$P(A,B) \leftarrow Q(A),R(B)$	$P(A,B) \leftarrow Q(A),R(B)$
	$P(A,B) \leftarrow Q(A,B),R(A,B)$
$P(A,B) \leftarrow Q(A,C),R(C,B)$	$P(A,B) \leftarrow Q(A,C),R(C,B)$
	$P(A,B) \leftarrow Q(A),R(A,B)$
	$P(A,B) \leftarrow Q(A,C),R(A,D),S(C,B),T(B,D),U(C,D)$

Fig. 3. Reductions of $\mathcal{K}^2_5$

5   Experiments

As explained in Sect. 1, entailment reduction can be too strong and can remove metarules necessary to make a hypothesis more specific. The contrast between entailment and derivation reduction was shown in the previous section, where in all cases the E-reductions are a subset of the D-reductions. However, as shown in Theorem 3.3, the MIL hypothesis space increases given more metarules, which suggests that we should use fewer metarules. In this section we experimentally explore this tradeoff between expressivity and efficiency. Specifically, we describe an experiment[5] that compares learning with the different reduced sets of metarules. We test the null hypothesis:

Null hypothesis 1: There is no difference in learning performance when using E-reduced and D-reduced sets of metarules

Materials. We use Metagol [5], the main MIL implementation, to compare learning with the E-reduced and D-reduced sets of metarules for the fragment $\mathcal{K}_5^2$. We also compare a third set which we call *D*-reduced*, which is the D-reduced set but without the irreducible metarule with 5 literals in the body. We compare the sets of metarules on the Michalski trains problems [17], where the task is to induce a hypothesis that distinguishes five eastbound trains from five westbound trains. To generate the experimental data, we first randomly generated 8 target train programs, where the programs are progressively more difficult measured by the number of literals.

Method. Our experimental method is as follows. For each target program:

1. Generate 10 training examples, half positive and half negative
2. Generate 200 testing examples, half positive and half negative

Task	E-reduction	D-reduction	D*-reduction
T1	95 ± 1	100 ± 0	100 ± 0
T2	99 ± 1	100 ± 0	100 ± 0
T3	56 ± 3	96 ± 2	96 ± 2
T4	69 ± 4	96 ± 2	96 ± 2
T5	59 ± 3	93 ± 3	93 ± 3
T6	50 ± 1	96 ± 3	96 ± 3
T7	68 ± 4	95 ± 2	95 ± 2
T8	54 ± 3	60 ± 3	90 ± 3

(a)

Task	E-reduction	D-reduction	D*-reduction
T1	0.01 ± 0	0 ± 0	0 ± 0
T2	0.01 ± 0	0 ± 0	0 ± 0
T3	431 ± 59	0.01 ± 0	0.01 ± 0
T4	300 ± 68	0 ± 0	0.01 ± 0
T5	427 ± 60	1 ± 0.3	1 ± 0.41
T6	600 ± 0	1 ± 0.41	1 ± 0.42
T7	917 ± 535	1 ± 0.27	1 ± 0.36
T8	487 ± 51	360 ± 67	26 ± 5

(b)

Fig. 4. (a) and (b) show the predictive accuracies (%) and learning times (seconds rounded to 2 decimal places) respectively when using different reduced sets of metarules on the Michalski trains problems

---

[5] All code and data used in the experiments are available at https://github.com/andrewcropper/ilp18-dreduce.

3. For each set of metarules m:
   (a) Learn a program p using the training examples and metarules m with a timeout of 10 min
   (b) Measure the predictive accuracy of p using the testing examples

We repeat the above method 20 times, and measure mean predictive accuracies, learning times, and standard errors.

Results. Figure 4(a) shows the predictive accuracies when learning with the different sets of metarules. In 6/8 tasks, the D-reduced set has higher predictive accuracies than the E-reduced set. The D-reduced and D*-reduced sets have similar levels of performance, except on the most difficult task 8. A McNemar's test on the D-reduced and D*-reduced accuracies confirmed the significance at the $p < 0.01$ level. On task 8, the D*-reduced set greatly outperforms the other two sets. The poor performance with the D-reduced set on task 8 is because

Target program

```
f(X):-has_car(X,C1),long(C1),two_wheels(C1),
    has_car(X,C2),long(C2),three_wheels(C2).
```

E-reduction program

```
f(A):-has_car(A,B),f1(A,B).
f1(A,B):-has_car(A,C),f2(C,B).
f2(A,B):-long(A),three_wheels(B).
```

D-reduction program

```
f(A):-f1(A),f2(A).
f1(A):-has_car(A,B),three_wheels(B).
f2(A):-has_car(A,B),roof_open(B).
```

D*-reduction program

```
f(A):-f1(A),f2(A).
f1(A):-has_car(A,B),three_wheels(B).
f2(A):-has_car(A,B),f3(B).
f3(A):-long(A),two_wheels(A).
```

Fig. 5. Example programs learned by Metagol when varying the metarule set. Only the D*-reduction program is success set equivalent to the target program (when restricted to the target predicate f/1). In all three cases Metagol discovered that if a carriage has three wheels then it is a long carriage, i.e. Metagol discovered that the literal *long(C2)* is redundant in the target program. In fact, if you unfold the D*reduction program to remove the invented predicates, then the resulting single clause program is one literal shorter than the target program.

Metagol often times out when using these metarules, which can be explained by the larger hypothesis space searched (Theorem 3.3). Specifically, when searching for a program with 3 clauses, the D-reduced space contains 4.27^{23} programs, whereas the D*-reduced space contains 1.51^{13} programs. When searching for a program with 4 clauses, the D-reduced space contains 3.21^{31} programs, whereas the D*-reduced space contains 3.72^{17} programs.

Figure 4(b) shows the learning times when learning using the different reduced sets of metarules. Again, the D-reduced set has lower learning times compared to the E-reduced set, and again the D*-reduced set outperforms the D-reduced set on the most difficult task 8. A paired t-test on the D-reduced and D*-reduced learning times confirmed the significance at the $p < 0.01$ level. Figure 5 shows the target program for task 8 and example programs learned by Metagol using the various reduced sets of metarules. In both cases, the null hypothesis is refuted, both in terms of predictive accuracies and learning times.

6   Conclusions and Further Work

We have introduced the derivation reduction problem (Definition 3.9), the problem of removing derivationally redundant clauses from a clausal theory. We have also introduced a derivation reduction algorithm, which we have used to reduce sets of metarules. We have shown that certain sets of metarules do not have finite reductions (Theorem 4.2), which has implications on completeness not only for MIL, but for any ILP system which relies on metarules. We also compared learning programs using the E-reduced and D-reduced sets of metarules. In general, using the D-reduced set outperforms the E-reduced set both in terms of predictive accuracies and learning times. We also compared a D*-reduced set, a subset of the D-reduced metarules, which, although derivationally incomplete, outperforms the other two sets in terms of predictive accuracies and learning times.

Limitations and Future Work. Theorem 3.2 shows that the derivation reduction problem is undecidable for general Horn theories. In future work, we wish to study the decidability of the derivation problem for other fragments of logic, such as function-free theories. For the decidable cases, we wish to identify more efficient reduction algorithms. Theorem 4.2 shows that certain fragments of Datalog do not have finite D-reductions. Future work should explore techniques to mitigate this result, such as exploring whether special metarules, such as a currying metarule [4], could alleviate the issue. We have compared D-reduction to E-reduction, but we would also like to compare other forms of reduction, such as theta-subsumption reduction [27]. We would also like to study other fragments of logic, including triadic logics. We have shown that, although incomplete, the D*-reduced set of metarules outperforms the other sets in our Michalski trains experiment. We would like to explore this incompleteness in more detail, such as determining the degree of incompleteness. Finally, we would like to run more experiments comparing the learning performance of the different sets of metarules on a wider variety of problems.

Acknowledgements. The authors thank Stephen Muggleton and Katsumi Inoue for helpful discussions on this topic.

Appendices

A   Exactly-Two-Connected Fragment

Theorem 4.1. $\mathcal{E}_\infty^2$ *has the same D-reduction as* $\mathcal{E}_2^2$.

Proof. Let us consider a clause $C \in \mathcal{E}_\infty^2$ such that C has at least three body literals. If C contains a monadic predicate, e.g. $P(x_1)$, then x_1 occurs in only one other literal $P_{x_1}(x_1, x_2)$ (up to the order of the variables and their names) that is dyadic because of the exactly-two-connected nature of C and its length. Replacing in C these two literals by a monadic pivot $P_p(x_2)$ generates a clause $C_1 \in \mathcal{E}_\infty^2$ smaller than C that can be resolved with the clause C_2 containing $P(x_1)$, $P_{x_1}(x_1, x_2)$ and $P_p(x_2)$ to derive C. Note that if one of $P(x_1)$ or $P_{x_1}(x_1, x_2)$ is the head of C then $P_p(x_2)$ is the head of C_1, otherwise, $P_p(x_2)$ is the head of C_2.

Let us now assume that C contains no monadic predicate. Then we can pick any variable x such that its two occurrences are in the body of C. There must be at least one such variable due to the length of C. Let us denote the two literals where x occurs by $P_1(x, x_1)$ and $P_2(x, x_2)$, up to the ordering of the variables in the literals that has no incidence on the proof. Let the clause C_1 be C without $\{P_1(x, x_1), P_2(x, x_2)\}$ and with the added pivot literal $P_p(x_1, x_2)$ in the body. This clause belongs to $\mathcal{E}_\infty^2$, is smaller than C and can be resolved with $C_2 = P_p(x_1, x_2) \leftarrow P_1(x, x_1), P_2(x, x_2)$ that also belongs to $\mathcal{E}_\infty^2$ to derive C. Hence any clause in $\mathcal{E}_\infty^2 \backslash \mathcal{E}_2^2$ can be derived from clauses in $\mathcal{E}_2^2$. Thus any D-reduction of $\mathcal{E}_2^2$ is also a D-reduction of $\mathcal{E}_\infty^2$

B   Two-connected fragment

Proposition 4.1. *There is no D-reduction of* $\mathcal{K}_5^2$ *in* $\mathcal{K}_2^2$.

Proof. Let $C = P_0(x_1, x_2) \leftarrow P_1(x_1, x_3), P_2(x_1, x_4), P_3(x_2, x_3), P_4(x_2, x_4),$ $P_5(x_3, x_4)$, where $C \in \mathcal{K}_5^2$. To derive C from two smaller clauses, these two smaller clauses C_1 and C_2 must form a partition of the literals in C if one excludes the pivot. Let us consider the possible partitions of C. Each of the two sets in the partition must contain at least two elements, otherwise one of C_1, C_2 would be as big as C, which we want to avoid. There are a total of 6 literals in C, thus the only partitions of interest are the ones with a 2–4 ratio and a 3–3 ratio, for a total of 25 cases (15 2–4 cases and half of the 20 3–3 cases since we do not care which clause gets which set of literals). Due to the symmetries of the problem, a great number of cases can be safely skipped, reducing the number of cases to consider to only 4.

1. Assume $P_0(x_1, x_2)$ and $P_1(x_1, x_3)$ are the only literals of C that belong to C_1. Then, for C_1 and C_2 to both be in any $\mathcal{K}_m^2$ where $m < 5$, the pivot needs to contain at least the variables x_1 (occurring only once in C_2) and x_2, x_3 (occurring only once in C_1). Since these clauses contain at most dyadic literals, this is not possible. All the 2–4 cases where there is one term variable that connects the two literals occurring in the smaller subset of size two, in either C_1 or C_2, are symmetrical to this one and thus also impossible to fulfill.

2. Assume $P_0(x_1, x_2)$ and $P_5(x_3, x_4)$ are the only literals of C that belong to C_1. Then, the pivot needs to contain all the four variables for C_1 and C_2 to belong to $\mathcal{K}_{m<5}^2$, which is not possible. All the remaining 2–4 cases are symmetrical to this one.

3. Assume $P_0(x_1, x_2)$, $P_1(x_1, x_3)$ and $P_2(x_1, x_4)$ are the only literals of C in C_1. Then, x_2, x_3 and x_4 must occur in the pivot, which is impossible. All the 3-3 cases where the three literals share a common variable are symmetrical.

4. Assume $P_1(x_1, x_2)$, $P_2(x_1, x_4)$ and $P_3(x_2, x_3)$ are the only literals of C in C_1. Then, all four variables must occur in the pivot, which is impossible. All the remaining 3-3 cases are symmetrical to this one.

Thus it is not possible to derive C from clauses in $\mathcal{K}_2^2$. For this reason, a D-reduction of $\mathcal{K}_5^2$ cannot be in $\mathcal{K}_2^2$.

Note that it cannot be in $\mathcal{K}_3^2$ nor $\mathcal{K}_4^2$ for the same reason.

Proposition B.1. *If a clause C is irreducible (i.e. it cannot be derived from clauses of strictly smaller size), has at least two literals in its body and all the term variables it contains occur three times then applying the following transformation on C produces a clause that is also irreducible.*

Replace two dyadic literals that share a variable in the body of C, denoted as $P_1(x_1, x_2)$ and $P_2(x_1, x_3)$ up to the order of the variables and their names, by the following set of literals: $P_1(x_1, x_4)$, $P_2(x_1, x_5)$, $P_3(x_4, x_5)$, $P_4(x_4, x_2)$, $P_5(x_5, x_3)$ where P_3, P_4, P_5, x_4 and x_5 are fresh predicate and term variables.

Proof. Let C be a irreducible clause containing the two literals $P_1(x_1, x_2)$ and $P_2(x_1, x_3)$ (without loss of generality) in which all variables occur exactly three times. Let C_{ext} be the result of the transformation of C where the two previously mentioned literals have been replaced by the set of literals $P_1(x_1, x_4)$, $P_2(x_1, x_5)$, $P_3(x_4, x_5)$, $P_4(x_4, x_2)$, $P_5(x_5, x_3)$ where P_3, P_4, P_5, x_4 and x_5 are fresh predicate and term variables. Assume that there exist two clauses C_{ext1} and C_{ext2} in $\mathcal{K}_\infty^2$ both smaller than C_{ext}, such that $C_{\text{ext1}}, C_{\text{ext2}} \vdash C_{\text{ext}}$. If C_{ext1} is made of a subset of the literals in $C_{\text{ext}} \backslash C$ (plus a pivot), then C_{ext1} is not two-connected because all these subsets leave three or more variables that occur only once. The corresponding literals for each case are described in Table 1 (the symmetrical cases are excluded). To illustrate how the table was built, we consider the case where C_{ext1} contains $P_1(x_1, x_4)$, $P_2(x_1, x_5)$, $P_3(x_4, x_5)$, $P_4(x_4, x_2)$, i.e. the second line of Table 1. Consider these four literals. The variable x_2 occurs exactly once. In addition, since the variables x_1 and x_5 occur only three times in C_{ext}, they also occur only once in C_{ext2}. In the table, variables that occur only once in C_{ext2} are followed by a star ($\star$). In total, there are three such variables, which is one too many for the pivot to include all of them as arguments. The cases where C_{ext2} is made only of the literals in $C_{\text{ext}}\backslash C$ plus the pivot are symmetrical to the ones in Table 1.

Table 1. Literals occurring only once in C_{ext1} or C_{ext2} when the given literal set is the body of C_{ext1} - the $\star$ symbol indicates a variable occurring only once in C_{ext2}

New literals in C_{ext1}	Single-occurrence variables
$P_1(x_1,x_4), P_2(x_1,x_5), P_3(x_4,x_5), P_4(x_4,x_2), P_5(x_5,x_3)$	$x_1\star, x_2\star, x_3\star$
$P_1(x_1,x_4), P_2(x_1,x_5), P_3(x_4,x_5), P_4(x_4,x_2)$	$x_1\star, x_2, x_5\star$
$P_1(x_1,x_4), P_2(x_1,x_5), P_4(x_4,x_2), P_5(x_5,x_3)$	$x_1\star, x_2, x_3, x_4\star, x_5\star$
$P_1(x_1,x_4), P_3(x_4,x_5), P_4(x_4,x_2), P_5(x_5,x_3)$	$x_1, x_2, x_3, x_5\star$
$P_1(x_1,x_4), P_2(x_1,x_5), P_3(x_4,x_5)$	$x_1\star, x_4\star, x_5\star$
$P_1(x_1,x_4), P_2(x_1,x_5), P_4(x_4,x_2)$	$x_1\star, x_2, x_4\star, x_5$
$P_1(x_1,x_4), P_3(x_4,x_5), P_4(x_4,x_2)$	x_1, x_2, x_5
$P_1(x_1,x_4), P_3(x_4,x_5), P_5(x_5,x_3)$	$x_1, x_3, x_4\star, x_5\star$
$P_1(x_1,x_4), P_4(x_4,x_2), P_5(x_5,x_3)$	$x_1, x_2, x_3, x_4\star, x_5$
$P_3(x_4,x_5), P_4(x_4,x_2), P_5(x_5,x_3)$	$x_2, x_3, x_4\star, x_5\star$
$P_1(x_1,x_4), P_2(x_1,x_5)$	$x_1\star, x_4, x_5$
$P_1(x_1,x_4), P_3(x_4,x_5)$	$x_1, x_4\star, x_5$
$P_1(x_1,x_4), P_4(x_4,x_2)$	$x_1, x_2, x_4\star$
$P_1(x_1,x_4), P_5(x_5,x_3)$	x_1, x_3, x_4, x_5
$P_3(x_4,x_5), P_4(x_4,x_2)$	$x_2, x_4\star, x_5$
$P_4(x_4,x_2), P_5(x_5,x_3)$	x_2, x_3, x_4, x_5

The remaining possibilities are when both C_{ext1} and C_{ext2} are made of a mix of the literals in $C_{\text{ext}}\backslash C$ and $C_{\text{ext}} \cap C$. In these cases, the contradiction appears by going from $C_{\text{ext1}}, C_{\text{ext2}} \vdash C_{\text{ext}}$ to $C_1, C_2 \vdash C$. For example, if $P_1(x_1,x_4)$ and $P_2(x_1,x_5)$ belong to C_{ext1} while the other literals from $C_{\text{ext}}\backslash C$ belong to C_{ext2}, then x_4 and x_5 occur only once in C_{ext1} (without pivot). There cannot be more than two such literals in the pivot-less $C_{\text{ext1}}, C_{\text{ext2}}$ pair or the pivot cannot take all of them as arguments so that they occur at least twice in C_{ext1} and C_{ext2} (with pivot), thus x_4 and x_5 are the only ones. Now consider C_1 and C_2, obtained respectively from C_{ext1} and C_{ext2} by deleting the five literals of $C_{\text{ext}}\backslash C$ from them and adding $P_1(x_1,x_2)$ and $P_2(x_1,x_3)$, i.e. the literals in $C\backslash C_{\text{ext}}$ into C_1. Before this transformation, the three occurrences of the variables x_2 and x_3 were located in C_{ext2}. Due to the deletion of literals, only two occurrences of each remain in C_2 and one occurrence of each is now in C_1. Hence both x_2 and x_3 occur only once in that case. Except for the variables x_4 and x_5 that are absent from C_1, C_2, the distribution of the remaining variables is unchanged when transforming C_{ext1}, C_{ext2} in C_1, C_2, hence these variables occur at least twice. Thus the pair C_1 C_2 derives C and C_1 and C_2 are both smaller than C, a contradiction.

Table 2. Transformation from (C_{ext1}, C_{ext2}) to (C_1, C_2) and corresponding evolution of the variables occurring only once

C_{ext1} ; C_{ext2}	Variables occurring once	C_1 ; C_2
$1, 2, 3, 4, 5$; $\emptyset$	$\emptyset$; $\emptyset$	$1, 2$; $\emptyset$
$1, 2, 3, 4$; 5	x_5 ; x_1	1 ; 2
$1, 2, 4, 5$; 3	x_4, x_5 ; $\emptyset$	$1, 2$; $\emptyset$
$1, 3, 4, 5$; 2	x_1, x_5 ; $\emptyset$	$1, 2$; $\emptyset$
$1, 2$; $3, 4, 5$	x_4, x_5 ; x_2, x_3	$1, 2$; $\emptyset$
$1, 3$; $2, 4, 5$	x_1, x_4, x_5 ; $* * *$	$* * *$; $* * *$
$1, 4$; $2, 3, 5$	x_4 ; $\emptyset$	1 ; 2
$1, 5$; $2, 3, 4$	x_1, x_4, x_5 ; $* * *$	$* * *$; $* * *$
$3, 4$; $1, 2, 5$	x_4, x_5 ; x_2	$\emptyset$; $1, 2$
$4, 5$; $1, 2, 3$	x_4, x_5 ; x_2, x_3	$\emptyset$; $1, 2$

By taking into account all the symmetries of the problem, there are only ten such cases to consider. They are summarized in Table 2. On the left-hand side of the table is the partition between C_{ext1} and C_{ext2} of the five literals in $C_{ext}\backslash C$. On the right-hand side of the table is the partition between C_1 and C_2 of the two literals in $C\backslash C_{ext}$. As was done in the previous example, C_1 and C_2 are obtained by removing the five literals in $C_{ext}\backslash C$ from C_{ext1} and C_{ext2} respectively and replacing them with the two literals in $C\backslash C_{ext}$ as indicated in the table. For readability, the literals are only referred to by their number. In the middle of the table are the variables that are known to occur only once in each case (in C_{ext1} and C_{ext2} on the left-hand side and in C_1 and C_2 on the right-hand side). In the cases where there are strictly less than two identified variables that occur only once, there may also be unknown variables that also occur only once, but these are preserved by the transformation and thus do not impact the reasoning. In most of the cases, it is possible to have at most two literals occurring only once on the right-hand side of the table, implying that C can be derived from two smaller clauses in $\mathcal{K}^2_\infty$, a contradiction. There are also two cases where the assumption that $C_{ext1}, C_{ext2} \in \mathcal{K}^2_\infty$ is not verified because there are already more than two variables that occur only once in the explicit parts of C_{ext1} and C_{ext2}. In such cases, there is nothing to verify so the right-hand side of the table is filled with asterisks (***).

Theorem 4.2. $\mathcal{K}^2_\infty$ *has no D-reduction.*

Proof. The clause $C = P_0(x_1, x_2) \leftarrow P_1(x_1, x_3), P_2(x_1, x_4), P_3(x_2, x_3),$ $P_4(x_2, x_4), P_5(x_3, x_4)$ in $\mathcal{K}^2_5$ was shown irreducible in the proof of Proposition 4.1.

It has five literals in its body and all of its term variables occur exactly three times. It can thus be transformed following Proposition B.1 into a bigger irreducible clause in $\mathcal{K}_8^2$. In fact, this transformation preserves all of its requirements (irreducibility, three occurrences of all variables, size of the body greater than three) and can thus be applied iteratively from C so as to generate irreducible clauses in $\mathcal{K}_\infty^2$ that are as big as one wants. For this reason, any D-reduced subset of $\mathcal{K}_\infty^2$ is infinite, thus $\mathcal{K}_\infty^2$ has no D-reduction.

References

1. Albarghouthi, A., Koutris, P., Naik, M., Smith, C.: Constraint-based synthesis of datalog programs. In: Beck, J.C. (ed.) CP 2017. LNCS, vol. 10416, pp. 689–706. Springer, Cham (2017). https://doi.org/10.1007/978-3-319-66158-2_44
2. Bradley, A.R., Manna, Z.: The Calculus of Computation: Decision Procedures with Applications to Verification. Springer, Heidelberg (2007). https://doi.org/10.1007/978-3-540-74113-8
3. Cropper, A., Muggleton, S.H.: Logical minimisation of meta-rules within meta-interpretive learning. In: Davis, J., Ramon, J. (eds.) ILP 2014. LNCS (LNAI), vol. 9046, pp. 62–75. Springer, Cham (2015). https://doi.org/10.1007/978-3-319-23708-4_5
4. Cropper, A., Muggleton, S.H.: Learning higher-order logic programs through abstraction and invention. In: Kambhampati, S. (ed.) Proceedings of the Twenty-Fifth International Joint Conference on Artificial Intelligence, IJCAI 2016, 9–15 July 2016, pp. 1418–1424. IJCAI/AAAI Press, New York (2016)
5. Cropper, A., Muggleton, S.H.: Metagol system (2016). https://github.com/metagol/metagol
6. Cropper, A., Muggleton, S.H.: Learning efficient logic programs. Mach. Learn., 1–21 (2018)
7. Emde, W., Habel, C., Rollinger, C.-R.: The discovery of the equator or concept driven learning. In: Bundy, A. (ed.) Proceedings of the 8th International Joint Conference on Artificial Intelligence, August 1983, pp. 455–458. William Kaufmann, Karlsruhe (1983)
8. Evans, R., Grefenstette, E.: Learning explanatory rules from noisy data. J. Artif. Intell. Res. **61**, 1–64 (2018)
9. Flener, P.: Inductive logic program synthesis with DIALOGS. In: Muggleton, S. (ed.) ILP 1996. LNCS, vol. 1314, pp. 175–198. Springer, Heidelberg (1997). https://doi.org/10.1007/3-540-63494-0_55
10. Fonseca, N., Costa, V.S., Silva, F., Camacho, R.: On avoiding redundancy in inductive logic programming. In: Camacho, R., King, R., Srinivasan, A. (eds.) ILP 2004. LNCS (LNAI), vol. 3194, pp. 132–146. Springer, Heidelberg (2004). https://doi.org/10.1007/978-3-540-30109-7_13
11. Garey, M.R., Johnson, D.S.: Computers and Intractability: A Guide to the Theory of NP-Completeness. W. H. Freeman, New York (1979)
12. Heule, M., Järvisalo, M., Lonsing, F., Seidl, M., Biere, A.: Clause elimination for SAT and QSAT. J. Artif. Intell. Res. **53**, 127–168 (2015)
13. Kaminski, T., Eiter, T., Inoue, K.: Exploiting answer set programming with external sources for meta-interpretive learning. In: 34th International Conference on Logic Programming (2018)

14. Kietz, J.-U., Wrobel, S.: Controlling the complexity of learning in logic through syntactic and task-oriented models. In: Inductive Logic Programming. Citeseer (1992)
15. Kowalski, R.A.: Predicate logic as programming language. In: IFIP Congress, pp. 569–574 (1974)
16. Langlois, M., Mubayi, D., Sloan, R.H., Turán, G.: Combinatorial problems for horn clauses. In: Lipshteyn, M., Levit, V.E., McConnell, R.M. (eds.) Graph Theory, Computational Intelligence and Thought. LNCS, vol. 5420, pp. 54–65. Springer, Heidelberg (2009). https://doi.org/10.1007/978-3-642-02029-2_6
17. Larson, J., Michalski, R.S.: Inductive inference of VL decision rules. SIGART Newslett. **63**, 38–44 (1977)
18. Liberatore, P.: Redundancy in logic I: CNF propositional formulae. Artif. Intell. **163**(2), 203–232 (2005)
19. Liberatore, P.: Redundancy in logic II: 2CNF and horn propositional formulae. Artif. Intell. **172**(2–3), 265–299 (2008)
20. Lin, D., Dechter, E., Ellis, K., Tenenbaum, J.B., Muggleton, S.: Bias reformulation for one-shot function induction. In: ECAI 2014–21st European Conference on Artificial Intelligence, 18–22 August 2014, Prague, Czech Republic - Including Prestigious Applications of Intelligent Systems (PAIS 2014), pp. 525–530 (2014)
21. Lloyd, J.W.: Foundations of Logic Programming. Springer, Heidelberg (2012). https://doi.org/10.1007/978-3-642-83189-8
22. Marcinkowski, J., Pacholski, L.: Undecidability of the horn-clause implication problem. In: 33rd Annual Symposium on Foundations of Computer Science, Pittsburgh, Pennsylvania, USA, 24–27 October 1992, pp. 354–362 (1992)
23. Muggleton, S.: Inverse entailment and progol. New Gener. Comput. **13**(3&4), 245–286 (1995)
24. Muggleton, S., Feng, C.: Efficient induction of logic programs. In: Algorithmic Learning Theory, First International Workshop, ALT 1990, Tokyo, Japan, 8–10 October 1990, Proceedings, pp. 368–381 (1990)
25. Muggleton, S.H., Lin, D., Tamaddoni-Nezhad, A.: Meta-interpretive learning of higher-order dyadic datalog: predicate invention revisited. Mach. Learn. **100**(1), 49–73 (2015)
26. Nienhuys-Cheng, S.-H., de Wolf, R.: Foundations of Inductive Logic Programming. LNCS, vol. 1228. Springer, Heidelberg (1997). https://doi.org/10.1007/3-540-62927-0
27. Plotkin, G.D.: Automatic methods of inductive inference. Ph.D. thesis, Edinburgh University, August 1971
28. Raedt, L.: Declarative modeling for machine learning and data mining. In: Bshouty, N.H., Stoltz, G., Vayatis, N., Zeugmann, T. (eds.) ALT 2012. LNCS (LNAI), vol. 7568, pp. 12–12. Springer, Heidelberg (2012). https://doi.org/10.1007/978-3-642-34106-9_2
29. De Raedt, L., Bruynooghe, M.: Interactive concept-learning and constructive induction by analogy. Mach. Learn. **8**, 107–150 (1992)
30. Schmidt-Schauß, M.: Implication of clauses is undecidable. Theor. Comput. Sci. **59**, 287–296 (1988)
31. Shapiro, E.Y.: Algorithmic Program Debugging. MIT Press, Cambridge (1983)
32. Wang, W.Y., Mazaitis, K., Cohen, W.W.: Structure learning via parameter learning. In: Proceedings of the 23rd ACM International Conference on Conference on Information and Knowledge Management, pp. 1199–1208. ACM (2014)

Large-Scale Assessment of Deep Relational Machines

Tirtharaj Dash[1(✉)], Ashwin Srinivasan[1(✉)], Lovekesh Vig[2],
Oghenejokpeme I. Orhobor[3], and Ross D. King[3]

[1] Department of CSIS, BITS Pilani, Goa Campus, Sancoale, Goa, India
{tirtharaj,ashwin}@goa.bits-pilani.ac.in
[2] TCS Innovation Labs, New Delhi, India
[3] Department of Computer Science, University of Manchester, Manchester, UK

Abstract. Deep Relational Machines (or DRMs) present a simple way
for incorporating complex domain knowledge into deep networks. In a
DRM this knowledge is introduced through relational features: in the
original formulation of [1], the features are selected by an ILP engine
using domain knowledge encoded as logic programs. More recently, in [2],
DRMs appear to achieve good performance without the need of feature-
selection by an ILP engine (the features are simply drawn randomly from
a space of relevant features). The reports so far on DRMs though have
been deficient on three counts: (a) They have been tested on very small
amounts of data (7 datasets, not all independent, altogether with few
1000s of instances); (b) The background knowledge involved has been
modest, involving few 10s of predicates; and (c) Performance assessment
has been only on classification tasks. In this paper we rectify each of these
shortcomings by testing on datasets from the biochemical domain involving 100s of 1000s of instances; industrial-strength background predicates
involving multiple hierarchies of complex definitions; and on classification
and regression tasks. Our results provide substantially reliable evidence
of the predictive capabilities of DRMs; along with a significant improvement in predictive performance with the incorporation of domain knowledge. We propose the new datasets and results as updated benchmarks
for comparative studies in neural-symbolic modelling.

1 Introduction

One of the most remarkable recent advances in the area of Machine Learning is a
resurgence of interest in neural networks, resulting from the automated construction of "deep networks" for prediction. Simplistically, Deep Learning is a rebrand-
ing of neural networks with multiple hidden layers. Mathematically speaking, it
is a composition of multiple simple non-linear functions trying to learn a hierarchy of intermediate features that most effectively aid the global learning task.
However, despite some spectacular successes, deep learning is thought unlikely to
be sufficient for many kinds of data analysis problems. The principal difficulties
appear to lie in the data and computational requirements to train such models.

© Springer Nature Switzerland AG 2018
F. Riguzzi et al. (Eds.): ILP 2018, LNAI 11105, pp. 22–37, 2018.
https://doi.org/10.1007/978-3-319-99960-9_2

This is especially the case if many hidden layers are needed to encode complex concepts (features). For many industrial processes, acquiring data can incur significant costs, and simulators be computationally very intensive.

Some of this difficulty may be alleviated if knowledge already available in the area of interest can be taken into account. Consider, for example, a problem in the area of drug design. Much may be known already about the target of interest, small molecules that have proved to be effective, what can and cannot be synthesized cheaply and so on. If these concepts are relevant to constructing a model for predicting good drugs, it seems both unnecessary and inefficient to require a deep network to re-discover them (the problem is actually worse: it may not even be possible to discover the concepts from first-principles, using the data available). It is therefore of significant practical interest to explore ways in which prior domain-knowledge could be used in deep networks to reduce data and computational requirements. This has led to a growing interest in the development of deep networks that are able to use and manipulate logical encodings of complex background knowledge. Combining neural and symbolic modelling is not a new idea, going back at least to KBANN [3]: see [4] for detailed ways of hybrid neural-symbolic models. Our interest here is in more recent research in combining deep networks and ILP, of which we are aware of at least 3 attempts. These are: (1) symbolic inference learner [5]; (2) Lifted Relational Neural Network (LRNN) [6]; and (3) ∂-ILP [7]. Each of these focuses on using the first-order representation directly by the neural network. The symbolic inference learner transfers first-order logical formulas into a variable-free representation that can be used to generate homogeneous equations functioning as input data to the neural network. LRNN transforms relational facts into a sequence of grounding neural layers such as ground atom layer, ground-rule layer, and aggregator layer. This allowed the neural network to capture minute internal relationships among the variables and showed considerable improvement over relational learners on a set of biologically relevant classification benchmarks. The ∂-ILP deals with training data over noisy domains. The central concept of ∂-ILP is a differentiable implementation of deduction through forward chaining on definite clauses. In contrast, the DRM represents a much simpler form of combination, based on ILP efforts in propositionalization, originating with LINUS [8]. It is our intent in this paper to set up some benchmarks with this simpler form of neural-symbolic models, which will eventually allow us to assess the utility of encoding the first-order representation directly. We will take LRNN [6] as an instance of the state-of-the-art of neural modelling with relational data[1].

The goals of this paper are threefold. First, we wish to establish a good baseline for comparison of neuro-symbolic models, both in terms of data and for prediction. For the former, we propose recently available datasets from the biochemical literature that provide significantly greater amounts of data and background knowledge than some of the usual benchmarks used in ILP. As a baseline predictor, we propose the use of simple neuro-symbolic models that draw on prior ILP work of combining neural networks with relational features.

---

[1] We have contacted the authors of [5] and [7] and are awaiting a response.

Secondly, using the baseline predictor, we wish to demonstrate the role that symbolic domain-knowledge can play in the performance of a neural network. Thirdly, where possible, we wish to compare the baseline-predictor against the state-of-the-art.

2   Deep Relational Machines for Prediction

Deep Relational Machines, or DRMs, proposed in [1], are deep neural networks with first-order Boolean functions at the the input layer ("function f1 is true if the instance x is a molecule containing a 7-membered ring connected to a lactone ring" — definitions of relations like 7-membered and lactone rings are expected to be present in the background knowledge). In [1] the functions are learned by an ILP engine. This follows a long line of research sometimes called *propositionalisation* in which features constructed by ILP have been used by other modelling methods like regression, decision-trees, SVMs, topic models, and multiplicative-weight linear threshold models [9–14], inspired by the original work in [8]. More recent relevant work is in [1,15]. In each of these, the final model is constructed in two steps: first, a set of features are obtained, and then, the final model is constructed using these features, possibly in conjunction with other features already available. Usually the models show significant improvements in predictive performance when an existing feature set is enriched in this manner. In [1], the deep network with ILP-features is shown to perform well, although the empirical evidence is limited. For the DRMs used in this paper, we dispense with the requirement for an ILP-based selection of input features, and adopt instead the randomised feature-selection approach used in [2]. For completeness, we reproduce the procedure for generating these features in Fig. 1.

The use of these features by a DRM is simple enough. First, we obtain a random set of features using the procedure in Fig. 1 and (training) data. No attempt is made at evaluating how good or useful the features are (this will be done by the network's backpropagation-based estimation of weights). Values of these features for the training data are computed, and an appropriate network structure and weights are identified. Since the features are defined in terms of the background predicates provided, domain knowledge and a logical interpreter (like a Prolog engine) are needed to evaluate their values (1, if true or 0 otherwise) for the data instances. Domain knowledge, therefore, is introduced into the network, albeit in a restricted way: when the network composes new features, it does not really perform the same operation as a true relational join, since the information about variables is lost. More on this later.

This apparently simple-minded approach was shown in [1,2] to be resulting in surprisingly effective predictive performance. But these reports have been limited in the following ways: (a) They have been tested on very small amounts of data (4 in [1]; 7 in [2] not all independent; altogether consisting of few 1000s of instances); (b) The background knowledge involved has been modest, involving few 10s of predicates; and (c) Performance assessment has been only on classification tasks. In this paper, we address each of these shortcomings.

$DrawFeatures(B, M, E, \mathcal{L}, d, MaxDraws)$:
1. Let F be $\langle \rangle$
2. Let $draws = 0$
3. Let $i = 1$
4. Let $Drawn$ be $\emptyset$
5. **while** $draws \leq MaxDraws$ **do**
   (a) Randomly draw with replacement an example $e_i \in E$
   (b) Let $\perp_d(B, e_i)$ be the most specific rule in the depth-limited mode language $\mathcal{L}_d(M)$ that subsumes $\perp(B, e_i)$ (the most-specific clause that entails e, given B)
   (c) Randomly draw a clause C_i s.t. $C_i \sqsubseteq \perp_d(B, e_i)$
   (d) **if** (C_i is not redundant given $Drawn$) **then**
      i. Let $C_i = (Class(x, c) \leftarrow Cp_i(x))$
      ii. Lef $f_i = (F_i(x) \leftarrow Cp_i(x))$
      iii. Update sequence F with f_i
      iv. $Drawn := Drawn \cup \{C_i\}$
      v. increment i
   (e) increment $draws$
6. **done**
7. return F

Fig. 1. The procedure from [2] for obtaining features within a mode language, given background knowledge and data. The construction of $\perp$ in Step 5b is as described in [16], and subsumption refers to Plotkin's θ-subsumption [17]. The redundancy test used in Step 5d is subsumption-equivalence (which is weaker than logical equivalence).

3   Empirical Assessment of DRMs

3.1   Aims

The aim of this empirical study is primarily to establish some baseline predictive performances for neuro-symbolic learning in relational domains. Our position is that a DRM with randomised selection of relational feature construction constitutes an appropriate baseline predictor.

Of course, baselines are intended for use as yardsticks for comparison. The experiments below, therefore, compare the performance of a state-of-the-art neuro-symbolic learner against the DRM baselines. The construction of the baselines also allows the investigation of a secondary goal, namely, the effect of inclusion of domain knowledge on the performance of a deep neural network.

3.2   Data

We use the 73 anti-cancer datasets for the study on classification and 50 QSAR datasets for our study on regression. The data are summarised in Fig. 2.

Task	Size		Features		Target Distributions
	Datasets	Examples	AB	$ABFR$	
Classification	73	$\approx$ 220,000	$\approx$ 3000	$\approx$ 4000	0.4 − 0.9 (% positives)
Regression	50	$\approx$ 18,000	$\approx$ 900	$\approx$ 2200	1.5 − 11.0 (predicted values)

Fig. 2. Summary of datasets. AB refers to relational features using only the atom ad bond structure of the molecules; $ABFR$ refers to features that use background knowledge of functional groups and rings, in addition to the atom-bond information (more on this below).

Classification Problems

The 73 datasets used here represent an extensive drug evaluation effort at the National Cancer Institute (NCI)[2]. The datasets represent experimentally determined effectiveness (anti-cancer activity: kill or inhibit) of a compound against a number of cell lines [18]. The datasets correspond to the concentration parameter GI50, which is the concentration that results in 50% growth inhibition. Some of the datasets have been used in various data mining studies such as in a study involving the use of graph kernels in machine learning [19], and in a recent study that combines relational-logic representations with neural network learning [6].

Each instance (a chemical compound) can be represented as a set of bond facts along with the anti-cancer activity (+ or −). A bond fact has arity 6 such as bond(CompoundID, Atom1, Atom2, Atom1Type, Atom2Type, BondType). For example, a compound can be explained as follows

class(m1, pos).bond(m1, 29, 26, car, car, ar). bond(m1, 14, 11, car, c3, 1). ...

Regression Problems

The 50 datasets here are obtained from ChEMBL database[3] which is managed by the European Bioinformatics Institute (EBI). The datasets consist of information on the drug targets, the structure of the tested chemical compounds, the bioactivities of these compounds on their targets. The drug targets are mainly proteins from a broad set of target families, e.g. kinases) [20]. We describe the structure of a chemical compound as a set of atom(CompoundID, Atom, AtomType) facts and a set of bond(CompoundID, Atom1, Atom2, BondType) facts. These are easily reorganised in the same form used for classification. That is, both atom/3 and bond/4 are represented together by bond/6 facts. The regression task is to predict the bioactivity of the compounds on their targets and are binding constants.

---

[2] https://www.cancer.gov/.
[3] https://www.ebi.ac.uk/chembl/.

3.3   Background Knowledge

We used the background knowledge used in [21,22] with minor modifications to avoid redundant computation and for tractable computation (essentially trading-off completeness for efficiency). The organisational levels of the background knowledge are as shown in Fig. 3. The functional groups [23] and ring

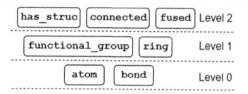

Fig. 3. Levels of organisation of the background knowledge

definitions used are much more elaborate than have been reported in the ILP literature. The definitions used were originally developed for tackling industrial-strength problems by the biotechnology company PharmaDM and consist of multiple hierarchies[4]. The functional group hierarchy consists of amide, amine, ammonium, ether, ester, non_amine_base, non_ammonium_acid, aliphatic_chain, ol, oxime, sulfide, nitrile, counter_ion, metal_ion, iminium_ion, imine, nitroso_group, nitro_group, halide, azide, phospate, phosphonate, phosphinate, misc_phosphor_group, acylhalide, oxide, aldehyde, diazo_group. Many of these functional groups consists of multiple sub-functional groups with 'is a' relationship. For example, hydroxylamine is a amine group. The background knowledge consists of information on accepting and donating groups. For example, methyl group is an inductive donating chemical group. Inductive accepting groups are alcohol, amine, halide, nitro group, methoxy group, acylhalide, acid_car, keton, aldehyde, and nitrile. The ring hierarchy consists of aromatic and non-aromatic rings, which are further divided into hetero or non-hetero rings.

For proprietary reasons, we are not able to show the actual definitions used. However, we are able to show the results of using the definitions, which are functional groups represented as functional_group(CompoundID, Atom, Length, Type) and rings described as ring(CompoundID, RingID, Atoms, Length, Type). For efficiency, we have restricted the background predicate definition of a ring to produce rings of maximum length 8.

The definitions of functional groups and rings are used to infer the presence of composite structures. In this paper, these are: the presence of fused rings, connected rings, and substructures. They are represented by the relations:

- fused(CompoundId, Struc1, Atoms1, Struc2, Atoms2): CompoundId contains a pair fused structures Struc1 and Struc2 with Atoms1 and Atoms2 respectively (that is, there is at least 1 pair of common atoms)
- connected(CompoundId, Struc1, Atoms1, Struc2, Atoms2): CompoundId contains a pair structures Struc1 and Struc2 that with Atoms1 and Atoms2 respectively that are not fused but connected by a bond between an atom in Struc1 and an atom in Struc2
- has_struc(CompoundId, Atoms, Length, Struc): CompoundId contains a structure Struc of length Length containing Atoms

---

[4] Due to the page limit, we don't show the hierarchy figure. This hierarchy is available on the web. Refer the Dataset availability section for more information.

In this paper, the definitions for bond/6 are collectively referred to as AB; and the definitions for bond/6 along with fused/5, connected/5 and has_struc/4 are collectively referred to as $ABFR$.

3.4   DRM Architecture

For the DRM, the inputs are boolean that encodes the relational features (AB or $ABFR$) and outputs are target values. Figure 4 is a diagrammatic representation of how the structure and parameters of the neural network are identified. The procedure to learn the deep network requires the setting of various parameters such as (a) number of hidden layers, (b) size[5] of each hidden layers, (c) loss function, (d) evaluation metric. Further discussion on parameter setting is as follows.

Parameters. We use the same procedure for selecting the structure of the deep network for both classification and regression problems except a few hyperparameters. Many of the hyperparameters are automatically decided by the optimizer. The choice of initial values remains as arbitrary since there is no theory in deep learning to guide in this aspect. The deep networks are fully connected multilayer perceptrons. The number of inputs in the deep net is the number of relational features obtained by the procedure described earlier (for the experiments here this is restricted to a maximum of 5000 features,

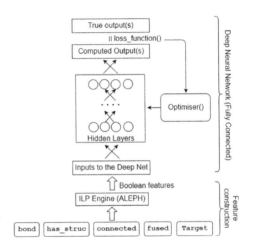

Fig. 4. Diagrammatic Representation of Deep Relational Machine (DRM)

obtained from clauses containing no more than 3 literals in the body). In principle, a neural net with a small number of hidden neurons should be sufficient to deal with learning the input–output mapping function: we allow networks varying from 1 to 4 hidden layers. The number of neurons in each hidden layer is from a small set (here $\{5, 10\}$). Therefore, network architectures have the following structures: (1) $IL - HL\{5, 10\} - OL$, (2) $IL - HL\{5, 10\} - HL\{5, 10\} - OL$, (3) $IL - HL\{5, 10\} - HL\{5, 10\} - HL\{5, 10\} - OL$, and (4) $IL - HL\{5, 10\} - HL\{5, 10\} - HL\{5, 10\} - HL\{5, 10\} - OL$. So, the number of networks evaluated for each problem is $(2 + 4 + 8 + 16) = 30$. For the classification problem, the hidden units (neurons) are rectified linear units and the output units use softmax activation. For the regression problem, both hidden and output units use linear activation. The dropout rate is fixed at 0.50. The number of maximum

---

[5] Size refers to the number of neurons.

training epochs is 1200 for classification and 5000 for the regression problem. The loss functions are cross-entropy (for classification) and mean-squared-error (mse) (for regression). We use an Adam Optimiser [24] with following parameters for learning the synaptic weights in the deep net. The learning rate is fixed at 0.001 and other parameters are $\beta_1 = 0.9$, $\beta_2 = 0.999$, $\epsilon = 10^{-8}$, $decay = 0$. The evaluation metrics are accuracy (for classification) and mse (for regression).

For a fair comparison with the state-of-the-art results, we chose an identical evaluation strategy as in [6,20] for the DRM. In the classification problem, the evaluation is based on a randomly drawn test set consisting of 30% of instances and in the regression problem, the evaluation is based on 10-fold cross-validation. The computational time spent on these evaluations (training and test) would not be a reasonable benchmark for comparison as there are several architectural parameters that can affect the computational time. Three most important parameters are: the number of HLs and sizes, size of IL and epoch. The computational complexity of the deep net is studied in earlier works such as [25].

3.5   State-of-the-Art

The state-of-the-art for the classification problems are the results reported on the use of lifted relational neural networks (LRNNs) [6]. The first layer of the LRNN is a set of fact neurons representing ground facts. The subsequent layers are atom neurons representing ground atoms, and rule neurons representing ground rules. The rules neurons can be further combined with the help of aggregator function at aggregator neurons which can further generate an atom neuron or output value. Each example was represented in terms of atom-bond features. These results use the equivalent of the AB representation used here.

The state-of-the-art for the regression problems are the results reported in extensive Meta-QSAR study [20]. Our interest in this paper is in the results reported for the neural network models, which use Boolean "fingerprint" (FP) features as inputs. The FP features used in these studies are pharmacophore features (FCFP4 fingerprint representation) of the compounds. Pharmacophoric features include all binding related structural or chemical properties of chemical compounds that are thought to be responsible for a specific pharmacological action. Chemical features, which are taken into account usually include hydrogen bond donor/acceptor, charge, hydrophobicity, and aromacity. In the Meta-QSAR study, these features (or pharmacophoric properties) were used to represent each chemical compound. In Meta-QSAR the number of such features is 1024 and is obtained by using the BIOVIA software [26]. We note that the FP features use 3-d information that is not part of the $ABFR$ representation. The FCFP4 fingerprint also includes boolean features representing presence/absence of molecular substructures.

3.6   Results

The results of the experiments[6] here are in Figs. 5 and 6. The principal qualitative conclusions from these tabulations are these:

1. For both classification and regression problems, DRM performance is mostly better the best reports in the literature, suggesting that the DRM benchmark is not just a straw man; and
2. The inclusion of background predicates makes a substantial difference to DRM performance, suggesting that DRMS are able to utilise domain knowledge to improve performance, without requiring an increase in data.

The appropriate test for a quantitative assessment of the differences observed is the Wilcoxon signed-rank test. Figure 7 tabulates some summary statistics of the differences observed in Figs. 5 and 6 ("wins" and "losses": the Wilcoxon test uses the actual differences associated with a win and a loss). The null hypothesis is that the predictors being compared have performance values from the same population (that is, differences in performance will be symmetrically distributed around 0). For the actual differences observed, the P-values are as tabulated in Fig. 7 which suggests the state-of-the-art is either no better than DRMs.[7] Also, the inclusion of background knowledge clearly makes a significant difference to the performance of a DRM.

Of more interest than to a practitioner is not the comparisons in Fig. 7, but how a DRM performs when provided with not just the relational features found by an ILP engine, but also other data available to it. We are able to assess the performance of such an "extended DRM" on the regression problems, by augmenting the ABFR features with the FP (fingerprint) features used in the QSAR study. We show the performance of the extended DRM on the bottom 30-percentile of results using a DRM with only ABFR features. The results in Fig. 8 suggests that extended DRMs may perform better than a neural network that uses only ILP-derived features.

Limitations of DRM. We turn now on how and why we expect DRM performance to be bettered, even when there is sufficient background knowledge. DRMs share the principal limitations of propositionalisation approaches to ILP problems, namely: (a) Much depends on the expressive power of the features used as input; (b) For any language with sufficient expressive power, it is intractable

---

[6] All the experiments (feature construction and deep learning) are conducted in Linux based machines with 64GB main memory, 16 processing cores, 2GB NVIDIA Graphics Processing Units. We used Python based Keras [27] with Tensorflow as backend [28] for implementing deep nets.

[7] We are adopting this more conservative stand despite low P values for two reasons. First, we note that LRNNs only use the equivalent of the AB representation: we would, therefore, expect their performance to improve if provided with relations in the $ABFR$ representation. Secondly, the reader is no doubt aware of the usual precautions when interpreting P-values obtained from multiple comparisons.

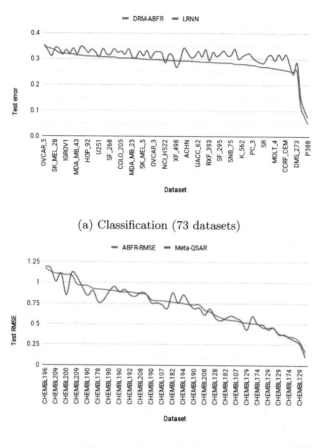

(a) Classification (73 datasets)

(b) Regression (50 datasets)

Fig. 5. DRM (*ABFR*) performance for classification and regression (X-axis: datasets, Y-axis error on test data). For classification, we show the test performance of LRNNs [6] and for regression, the test performance of neural-networks results reported in the Meta-QSAR study, using fingerprint features. (We have not shown error bars for clarity: but these are small, given the sizes of test-sets involved.)

to provide all features within the language; and (c) Recursive definitions for prediction are not necessary, and that the background knowledge is assumed to be sufficient. Of these, we set aside (c) as being a constraint inherent to this form of modelling, and focus instead on the first two limitations.

Practitioners of ILP will be well aware of relational composition of features by sharing existential variables. Thus, in the well-known train-spotting problem posed by Michalski, let us assume that we have the features $F_1 : \forall x(East(x) \leftarrow \exists y(HasCar(x, y), Short(y)))$ and $F_2 : \forall x(East(x) \leftarrow \exists y(HasCar(x, y), Closed(y)))$. Then, depending on the data, the DRM's

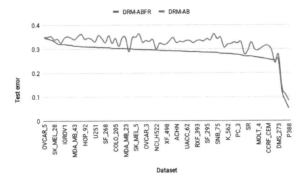

Fig. 6. Degradation of DRM performance with insufficient background knowledge (using AB instead of ABFR). The results for regression are similar.

Task	Comparison		
	versus	Win ratio (%)	P-value
Classification	DRM(AB) vs LRNN [6]	12/73 (17%)	< 0.0001
	DRM($ABFR$) vs LRNN [6]	66/73 (90%)	< 0.0001
Regression	DRM(AB) vs Meta-QSAR [20]	3/50 (6%)	< 0.0001
	DRM($ABFR$) vs Meta-QSAR [20]	22/50 (44%)	= 0.0582

Fig. 7. Quantitative comparison of methods. In a comparison of X vs Y, a "win" denotes the number of times the error of X is lower than Y

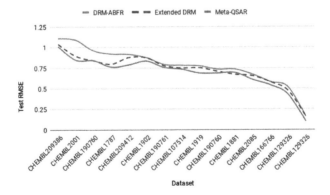

Fig. 8. Performance of Extended DRM: Effect of feature enrichment in DRM for worst and best performing datasets for DRM($ABFR$). All the 15 X-axis labels are shown.

internal layer may not be able to distinguish correctly between F : $\forall x(East(x) \leftarrow \exists y(HasCar(x, y), Short(y), Closed(y)))$ and F' : $\forall x(East(x) \leftarrow \exists y, z(HasCar(x, y), HasCar(x, z), Short(y), Closed(z)))$. This means that to correctly capture shared relationships, we have to ensure that there we include such features at the input layer (in this example, F will have to be provided as an input feature). Neural models that attempt explicitly to capture relationships among variables will not suffer from this limitation (separate internal nodes would represent F and F' for example, given F_1 and F_2 as input features). In [12] classes of features with varying expressive power were identified. Figure 9 shows a significant drop in DRM performance when input features are drawn from the class of "simple" features (see (all features in the unrestricted class of features can be constructed from some combination of features from the simple class: see [12,29]. This suggests that DRMs require features from a fairly expressive class: we conjecture that features provided to the DRM have to be at least from the class of *independent* features identified in [12] for them to have reasonable performance. This brings in the second of the limitations listed above. Despite recent advances in commodity hardware capabilities, the number of input features for the datasets here for the class of independent features can range from the 10s of 1000s to the 100s of 1000s, even when features are restricted to containing no more than 3 literals, as was done here. This is beyond the routine capabilities of the existing hardware support for deep networks, and some form of selection appears inevitable, along with the resulting limitations that result. Current commodity hardware does not allow us to practically use more features than a few thousand.

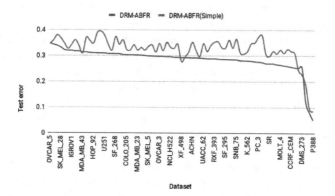

Fig. 9. Degradation of DRM performance when expressivity of features is decreased from an unrestricted class to the class of simple features

4   Concluding Remarks

In this paper, it is our intent to establish some benchmarks for comparative study in the emerging area of neural-network models for relational problems. The results here present substantial statistical evidence that: (a) Despite their apparent simplicity, the predictive performance of DRMs represent substantial high-water marks for relational problems of classification and regression (but more on this below); (b) a DRM's performance improves significantly with the inclusion of domain knowledge; and (c) DRM's performance can degrade significantly if features are not drawn from a sufficiently expressive language.

More generally, within the ILP literature, the continued utility of some established datasets on structure-activity prediction has been questioned [30]. Problems like the prediction of mutagenesis allowed ILP systems to move from determinate to non-determinate background knowledge. The datasets here, ostensibly also dealing with structure-activity relations, serve a different purpose. Here the emphasis is on a scale: we want to be able to test hypotheses on large amounts of data; we want to models to use large amounts of background knowledge, and we want to address prediction problems that are both nominal and numeric. We suggest that the problems and data used in this paper could replace mutagenesis and related tasks as ILP benchmarks for the future. We do not, of course, suggest that these datasets act as benchmarks for problems requiring either the construction of recursive definitions or invention of new background knowledge.

There are several ways in which the work here can be extended. First, the comparisons against the literature can be done better or done differently. Better by obtaining results from very recent techniques like ∂-ILP, which do not need propositionalisation.[8] The comparison against LRNN reported here is also not fair, since that method does not have access to the large quantities of background knowledge we have used: we would expect LRNN to perform better if this knowledge was provided to it. The comparisons could be done differently for the regression problems, by augmenting the DRM's relational features with those used in the Meta-QSAR comparison. If this is done for each of the prediction techniques used in that comparative study, we would be in a position to judge the utility of relational features for each of those prediction techniques. Also, we have not considered here how the performance changes with the number of features and number of inputs. This has to be explored. Since our intention was to establish a benchmark for neuro-symbolic learning, we have not really examined other non-neural learning algorithms such as random forest (RF) given the same features. It would be general machine learning interest on how RF perform with the same set of features, and how standard ILP algorithms such TILDE does, given the same background knowledge. Second, the choice of features can be better than the simple random sample we have used. In [31], a sampling technique is described that with high probability will result in high-utility features. It is naturally relevant to investigate the performance of DRMs with features drawn with this form of sampling. Finally, the problems here have only been concerned

---

[8] We have contacted the authors proposing ways to conduct this comparison.

with discriminatory models. It is of interest, especially for optimisation problems like those described in [32], to examine the performance of generative deep networks with relational features as inputs.

Dataset Availability

The datasets for *ABFR* features (in ARFF format) for both classification and regression problems are available at https://github.com/tirtharajdash/ILP2018_DRM. The hierarchy used in the background knowledge is also available in this link.

Acknowledgments. A.S. is a Visiting Professorial Fellow, School of CSE, UNSW Sydney. A.S. is supported by the SERB grant EMR/2016/002766. RDK is supported by Indian National Science Academy's Dr. V. Ramalingaswamy Chair award. We thank the following for their invaluable assistance: researchers at the DTAI, University of Leuven, for suggestions on how to use the background knowledge within DMAX; Ing. Gustav Sourek (Czech Technical University, Prague) and Dr. Ivan Olier Caparroso (Liverpool John Moores University, UK) for providing the dataset information and scores.

References

1. Lodhi, H.: Deep relational machines. In: Lee, M., Hirose, A., Hou, Z.-G., Kil, R.M. (eds.) ICONIP 2013. LNCS, vol. 8227, pp. 212–219. Springer, Heidelberg (2013). https://doi.org/10.1007/978-3-642-42042-9_27
2. Vig, L., Srinivasan, A., Bain, M., Verma, A.: An Investigation into the role of domain-knowledge on the use of embeddings. In: Lachiche, N., Vrain, C. (eds.) ILP 2017. LNCS (LNAI), vol. 10759, pp. 169–183. Springer, Cham (2018). https://doi.org/10.1007/978-3-319-78090-0_12
3. Towell, G.G., Shavlik, J.W.: Knowledge-based artificial neural networks. Artif. Intell. **70**(1–2), 119–165 (1994)
4. d'Avila Garcez, S., Broda, K.B., Gabbay, D.M.: Neural-symbolic Learning Systems: Foundations and Applications. Springer, London (2012). https://doi.org/10.1007/978-1-4471-0211-3
5. Gust, H., Hagmayer, Y., Kuhnberger, K.U., Sloman, S.: Learning symbolic inferences with neural networks. In: Proceedings of the Annual Meeting of the Cognitive Science Society, vol. 27 (2005)
6. Sourek, G., Aschenbrenner, V., Zelezny, F., Kuzelka, O.: Lifted relational neural networks. arXiv preprint arXiv:1508.05128 (2015)
7. Evans, R., Grefenstette, E.: Learning explanatory rules from noisy data. J. Artif. Intell. Res. **61**, 1–64 (2018)
8. Lavrač, N., Džeroski, S., Grobelnik, M.: Learning nonrecursive definitions of relations with linus. In: Kodratoff, Y. (ed.) EWSL 1991. LNCS, vol. 482, pp. 265–281. Springer, Heidelberg (1991). https://doi.org/10.1007/BFb0017020
9. Faruquie, T.A., Srinivasan, A., King, R.D.: Topic models with relational features for drug design. In: Riguzzi, F., Železný, F. (eds.) ILP 2012. LNCS (LNAI), vol. 7842, pp. 45–57. Springer, Heidelberg (2013). https://doi.org/10.1007/978-3-642-38812-5_4

10. Joshi, S., Ramakrishnan, G., Srinivasan, A.: Feature construction using theory-guided sampling and randomised search. In: Železný, F., Lavrač, N. (eds.) ILP 2008. LNCS (LNAI), vol. 5194, pp. 140–157. Springer, Heidelberg (2008). https://doi.org/10.1007/978-3-540-85928-4_14

11. Ramakrishnan, G., Joshi, S., Balakrishnan, S., Srinivasan, A.: Using ILP to construct features for information extraction from semi-structured text. In: Blockeel, H., Ramon, J., Shavlik, J., Tadepalli, P. (eds.) ILP 2007. LNCS (LNAI), vol. 4894, pp. 211–224. Springer, Heidelberg (2008). https://doi.org/10.1007/978-3-540-78469-2_22

12. Saha, A., Srinivasan, A., Ramakrishnan, G.: What kinds of relational features are useful for statistical learning? In: Riguzzi, F., Železný, F. (eds.) ILP 2012. LNCS (LNAI), vol. 7842, pp. 209–224. Springer, Heidelberg (2013). https://doi.org/10.1007/978-3-642-38812-5_15

13. Specia, L., Srinivasan, A., Joshi, S., Ramakrishnan, G., das Graças Volpe Nunes, M.: An investigation into feature construction to assist word sense disambiguation. Mach. Learn. **76**(1), 109–136 (2009). https://doi.org/10.1007/s10994-009-5114-x

14. Srinivasan, A., King, R.D.: Feature construction with inductive logic programming: a study of quantitative predictions of biological activity by structural attributes. In: Muggleton, S. (ed.) ILP 1996. LNCS, vol. 1314, pp. 89–104. Springer, Heidelberg (1997). https://doi.org/10.1007/3-540-63494-0_50

15. França, M.V.M., Zaverucha, G., Garcez, A.: Neural relational learning through semi-propositionalization of bottom clauses. In: AAAI Spring Symposium Series (2015)

16. Muggleton, S.: Inverse entailment and progol. New Gener. Comput. **13**(3–4), 245–286 (1995)

17. Plotkin, G.: Automatic Methods of Inductive Inference. Ph.D. thesis, Edinburgh University, August 1971

18. Marx, K.A., O'Neil, P., Hoffman, P., Ujwal, M.: Data mining the NCI cancer cell line compound GI50 values: identifying quinone subtypes effective against melanoma and leukemia cell classes. J. Chem. Inf. Comput. Sci. **43**(5), 1652–1667 (2003)

19. Ralaivola, L., Swamidass, S.J., Saigo, H., Baldi, P.: Graph kernels for chemical informatics. Neural Netw. **18**(8), 1093–1110 (2005)

20. Olier, I., Sadawi, N., Bickerton, G.R., Vanschoren, J., Grosan, C., Soldatova, L., King, R.D.: Meta-QSAR: a large-scale application of meta-learning to drug design and discovery. Mach. Learn., pp. 1–27 (2018)

21. Van Craenenbroeck, E.; Vandecasteele, H.D.L.: Dmax's functional group and ring library (2002). https://dtai.cs.kuleuven.be/software/dmax/

22. Ando, H.Y., Dehaspe, L., Luyten, W., Van Craenenbroeck, E., Vandecasteele, H., Van Meervelt, L.: Discovering h-bonding rules in crystals with inductive logic programming. Mol. Pharm. **3**(6), 665–674 (2006)

23. Grave, K.D., Costa, F.: Molecular graph augmentation with rings and functional groups. J. Chem. Inf. Model. **50**(9), 1660–1668 (2010)

24. Kingma, D.P., Ba, J.: Adam: A method for stochastic optimization. arXiv preprint arXiv:1412.6980 (2014)

25. Bianchini, M., Scarselli, F.: On the complexity of shallow and deep neural network classifiers. In: ESANN (2014)

26. Rogers, D., Hahn, M.: Extended-connectivity fingerprints. J. Chem. Inf. Model. **50**(5), 742–754 (2010)

27. Chollet, F., et al.: Keras (2015). https://keras.io

28. Abadi, M., Agarwal, A., et al.: TensorFlow: Large-scale machine learning on heterogeneous systems (2015), Software available from tensorflow.org. https://www.tensorflow.org/

29. McCreath, E., Sharma, A.: LIME: a system for learning relations. In: Richter, M.M., Smith, C.H., Wiehagen, R., Zeugmann, T. (eds.) ALT 1998. LNCS (LNAI), vol. 1501, pp. 336–374. Springer, Heidelberg (1998). https://doi.org/10.1007/3-540-49730-7_25

30. Lodhi, H., Muggleton, S.: Is mutagenesis still challenging. In: Proceedings of the 15th International Conference on Inductive Logic Programming, ILP, pp. 35–40. Citeseer (2005)

31. Dash, T., Joshi, R.S., Baskar, A., Srinivasan, A.: Some distributional results for discrete stochastic search. In: Submitted to Asian Conference on Machine Learning (ACML) (2018)

32. Srinivasan, A., Ramakrishnan, G.: Parameter screening and optimisation for ILP using designed experiments. J. Mach. Learn. Res. **12**, 627–662 (2011). http://portal.acm.org/citation.cfm?id=1953067

How Much Can Experimental Cost Be Reduced in Active Learning of Agent Strategies?

Céline Hocquette[(✉)] and Stephen Muggleton

Department of Computing, Imperial College London, London, UK
{celine.hocquette16, s.muggleton}@imperial.ac.uk

Abstract. In science, experiments are empirical observations allowing for the arbitration of competing hypotheses and knowledge acquisition. For a scientist that aims at learning an agent strategy, performing experiments involves costs. To that extent, the efficiency of a learning process relies on the number of experiments performed. We study in this article how the cost of experimentation can be reduced with active learning to learn efficient agent strategies. We consider an extension of the meta-interpretive learning framework that allocates a Bayesian posterior distribution over the hypothesis space. At each iteration, the learner queries the label of the instance with maximum entropy. This produces the maximal discriminative over the remaining competing hypotheses, and thus achieves the highest shrinkage of the version space. We study the theoretical framework and evaluate the gain on the cost of experimentation for the task of learning regular grammars and agent strategies: our results demonstrate the number of experiments to perform to reach an arbitrary accuracy level can at least be halved.

Keywords: Bayesian meta-interpretive learning · Active learning
Agent-based modelling

1 Introduction

Once a honeybee has found a rich source of pollen, it shares its location with other members of the colony by executing a particular figure called waggle dance [16]. It guides the search for other bees toward flowers yielding nectar and pollen and thus enhances the efficiency of the colony foraging strategy.

More broadly, strategies are general programs aimed at achieving particular goals from a multiplicity of initial states. When a scientist models animal behaviours or other strategies, the learning process generally requires selecting and conducting many experiments, with associated costs. Thus, learning efficiency relies on the sum of the costs of the performed experiments. We investigate in this work how much the experimental cost can be reduced with active

---

The original version of this chapter was revised: The authors affiliation was corrected. The correction to this chapter is available at https://doi.org/10.1007/978-3-319-99960-9_11

© Springer Nature Switzerland AG 2018
F. Riguzzi et al. (Eds.): ILP 2018, LNAI 11105, pp. 38–53, 2018.
https://doi.org/10.1007/978-3-319-99960-9_3

learning to learn agent strategies. An active learner is allowed to actively choose the experiments to perform to acquire knowledge during the learning process. Furthermore, in real-world situations, strategies should be resource-efficient to be beneficial for agents. Therefore, we additionally want to converge toward efficient strategies.

waggle dance

initial state: [position(5),hive_position(5),flower_position(8), waggle_dance(east),energy(5), weight(0)]
final state: [position(8),hive_position(5),flower_position(8), waggle_dance(east),energy(2), weight(1)]

waggle dance

initial state: [position(5),hive_position(5),flower_position(1), waggle_dance(west),energy(9), weight(0)]
final state: [position(?),hive_position(5),flower_position(1), waggle_dance(west),energy(?), weight(?)]

(a) First observation: the bee starts at the hive with no weight carried and ends up at the flower carrying pollen

(c) Second observation, no matter its outcome, it is discriminative for the competing hypotheses of Figure 1b

Hypothesis 1	Hypothesis 2
f(A,B):-f1(A,C),grab(C,B). f1(A,B):-until(A,B,at_flower,move_right).	f(A,B):-f2(A,C),grab(C,B). f2(A,B):-until(A,B,at_flower,f1). f1(A,B):-ifthenelse(A,B,waggle_east,move_right,move_left).

(b) Two competing hypotheses for the first observation of Figure 1a

Fig. 1. Observations of a bee behaviour

In Sect. 6, we learn a general strategy for a bee to find pollen in an environment. Learnt strategies are logic programs built from observations of bee behaviour. Observations are labelled as positive if the goal is fulfilled and negative otherwise. Figure 1a represents a positive observation: the waggle dance indicates that a flower is at the right of the hive, the bee flies in this direction and finds pollen. Several hypotheses can be inferred from it, among them the two represented in Fig. 1b. To discriminate between them, the experiment of Fig. 1c could be performed. The flower is now on the left, which is indicated by the waggle dance. No matter its outcome, positive or negative, it would eliminate one of these two hypotheses. Therefore, it is an informative query.

Meta-Interpretive Learning (MIL) has been demonstrated to be a suitable paradigm to learn strategies since it supports predicate invention and the learning of recursive programs [22,24]. Given the observations so far, consistent hypotheses are built from a set of metarules and the background knowledge. A Bayesian posterior distribution is implemented over the hypothesis space [23] and introduces a bias toward hypotheses with lowest complexity. The learner computes at each iteration the entropies of the possible experiments given the current hypothesis space and the prior distribution. The instance with maximum entropy is selected: it is the most discriminative between the remaining competing hypotheses. This process is resumed and more experiments are performed until some target accuracy is reached.

Specifically, our contributions are the introduction of a framework for learning efficient agent strategies with active learning and for reducing the associated cost of experimentation. We describe its implementation. We also evaluate theoretically the expected gain in entropy, and demonstrate experimentally that

Bayesian MIL Active Learning converges faster toward efficient agent strategies than a passive learner in the same conditions.

This article is organised as follows. Section 2 reviews some related work. Section 3 describes the framework used in this paper together with the learning protocol. Section 4 details a theoretical analysis. Section 5 describes the implementation. Section 6 reports experiments in learning regular grammars and bee strategies. Finally, we conclude and discuss further work in Sect. 7.

2   Related Work

Active Learning. Active Learning is a protocol in which the learner is able to choose the data from which it learns by accessing an oracle. It contrasts with passive learning for which the labeled data is selected at random. The objective in active learning is to learn a model with high accuracy while ideally making fewer queries than the number of random data required by a passive learner to achieve the same accuracy level. It has been widely studied for identifying classifiers [27] and different query strategy frameworks have been introduced.

In the membership query setting, the learner is allowed to ask for the label of any points of the instance space, even artificially generated ones [1,2]. However, newly synthesized instances may be uninterpretable by human oracles. An alternative is stream-based selective sampling: the learner can sample from the instance distribution and decide whether to label or discard each sample instance [12]. A variant is to directly sample from a subpart of the instance space that is the most informative [4]. We focus in this work on pool-based active learning: the learner has access to a large number of initial unlabelled data points, and to an oracle which can provide the label of any of these points on request [20].

Several measures have been suggested for evaluating the shrinkage of the hypothesis space during the learning process and thus measuring the benefits of active learning over passive learning. The main ones are the diameter of the version space [11,29], the measure of the region of disagreement [13,14], the metric entropy [18] and the size of the version space [10,21] which inspired this paper. We will more specifically operate in a Bayesian setting [10,12] that benefits from a prior distribution over the hypothesis space.

Active Learning have been widely used for classification, although there are different applications: version space approaches have been considered for object detection in computer vision [26]. Similarly, the system presented in this article is based upon active learning for devising experiments to rule out hypotheses from the version space. However, our approach is different from the work presented above since we use active learning within the construction of logic programs and for learning agent strategies in a Bayesian setting.

Decision Trees. A search strategy can be represented by a tree whose internal nodes are experiments and whose leaves are hypotheses: minimizing the number of queries means building a tree of minimum average size. In that case, it has been shown that the performances of a greedy strategy are not worst than any other strategy for minimizing the number of label queries [10]. Moreover, the expected depth of any binary decision tree is lower bounded by the entropy of the prior distribution [5].

Combining Active Learning with Inductive Logic Programming. In [28], Inductive Logic Programming (ILP) has been combined with Active Learning for two non-classification tasks in natural language processing: semantic parsing and information extraction. Also, a closed loop Machine Learning system for Scientific Discovery applications is described in [3,17]: a robot scientist is introduced, it autonomously proposes and performs a sequence of experiments which minimises the expected cost of experimentation for converging upon an accurate hypothesis generated with ILP. Conversely, our work aims at learning efficient agent strategies.

Learning Efficient Strategies. A general framework for learning optimal resource complexity robot strategies is presented in [6]. It has been extended into *Metaopt* [8], an ILP system that learns minimal cost logic programs by adding a general cost function into the meta-interpreter. By contrast, our work focuses on another aspect of the learning efficiency: we investigate how to reduced experimental costs for learning efficient agent strategies.

Relational Reinforcement Learning. A challenge in reinforcement learning is the exploration/exploitation trade-off. In [19], the authors present relational exploration strategies: the generalisation of learnt knowledge over unobserved instances in relational worlds allows a generalisation of the notion of known states compared to propositional settings. It can also applied to largest domains. In [25], Active Learning is used to select actions to perform for reaching states that will enforce a revision of the current model. It is shown that the integration of Active Learning improves learning speed: an accurate action model is obtained after performing much less actions than when using random exploration only.

To the authors' best knowledge, this is the first time active learning is integrated with Bayesian MIL to devise a sequence of experiments to perform for learning efficient strategies with reduced experimental costs.

3   Theoretical Framework

3.1   Notations

Let $\mathcal{X}$ be the instance space, and $\mathcal{H}$ a concept class over the instance space $\mathcal{X}$. We consider a probability distribution $\Pi_{\mathcal{X}}$ over the instance space $\mathcal{X}$ and a probability distribution $\Pi_{\mathcal{H}}$ over the hypothesis space $\mathcal{H}$. We assume that the target hypothesis $\bar{H}$ is drawn from $\mathcal{H}$ and according to $\Pi_{\mathcal{H}}$. We call $E_m = \{e_0, ..., e_m\}$ the set of examples selected up to the iteration m. The version space V_m is the set of hypotheses $H \in \mathcal{H}$ consistent with E_m, therefore $V_m \subset \mathcal{H}$.

3.2   Meta-Interpretive Learning (MIL)

MIL is a form of ILP [22,24]. The learner is given a set of examples E and a background knowledge B composed of a set of Prolog definitions B_p and metarules M such that $B = B_p \cup M$. The goal is to generate a hypothesis H such that $B, H \models E$. The proof is based upon an adapted Prolog meta-interpreter. It first attempts to prove the examples considered deductively. Failing this, it unifies the head of a metarule with the goal, and saves the resulting meta-substitution. The body and then the other examples are similarly proved. The meta-substitutions recovered for each successful proofs are saved and can be used into further proofs by substituting them into their corresponding metarules. For example, the first clause of the learned hypothesis on Fig. 1 `f(A,B):-f1(A,C),grab(C,B).` has been derived from the metarule *chain rule* detailed in Fig. 2a and by applying the meta-substitution `[f/2,f1/2,grab/2]`.

Two key features of MIL are that it supports predicate invention and the learning of recursive programs. The former enables decomposition of the learned logic program into new sub-actions. The latter allows to learn more general programs and with shorter lengths. Both makes MIL well suited for learning strategies.

The choice of metarules induces a declarative bias on the hypothesis space since it determines the structure of learnable programs: an appropriate choice helps minimising the number of clauses in the consistent hypotheses [7]. Also, the use of higher-order Abstractions supports learning more compact programs [9]. We focus in this work on learning logic programs built from the metarules *chain rule*, *precondition* and *postcondition*, whose description is available on the Fig. 2a. Indeed, this set of metarules is enough to learn the class of dyadic logic programs investigated in this paper. The first experiment tackles the task of learning regular grammars, and metarules for finite state acceptors can be expressed with *chain rule* and *postcondition* only, as shown on Fig. 2b. The second experiment considers the task of learning agent strategies. Fluents are treated as monadic predicates which apply to a situation, while actions are dyadic predicates which transform one situation to another. We will use $Metagol_{AI}$ which supports Abstractions and Inventions [9]. We use the two abstractions *until/4* and *ifthenelse/5* (Fig. 2b) to reduce the complexity of the learned programs: *until/4* represents a recursive call to the action Ac while some condition $Cond$ is not fulfilled and *ifthenelse/5* expresses a choice between the actions $Then$ and $Else$ based upon the realisation of the condition $Cond$. Similarly, these Abstractions can be expressed with the *chain rule*, *precondition* and *postcondition* only as shown on the Fig. 2b.

3.3   Complexity of an Hypothesis

The hypotheses generated with MIL differ by their complexity. We distinguish two notions of complexity for a logic program H. The textual complexity relies on Occam's principle and represents the length $l(H)$ of H measured as its number of clauses. However, textually smaller programs are not necessarily the more

Name	Metarule
chain rule	$P(A, B) \leftarrow Q(A, C), R(C, B).$
precondition	$P(A, B) \leftarrow Q(A), R(A, B).$
postcondition	$P(A, B) \leftarrow Q(A, B), R(B).$

(a) General metarules

Exp.	Name	Metarule
1	*acceptor*	$Q(A, B) \leftarrow eq(A, B), acceptor(B).$
	delta	$Q0(A, B) \leftarrow zero(A, C), Q1(C, B).$
		$Q0(A, B) \leftarrow one(A, C), Q1(C, B).$
2	*until*	$until(A, B, Cond, Ac) \leftarrow Ac(A, B), Cond(B).$
		$until(A, B, Cond, Ac) \leftarrow F(A, C), until(C, B, Cond, Ac).$
	ifthenelse	$Ifthenelse(A, B, Cond, Then, Else) \leftarrow Cond(A), Then(A, B).$
		$Ifthenelse(A, B, Cond, Then, Else) \leftarrow Else(A, C), eq(C, B).$

(b) Metarules used in the experiments

Fig. 2. Metarules considered: the class of dyadic logic program studied in this work can be expressed with *chain rule*, *precondition* and *postcondition* only

efficient. The resource complexity $r(H)$ of an agent strategy [6] represents the amount of resources (eg: energy) consumed by the agent while executing the strategy, and can be evaluated as the sum of the actions costs in applying H to transform an initial state into a final state. In the following, we will combine the textual complexity with the resource complexity to learn efficient strategies in terms of a global complexity:

$$c(H) = l(H) + r(H)$$

3.4   Bayesian Prior Distribution

The preference for hypotheses with lowest complexity is encoded in a prior distribution which induces a bias over the hypothesis space and favors more efficient strategies. We consider the framework described in [23]. A Bayesian prior probability is defined for any H in $\mathcal{H}$ from the complexity $c(H)$ as follows and for $\frac{1}{a} = \sum_{i=1}^{\infty} \frac{1}{i^2} = \frac{\pi^2}{6}$ normalisation constant:

$$\Pi_{\mathcal{H}}(\{H \mid c(H) = k\}) = \frac{a}{k^2}$$

Moreover, given a background knowledge B and a set of examples E, the likelihood of E is:

$$p(E \mid B, H) = \begin{cases} 1 \text{ if } B, H \models E \\ 0 \text{ else} \end{cases}$$

According to Bayes's theorem, the posterior is then given by:

$$p(H \mid B, E) = \frac{\Pi_{\mathcal{H}}(H) p(E \mid B, H)}{c}$$

The denominator c is a normalization constant. Therefore, the posterior $p(H \mid B, E)$ is proportional to the prior $\Pi_{\mathcal{H}}(H)$. The MAP hypothesis H_{MAP} is defined as $H_{MAP} = \underset{H}{\text{argmax}}(p(H \mid B, E))$.

3.5   Active Learning

A set of N instances is initially sampled from $\mathcal{X}$. The active learner conducts at each iteration $m + 1$ an experiment in which it chooses the next instance e_{m+1} among this set and observes its label returned by an oracle. This information helps discriminating between the competing hypotheses built as described previously since it rules out some proportion of the version space V_m that is not consistent with it. The shrinkage of the hypothesis space is measured by the ratio $\frac{\Pi_{\mathcal{H}}(V_{m+1})}{\Pi_{\mathcal{H}}(V_m)}$. We associate to each sampled instance e a probability p_e:

$$p(e) = \frac{\min(\Pi_{\mathcal{H}}(\{H \in V_m \mid H(e) = 1\}), \Pi_{\mathcal{H}}(\{H \in V_m \mid H(e) = 0\})}{\Pi_{\mathcal{H}}(V_m)}$$

This value represents the minimal reduction ratio over the version space induced by the query of the instance e. Moreover, it was noted in [21] that in general, the optimal query strategy is to select an instance covered by half of the the version space. Indeed, no matter its true label, it would halve the version space. Therefore, the query strategy chosen is to select the instance e_m for which $p(e)$ is the closest to $\frac{1}{2}$, that is for which the entropy $ent(p(e))$ is maximal:

$$e_m = \underset{e}{\text{argmax}}(ent(p(e))) \text{ with } ent(p(e)) = -p(e)log(p(e)) - (1-p(e))log(1-p(e))$$

From an information-theory point of view, the expected entropy of $p(e_m)$ is the expected information gain from the label of e_m [15]. In that case, the instance selected is the most informative from the learner's point of view, since it is the most discriminative given the current version space. However, active learning with entropy based querying strategy can be used with different kind of hypotheses and therefore is not specific to ILP.

3.6   Learning Protocol

The learning protocol is summarised in the Figs. 3 and 4 and represents how the learner acquires information. First, a pool of N instances is randomly sampled. The training set is initialised with one positive instance randomly selected. At each iteration, a fresh new set of K hypotheses consistent with the examples of the training set is sampled. The entropy of each instance from the pool is computed given the set of sampled hypotheses. The instance with maximum entropy is selected. An oracle provides its label, and it is added to the training set. This process is resumed until the maximum number of iterations is reached.

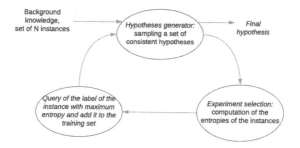

Fig. 3. Diagram of the framework studied: active learning is integrated within the MIL framework

```
Inputs: oracle O, N, K, I
1. Sample N instances from the instance space
2. Initialization: randomly select a positive initial instance
3. While the number of experiments is lower than I:
 - Sample K hypotheses from the hypotheses space
 - Select the instance with maximum entropy
 - Query its label to the oracle O and add it to the training set
Output: hypothesis H with the lowest complexity from the sampled set
```

Fig. 4. Pseudo-code of the framework studied

4   Theoretical Analysis

We evaluate the instantaneous expected gain on entropy, which represents the expected reduction of the hypothesis space at one iteration. We assume that the target hypothesis $\bar{H}$ is drawn from $\mathcal{H}$. Each instance e from $\mathcal{X}$ is associated a probability $p(e)$. We consider an arbitrary probability distribution $\mathcal{D}$ over $\mathcal{X}$ at some iteration m, that is bounded in $[0, \frac{1}{2}]$.

Lemma 1. *A set of N instances $\{x_1, ... x_N\}$ is randomly sampled from the instance space $\mathcal{X}$. The active learner selects the instance x_i with maximum entropy among this sample set of size N. Then, the probability of selecting an instance with maximal entropy on $\mathcal{D}$ is N times the one of a passive learner in the same conditions.*

Proof. Let's take $\epsilon > 0$, p_ϵ is set to the probability number in $[0, \frac{1}{2}]$ such that a ϵ-proportion of the instance space has a probability greater or equal to p_ϵ. Let's call $p(x_i)$ the probability of the instance selected. Then $p(x_i) < p_\epsilon$ if and only if every instance from the sample set has a probability smaller than p_ϵ. The instances being independently sampled, it can be written as following:

$$p(p(x_i) < p_\epsilon) = p(p(x_1) < p_\epsilon, ..., p(x_N) < p_\epsilon) = \prod_{k=1}^{N} p(p(x_k) < p_\epsilon) = (1 - \epsilon)^N$$

Then, the probability for an active learner to select an instance with probability at least p_ϵ is, from the binomial theorem:

$$p_{active}(p(x_i) \geq p_\epsilon) = 1 - (1 - \epsilon)^N = 1 - \sum_{k=0}^{N} \binom{n}{k}(-\epsilon)^k = N\epsilon - o(\epsilon)$$

By comparison, the probability for a passive learner to select an instance with probability at least p_ϵ simply is:

$$p_{passive}(p(x_i) \geq p_\epsilon) = \epsilon$$

Therefore, the probability of selecting an instance with maximal entropy on $\mathcal{D}$ is N times bigger for the active learner.

5   Implementation

5.1   Sampling a Set of Hypotheses

To cope with very large or potentially infinite hypothesis spaces, a set of consistent hypotheses is sampled at each iteration. This sample set is used both to measure the accuracy and to evaluate the entropies.

We use a process called Regular Sampling [23] which limits the number of duplicates while maintaining a good sampling efficiency. A set of probability fractions p_i is generated from the first K integers and with the following two properties: it is evenly distributed in $[0, 1]$ and it is isomorphic to $\mathbb{N}$ for K infinite. Consistent hypotheses are ordered in SLD order within the derivation tree. Samples are selected from the tree leafs and following the probability fractions generated. At each node of the tree, the different branches are given equal weights, and are associated a cumulative posterior probability computed as the sum of the posterior probabilities of the hypotheses on the left side. Starting from the top node, we browse through the tree and selects at each node the branch whose cumulative posterior probability interval $[min, max]$ contains the sampling probability fraction p_i. This latter is then updated as $(p_i - min)(max - min)$, and the process is repeated within the sub-tree selected. At the end, Regular Sampling reproduces sampling without replacement due to the distribution of the sequence of fractions, and provides a sample set representative of the current version space. A set of at most K hypotheses is dynamically sampled according to this process. The first K fractions and corresponding hypotheses are generated. If all of them are inconsistent with the examples selected so far, a new set of hypotheses is sampled from the next K natural numbers, and so forth until at least one consistent hypothesis is returned. After removing potential duplicates, this sampled set is saved for evaluating the accuracy and the entropies.

5.2   Computing the Entropies

As a next step, the entropies are computed from the sampled hypotheses. For every instance initially sampled from the instance space, we compute the proportion of sampled hypotheses that predict a positive label and weight it according to the hypotheses prior distribution. The entropy is derived from this probability. Finally, the instance with the highest entropy is selected. If several instances reach the maximum, one of them is selected at random.

6   Experiments

6.1   Experimental Hypothesis

This section describes two experiments for evaluating the benefits of Bayesian Meta-Interpretive Active Learning over the speed of convergence when learning efficient agent strategies[1]. Thus, we investigate the following research hypothesis:

Research Hypothesis: *Bayesian Meta-Interpretive Active Learning requires a smaller sample complexity for learning efficient agent strategies.*

For the sake of comparison, we consider a passive learner which randomly selects one instance at each iteration. Therefore, we associate to the previous research hypothesis the following null hypothesis that we will test:

Null Hypothesis: *Bayesian MIL Active Learning can not converge faster toward efficient strategies than Bayesian MIL Passive learning.*

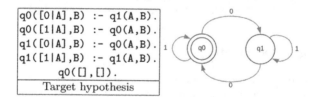

Fig. 5. Example of target hypothesis learned and corresponding FSA, the parity grammar

---

[1] Code for these experiments available at https://github.com/celinehocquette/Bayesian-MIL-active-learning.git.

6.2   Learning Regular Grammars

We learn regular languages, which are equivalent to deterministic Finite State Automata (FSA). Generally speaking, FSA represent sequences of actions depending on a sequence of events and an input state. Thus, they consist of compact ways of representing strategies. We additionally require target grammars to have a generality $g(H) = \Pi_{\mathcal{X}}(\{x \mid H(x) = 1\})$ between $\frac{1}{3}$ and $\frac{2}{3}$ such that the initial probability for an instance to be positive is $\frac{1}{2}$ on average. This also ensures that trivial grammars are not considered. An example of a target hypothesis and its corresponding automaton are represented on Fig. 5: the parity grammar accepts any string with an even number of 0.

Materials and Methods. Target grammars are generated with *Metagol*, from a set of sequences regularly sampled from Σ^* and for $\Sigma = \{0, 1\}$. The number of states $n \geq 3$ is generated according to an exponential decay distribution with mean 4. The generality of the hypothesis returned is measured against a set of 40 newly regularly sampled instances. These steps are repeated until a grammar with generality in $[\frac{1}{3}; \frac{2}{3}]$ is returned. A new number of states is similarly generated to bound the search space.

The metarules provided are *acceptor/1* and *delta/3* described previously in Fig. 2. The complexity of the hypotheses is set to their length $l(H)$, and the prior is computed by $\frac{1}{l(H)^2}$. For each target grammar, 150 training instances are initially regularly sampled from Σ^*: a threshold on the probability fraction used for sampling is randomly generated for each instance, thus their length is bounded. Another 50 instances are similarly sampled for testing.

At each iteration, 50 hypotheses are regularly sampled. The accuracy is measured as the average accuracy of all sampled hypotheses over the testing set. The results presented in the Fig. 7 have been averaged over 50 trials.

6.3   Learning a Bee Strategy

We learn the strategy introduced in section 1 and that describes a bee strategy for finding pollen following information given by a waggle dance. The target strategy is represented in the Fig. 6: until the bee reaches the flower, it flies in the direction given by the waggle dance, and then grabs pollen.

```
        f(A,B):- f2(A,C),grab(C,B).
        f2(A,B):- until(A,B,at_flower,f1).
f1(A,B):- ifthenelse(A,B,waggle_east,move_right,move_left).
```
Target hypothesis

Fig. 6. Target hypothesis describing a bee strategy for finding pollen in an environment

Materials and Methods. The world is a one-dimensional space of size 10. The state of the world is described by a list of facts: *position/1,flower_position/1,hive_position/1* describe respectively the bee, the flower and the hive position, *waggle_dance/1* gives the direction indicated by the waggle dance, *energy/1* and *weight/1* represent the energy left for the bee and the weight it carries. Actions are dyadic predicates that modify the state of the world. The primitive actions are as follows: *move_right/2*, *move_left/2*, *grab/2*, they all have a cost of one unit of energy. The metarules used are the chain rule and two abstractions *until/4* and *ifthenelse/5* (Fig. 2). For any hypothesis H with length $l(H)$, the resource complexity $r(H)$ is measured against the examples selected so far, and the prior of H is defined as $\frac{1}{l(H)+r(H)}$. The maximum length of an hypothesis is set to 3. The hive is located in the middle position of the environment. A flower is randomly positioned, and a waggle dance indicates if it is east or west of the hive. In the initial state, the bee is at the hive with no pollen carried. It has some amount of energy randomly generated between 0 and 30. In the final state, it is on the flower with one or zero unit of pollen carried. Positive examples are pairs of states for which the task of finding pollen is fulfilled and with a positive amount of energy in the final state. Negative examples are pairs of states for which the task is not fulfilled or resulting in a negative amount of energy in the final state. Training and test sets are respectively made of 20 and 40 examples, half positive and half negative. The results presented in the Fig. 8 have been averaged over 20 trials.

6.4 Results and Discussion

The results are presented in Figs. 7 and 8. The learning process takes between 10 min and a couple of hours for the grammar experiment according to the complexity of the target hypothesis, and around a few seconds for each run for the bee experiment. The entropy (Figs. 7a and 8a) is smaller and less regular for passive learning, which is above all visible for a small number of iterations (smaller than 10). In both cases the entropy is globally decreasing as the version space shrinks. The difference between the two curves represents the gain over the reduction of the version space. However, the entropy is smaller to 1: the number of hypotheses is not halved at each iteration as in the ideal case, even for active learning. The number of sampled hypotheses is represented on Figs. 7b and 8b, it is decreasing with the number of iterations, eventually converging to one hypothesis. The decay rate gets smaller as the entropy drops, and is greater for active learning. The complexity of the MAP hypothesis (Fig. 7c and 8c) increases with the number of iterations both for passive and active learning. Indeed, the search is conducted such that the least complex hypotheses consistent with the examples are preferred. Therefore, the prior of the MAP hypotheses is increasing as the training set grows. Finally, the accuracy (Fig. 7d and 8d) increases, starting between 0.6 and 0.7 (the default accuracy is 0.5, and the learning process starts with one positive instance for initialisation). It eventually converges toward 1 for the bee experiment. The convergence is longer and not guaranteed at every run for the grammar experiment, since the hypothesis space is bounded: a number of

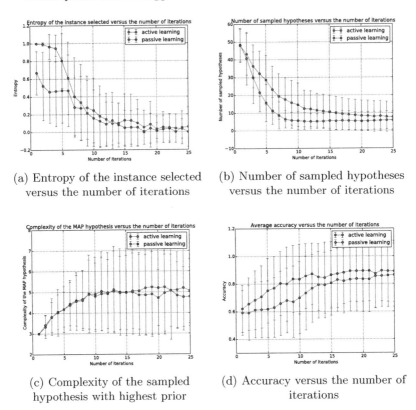

(a) Entropy of the instance selected versus the number of iterations

(b) Number of sampled hypotheses versus the number of iterations

(c) Complexity of the sampled hypothesis with highest prior

(d) Accuracy versus the number of iterations

Fig. 7. Learning a regular grammar with Bayesian MIL: comparison between active and passive learning; the convergence is faster for active learning.

states maximum is generated before the learning process. Figure 9 compares the number of queries required to reach some accuracy level for active and passive learning, it suggests that less iterations are required to achieve good performances, and that experimental costs can at least be halved with active learning. A Mann-Whitney U test indicates that the results are significant at a 0.01 level.

According to Lemma 1, the size N of the pool of instance initially sampled should be big enough to ensure that instances with high entropy can always be found. Increasing this number lifts up the entropy of the instance selected, and therefore accelerate the convergence. The number K of hypotheses sampled should be big enough to ensure that the sample set is representative of the hypothesis space, and thus relies on the initial size of the version space. Even though these results seem encouraging, the empirical evaluation has been performed on a small domain and focuses on artificial problems. We plan to demonstrate the scalability of this approach on real-world datasets as future work.

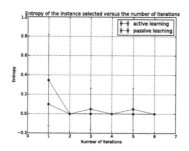

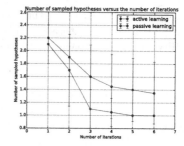

(a) Entropy of the instance selected versus the number of iterations

(b) Number of sampled hypotheses versus the number of iterations

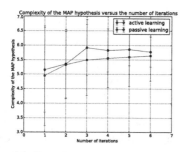

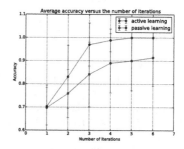

(c) Complexity of the sampled hypothesis with highest prior

(d) Accuracy versus the number of iterations

Fig. 8. Learning a bee strategy with Bayesian MIL: comparison between active and passive learning; the convergence is faster for active learning.

Accuracy	Active learning	Passive learning
0.75	5	12
0.80	7	15
0.85	11	22

(a) FSA

Accuracy	Active learning	Passive learning
0.80	2	3
0.90	3	6

(b) Bee experiment

Fig. 9. Number of iterations required to reach some accuracy level for active and passive learning: experimental costs can be halved with active learning.

7 Conclusion and Future Work

This article extends previous work on Meta-Interpretive Learning by integrating active learning for learning efficient agent strategies. We study how automated experimentation can help reducing the experimental costs required to reach some accuracy level. Mainly, we show over two examples that one can expect to halve the experimental costs with active learning and compared to passive learning. We believe that this approach is of interest in several AI domains such as robotics or agent-based modelling and could have a wide range of applications.

A limitation of this article is the lack of theoretical bounds on the sample complexity, which we characterise as future work. We also want to demonstrate the scalability of this approach by considering real-world datasets. A next step is to use this framework to uncover novel logic programs instead of known target hypotheses, to demonstrate that it supports scientific knowledge discovery. Another future line of work is to improve the sampling process over the instance space. So far, instances are sampled before the learning. A fresh new sample set of instances could be generated at each iteration, the sampling distribution being updated given the knowledge acquired so far. Also, instances could eventually be synthesised. Next, we want to study other query strategies. Finally, experiments are so far the observation of a binary output for a particular set-up, which could be extended to probabilistic observations.

References

1. Angluin, D.: Queries and concept learning. J. Autom. Reason. **2**(4), 319–42 (1988)
2. Angluin, D.: Queries revisited. Theor. Comput. Sci. **313**(2), 175–194 (2004)
3. Bryant, C.H., Muggleton, S.H., Oliver, S.G., Kell, D.B., Reiser, P., King, R.D.: Combining inductive logic programming, active learning and robotics to discover the function of genes. Electron. Trans. Artif. Intell. **5**–**B1**(012), pp. 1–36 (2001)
4. Cohn, D., Atlas, L., Ladner, R.: Improving generalization with active learning. Mach. Learn. **15**(2), 201–221 (1994)
5. Cover, M.T., Thomas, J.A.: Elements of Information Theory. Wiley (2006)
6. Cropper, A., Muggleton, S.H.: Learning efficient logical robot strategies involving composable objects. In: IJCAI 2015, pp. 3423–3429 (2015)
7. Cropper, A., Muggleton, S.H.: Logical minimisation of meta-rules within meta-interpretive learning. In: Davis, J., Ramon, J. (eds.) ILP 2014. LNCS (LNAI), vol. 9046, pp. 62–75. Springer, Cham (2015). https://doi.org/10.1007/978-3-319-23708-4_5
8. Cropper, A., Muggleton, S.H.: Learning efficient logic programs. Mach. Learn. (2018)
9. Cropper, A., Muggleton, S.H.: Learning higher-order logic programs through abstraction and invention. In: IJCAI 2016, pp. 1418–1424 (2016)
10. Dasgupta, S.: Analysis of a greedy active learning strategy. Adv. Neural Inf. Process. Syst. **17**, 337–344 (2005)
11. Dasgupta, S.: Coarse sample complexity bounds for active learning. In: Proceedings of the 18th International Conference on Neural Information Processing Systems, pp. 235–242 (2005)
12. Freund, Y., Seung, H.S., Shamir, E., Tishby, N.: Selective samping using the query by committee algorithm. Mach. Learn., pp. 1551–1557 (1997)
13. Hanneke, S.: A bound on the label complexity of agnostic active learning. In: ICML (2007)
14. Hanneke, S.: Theory of disagreement-based active learning. Found. Trends Mach. Learn. **7** (2014)
15. Haussler, D., Kearns, M., Schapire, R.E.: Bounds on the sample complexity of bayesian learning using information theory and the VC dimension. Mach. Learn. **14**, 83–113 (1994)
16. von Frisch, K.: The dance language and orientation of bees. The Belknap Press of Harvard University Press, Cambridge, Massachussets (1967)

17. King, R.D., et al.: Functional genomic hypothesis generation and experimentation by a robot scientist. Nature **427**, 247–252 (2004)
18. Kulkarni, S.R., Mitter, S.K., Tsitsiklis, J.N.: Active learning using arbitrary binary valued queries. Mach. Learn. **11**, 23–35 (1993)
19. Lang, T., Toussaint, M., Kersting, K.: Exploration in relational worlds. In: Balcázar, J.L., Bonchi, F., Gionis, A., Sebag, M. (eds.) ECML PKDD 2010. LNCS (LNAI), vol. 6322, pp. 178–194. Springer, Heidelberg (2010). https://doi.org/10.1007/978-3-642-15883-4_12
20. Lewis, D., Gale, W.: A sequential algorithm for training text classifiers. In: Croft, B.W., van Rijsbergen, C.J. (eds.) SIGIR 1994, pp. 3–12. ACM/Springer, London (1994). https://doi.org/10.1007/978-1-4471-2099-5_1
21. Mitchell, T.M.: Version Spaces: An Approach to Concept Learning. PhD Thesis (1978)
22. Muggleton, S.H., Lin, D.: Meta-interpretive learning of higher-order dyadic datalog: predicate invention revisited. In: Proceedings of the 23rd International Joint Conference Artificial Intelligence, pp. 1551–1557 (2013)
23. Muggleton, S.H., Lin, D., Chen, J., Tamaddoni-Nezhad, A.: MetaBayes: bayesian meta-interpretative learning using higher-order stochastic refinement. In: Zaverucha, G., Santos Costa, V., Paes, A. (eds.) ILP 2013. LNCS (LNAI), vol. 8812, pp. 1–17. Springer, Heidelberg (2014)
24. Muggleton, S.H., Lin, D., Pahlavi, N., Tamaddoni-Nezhad, A.: Meta-interpretive learning: application to grammatical inference. Mach. Learn. **94**, 25–49 (2014)
25. Rodrigues, C., Gérard, P., Rouveirol, C., Soldano, H.: Active learning of relational action models. In: Muggleton, S.H., Tamaddoni-Nezhad, A., Lisi, F.A. (eds.) ILP 2011. LNCS (LNAI), vol. 7207, pp. 302–316. Springer, Heidelberg (2012). https://doi.org/10.1007/978-3-642-31951-8_26
26. Roy, S., Namboodiri, V.P., Biswas, A.: Active learning with version spaces for object detection. ArXiv e-prints, November 2016
27. Settles, B.: Active learning literature survey. **52**, July 2010
28. Thompson, C.A., Califf, M.E., Mooney, R.J.: Active learning for natural language parsing and information extraction. In: Proceedings of the 16th International Conference on Machine Learning, ICML 1999, pp. 406–414. Morgan Kaufmann Publishers Inc. (1999)
29. Tosh, C., Dasgupta, S.: Diameter-based active learning. CoRR, abs/1702.08553 (2017)

Diagnostics of Trains with Semantic Diagnostics Rules

Evgeny Kharlamov[1], Ognjen Savković[2(✉)], Martin Ringsquandl[3],
Guohui Xiao[2], Gulnar Mehdi[3], Elem Güzel Kalayc[2], Werner Nutt[2],
Mikhail Roshchin[3], Ian Horrocks[1], and Thomas Runkler[3]

[1] University of Oxford, Oxford, UK
[2] Free University of Bozen-Bolzano, Bolzano, Italy
`ognjen.savkovic@unibz.it`
[3] Siemens AG, Corporate Technology, Munich, Germany

Abstract. Industry today employs rule-based diagnostic systems to minimize the maintenance cost and downtime of equipment. Rules are typically used to process signals from sensors installed in equipment by filtering, aggregating, and combining sequences of time-stamped measurements recorded by the sensors. Such rules are often data-dependent in the sense that they rely on specific characteristics of individual sensors and equipment. This dependence poses significant challenges in rule authoring, reuse, and maintenance by engineers especially when the rules require domain knowledge. In this work we propose an approach to address these problems by relying on the well-known Ontology-Based Data Access approach: we propose to use ontologies to mediate the sensor signals and the rules. To this end, we propose a semantic rule language, *SDRL*, where signals are first class citizens. Our language offers a balance of expressive power, usability, and efficiency: it captures most of Siemens data-driven diagnostic rules, significantly simplifies authoring of diagnostic tasks, and allows to efficiently rewrite semantic rules from ontologies to data and execute over data. We implemented our approach in a semantic diagnostic system and evaluated it. For evaluation we developed a use case of rail systems at Siemens and conducted experiments to demonstrate both usability and efficiency of our solution.

1 Introduction

Rule Based Diagnostics with Signal Processing Rules. Intelligent *diagnostic systems* play an important role in industry since they help to maximise equipment's up-time and minimise its maintenance and operating costs. Railway engineering companies like Siemens often rely on *rule-based* diagnostics to analyse rail systems by checking that, e.g., train service braking can be released normally; there are no axle or other equipment operating faults [17] or there is no performance degradation. For this purpose diagnostic engineers create and use complex diagnostic rule-sets to detect abnormalities during equipment run time

F. Riguzzi et al. (Eds.): ILP 2018, LNAI 11105, pp. 54–71, 2018.
https://doi.org/10.1007/978-3-319-99960-9_4

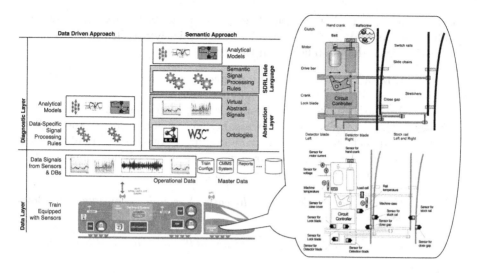

Fig. 1. Left: General scheme of train diagnostics with signal-processing rules, that depicts two approaches: data driven (commonly used in practice nowadays) and semantic driven (our proposal), that both rely on the same data: sensor signals, train configurations, reports, etc. Right: details of a control system for train breaks; the upper part explains the components of the system and the lower part shows the sensors installed in the system.

and sophisticated analytical models to combine these with models of physical aspects of equipment such as thermodynamics and energy efficacy.

An important class of rules that are commonly used in Siemens for rule-based train and railway diagnostics are *signal processing rules* (SPRs). SPRs allow to filter, aggregate, combine, and compare *signals*, that are time stamped measurement values, coming from sensors installed in equipment and trigger error or notification messages when a certain criterion has been met. Thus, sensors report temperature, pressure, vibration and other relevant parameters of equipment and SPRs process this data and alert whenever a certain pattern is detected. Rule-based diagnostics with SPRs can be summarises as in Fig. 1 (left), where the *data layer* consists of two parts: *master data* that contains train engineering specifications, results of previous diagnostic tasks, and diagnostic event data, and *operational data* that contains recorded signals from sensors installed in a train; and the *diagnostic layer* consists of SPRs and analytical models. Also, on the right of the figure, in the cloud, there are details of a control system for train breaks: the upper part explains the components of the system and the lower part shows the sensors installed in the system.

Data Dependency of Signal Processing Rules. SPRs that are currently offered in typical diagnostic systems (and in Siemens) are highly *data dependent* in the sense that

– data about specific characteristic like speed, capacity, and identifiers of individual sensors and pieces of equipment are explicitly encoded in SPRs and
– schema of such data is reflected in the SPRs.

As the result, for a typical simple train diagnostic task an engineer has to write from dozens to hundreds of SPRs with hundreds of sensor tags, component codes, sensor and threshold values and equipment configs and design data.

For example, a typical Siemens train has about 4000 sensors and a diagnostic task to detect whether the service braking is released normally in each car of given locomotive can be captured with 680 SPRs. We now illustrate this diagnostic tasks and SPRs on a running example.

Example 1 (Running Example: Breaks Released Normally). Consider the following diagnostic task:

Verify that service breaking is released normally in each car of locomotive L1.

Informally, to check this one has to make sure that: *(i)* all door sensors indicate that the car doors are ok, and the main train line pressure is trending upwards for more then 33 s; *(ii)* then, during this interval, the restart pressure of the main compressor is below the maximum allowed pressure of the breaking system; *(iii)* finally, after 0.2 s, break release rate is normal, break valves are closed and air breaks are released.

Each of the above task can be checked by analyzing the train sensors. For instance, let us assume that the locomotive L1 has door sensors SKNF_X01, SKNF_X02, SKNF_X03 and SKNF_X04, and let MNPRSS be the sensor that measures the main train pressure. Further, let us assume that Task (i) is verified as *ok* if the sum of the above sensors values is equal to 16. Then, the following data dependent SPR written in a syntax similar to the one of Siemens SPRs can be used verify the task:

$$\$\mathsf{CarDoorsOK} = \mathtt{truth}\,(\mathtt{sum}\,(\mathsf{SKNF\_X01}, \mathsf{SKNF\_X02}, \qquad (1)$$
$$\mathsf{SKNF\_X03}, \mathsf{SKNF\_X04}) : \mathtt{value}(=, 16)\quad \&\&$$
$$\mathtt{trend}(\mathsf{MNPRSS}, 'up') : \mathtt{duration}(>, 0.33s))$$

Here $CarDoorsOK is a Boolean variable. Similarly, one can write data-dependent SPRs for tasks *(ii)* and *(iii)*. Complete encoding of the rules that check if breaking is released normally for an average Siemens train requires to write around 300 SPRs some of which are as in the running example. Many of these SPRs are differ only on specific sensor identifiers and the number of speed signals to aggregate. Adapting these SPRs to another locomotive will also require to change a lot of identifiers. For example, in another locomotive L2 may have five door sensors STTF_01, STTF_02, STTF_03, STTF_05 and STTF_05 which sum of the values should be equal to 25. Thus, the rules for L2 would be as above but with these new sensors ids and threshold values. □

Challenges. The data dependence of SPRs poses significant challenges for diagnostic engineers in *(i)* authoring, and then *(ii)* reuse, and *(iii)* maintenance of SPRs. These challenges are common for large enterprises and Siemens is not an exception. Indeed, *authoring* such rules is time consuming and error prone, e.g., while aggregating the signals from card doors from a given car one has find among car doors signals relevant ones and ensure that *all* the relevant signals are included in the aggregation while other signals, e.g., temperature signals, are not included. Finding this information is hard since relevant data is scattered across multiple databases. As the result, in the overall time that a Siemens engineer spends on diagnostics up to 80% is devoted to rule authoring where the major part of this time is devoted to data access and integration [12].

Reuse of such rules is limited since they are too specific to concrete equipment and in many cases it is easier to write a new rule set than to understand and adapt an existing one. As the result, over the years Siemens has acquired a huge library of SPRs with more than 200,000 rules and it constantly grows. Finally, *maintenance* of such SPRs is also challenging and require significant manual work.

Semantics Enhancement and Requirements. Semantic technologies can help in addressing the challenges with authoring, reuse, and maintenance of SPRs. An *ontology* can be used to abstractly represent sensors and background knowledge about trains including locations of sensors, structure and characteristics of trains. Then, in the spirit of *Ontology Based Data Access* (OBDA) [16], the ontology can be 'connected' to the data about the actual train, their sensors and signals with the help of declarative *mapping specifications*. OBDA has recently attracted a lot of attention by the research community: a solid theory has been developed, e.g. [6,18], and a number of mature systems have been implemented, e.g. [4,5]. Moreover, OBDA has been successfully applied in several industrial applications, e.g. [9].

Adopting OBDA for rule-based diagnostics in Siemens, however, requires a rule based language for SPRs that enjoys the following features:

(i) Signals orientation: The language should treat signals as first class citizens and allow for their manipulation: to filter, aggregate, combine, and compare signals;

(ii) Expressiveness: The language should capture most of the features of the Siemens rule language used for diagnostics;

(iii) Usability: The language should be simple and concise enough so that the engineers can significantly save time in specifying diagnostic tasks;

(iv) Efficiency: The language should allow for efficient execution of diagnostic tasks.

To the best of our knowledge no rule language exists that fulfils all these requirements (see details in Sect. 5).

Our Contributions. In this work we propose to extend the traditional data driven approach to diagnostics with an OBDA layer and a new rule language to what we call *Semantic Rule-based Diagnostics*. Our approach is schematically depicted in Fig. 1 (right). To this end we propose a language *SDRL* (Semantic Diagnostic Rule Language) for SPRs that enjoys the four requirements above. Our language allows to write SPRs and complex diagnostic tasks in an abstract fashion and to exploit both ontological vocabulary and queries over ontologies to identify relevant sensors and data values. We designed the language in such a way that, on the one hand, it captures the main signal processing features required by Siemens train diagnostic engineers and, on the other hand, it has good computational properties. In particular, *SDRL* allows for rewriting [6] of diagnostic rule-sets written over OWL 2 QL ontologies (that are the W3C standard for OBDA) into multiple data-dependent rule-sets with the help of ontologies and OBDA mappings. This rewriting allows to exploit standard infrastructure, including the one of Siemens, for processing data-dependent SPRs.

We implemented *SDRL* and a prototypical Semantic Rule-based Diagnostic system. We deployed our implementation in Siemens over 100 S trains and evaluated the deployment with encouraging results. We evaluated usability of our solution with Siemens engineers by checking how fast they are in formulating diagnostic tasks in *SDRL*. We also evaluated the efficiency of our solution in processing diagnostic tasks over train signals in a controlled environment. Currently, our deployment is not included in the production processes, it is a prototype that we plan to evaluate and improve further before it can be used in production.

Structure of the Paper. In Sect. 2 we introduce our signal processing rule language *SDRL*; in Sect. 3 we describe how we implemented and deployed our solution in Siemens; in Sect. 4 we report on two evaluations of our solution; in Sect. 5 we compare our solution to other approaches; and in Sect. 6 we conclude.

2   Signal Processing Language *SDRL*

In this section we introduce our signal processing language *SDRL*. It has three components: *(i)* Basic signals that come from sensors; *(ii) Knowledge Bases* (KBs) that capture background knowledge of equipment and signals as well as concrete characteristics of the equipment that undergoing diagnostics, and *(iii)* Signal processing expressions that manipulate basic signals using mathematical functions and queries over KBs.

Signals. In our setting, a *signal* is a first-class citizen. A signal s is a pair (o_s, f_s) of a *sensor id* o_s and a *signal function* f_s defined on $\mathbb{R}$ to $\mathbb{R} \cup \{\bot\}$, where $\bot$ denotes the absence of a value. A *basic signal* is a signal which reading is obtained from a single sensor (e.g., in a train) for different time points. In practice, it may happen that a signal have a periods without identified values.

$C =$	Concept C contains
Q	all signal ids return by Q evaluated over the KB.
$\alpha \circ C_1$	one signal s' for each signal s in C_1 with $f_{s'} = \alpha \circ f_s$.
$C_1 : value(\odot, \alpha)$	one signal s' for each signal s in C_1 with $f_{s'}(t) = \alpha \odot f_s(t)$ if $f_s(t) \odot \alpha$ at time point t; otherwise $f_{s'}(t) = \bot$.
$C_1 : duration(\odot, t')$	one signal s' for each signal s in C_1 with $f_{s'}(t) = f_s(t)$ if exists an interval I s.t.: f_s is defined I, $t \in I$ and $size(I) \odot t'$; otherwise $f_{s'}(t) = \bot$.
$\{s_1, \ldots, s_m\}$	all enumerated signal $\{s_1, \ldots, s_m\}$.
$C = \text{agg } C_1$	one signal s' with $f_{s'}(t) = \text{agg}_{s \in C_1} f_s(t)$, that is, s' is obtained from all signals in C_1 by applying the aggregate agg at each time point t.
$C_1 : align \ C_2$	a signal s_1 from C_1 if: exists a signal s_2 from C_2 that is aligned with s_1, i.e., for each interval I_1 where f_{s_1} is defined there is an interval I_2 where f_{s_2} is defined s.t. I_1 aligns with I_2.
$C_1 : trend(\text{direction})$	one signal s' for each signal s in C_1 with $f_{s'}(t) = f_s(t)$ if exists an interval I around t s.t.: f_s is defined I, and f_s is an increasing (decreasing) function on I for direction=up (=down resp.)

Fig. 2. Meaning of signal processing expressions. For the interval I, $size(I)$ is its size. For intervals I_1, I_2 the *alignment* is: "I_1 *within* I_2" if $I_1 \subseteq I_2$; "I_1 *after*[t] I_2" if all points of I_2 are after I_1 and the start of I_2 is within the end of I_1 plus period t; "I_1 *before*[t] I_2" if "I_2 *start*[t] I_1".

Also, such periods are obtained when combining and manipulating basic signals. We say that a signal s is *defined* on a real interval I if it has a value for each point of the interval, i.e., $\bot \notin f_s(I)$. For technical reasons we introduce *undefined* signal function $f_\bot$ that maps all reals into $\bot$. In practice signals are typically step functions over time intervals since they correspond to sensor values delivered with some frequency. In our model, we assume that we are given a finite set of basic signals $\mathcal{S} = \{s_1, \ldots, s_n\}$.

Knowledge Bases and Queries. A Knowledge Base $\mathcal{K}$ is a pair of an *ontology* $\mathcal{O}$ and a *data set* $\mathcal{A}$. An *ontology* describes background knowledge of an application domain in a formal language. We refer the reader to [6] for detailed definitions of ontologies. In our setting we consider ontologies that describe general characteristics of equipment which includes partonomy of its components, characteristics and locations of its sensors, etc. As an example consider the following ontological expression that says that DoorSensor is a kind of PressureSensor:

$$\text{SubClassOf(DoorSensor PressureSensor).} \tag{2}$$

Data sets of KBs consist of *data assertions* enumerating concrete sensors, trains, and their components. The following assertions says that sensors SKNF_X01, SKNF_X02, SKNF_X03 and SKNF_X04 are all door sensors:

$$\text{ClassAssertion(DoorSensor SKNF\_X01),}$$
$$\text{ClassAssertion(DoorSensor SKNF\_X02),}$$

$$\text{ClassAssertion}(\text{DoorSensor } \text{SKNF\_X03}),$$
$$\text{ClassAssertion}(\text{DoorSensor } \text{SKNF\_X04}). \tag{3}$$

In order to enjoy favorable semantic and computational characteristics of OBDA, we consider well-studied ontology language OWL 2 QL that allows to express subclass (resp. sub-property) axioms between classes and projections of properties (resp. corollary between properties). We refer the reader to [6] for details on OWL 2 QL.

To query KBs we rely on conjunctive queries (CQs) and certain answer semantics that have been extensively studied for OWL 2 QL KBs and proved to be tractable [6]. For example, the following CQ is returning all main car sensors by asking for the door senors that are located in the cabin or platform:

$$\text{MainCarDoors}(x) \leftarrow \text{doorSensor}(x) \wedge \text{locatedIn}(x, y) \wedge$$
$$(\text{PlatformAccessArea}(y) \vee \text{CabinAccessArea}(y)) \tag{4}$$

(To be precise, the above contains disjunction in the body thus it can be represented as a union of two CQs).

Signals Processing Expressions. We introduce signal expressions that filter and manipulate basic signals and create new more complex signals. Intuitively, in our language we group signals in ontological concepts and signal expression are defined on the level of concepts. Then, a *signal processing expression* is recursively defined as follows:

$$
\begin{array}{llll}
C & = & Q & | \quad \{s_1, \ldots, s_m\} & | \\
& & \alpha \circ C & | \quad C_1 : value(\odot, \alpha) & | \\
& & \text{agg } C_1 & | \quad C_1 : duration(\odot, t) & | \\
& & C_1 : align\ C_2 & | \quad C_1 : trend(direction).
\end{array}
$$

where C is a concept, Q is a CQ with one output variable, $\circ \in \{+, -, \times, /\}$, $\text{agg} \in \{\text{min}, \text{max}, \text{avg}, \text{sum}\}$, $\alpha \in \mathbb{R}$, $\odot \in \{<, >, \leq, \geq\}$, $align \in \{within, after[t], before[t]\}$, t is a period, and $direction \in \{\text{up}, \text{down}\}$.

The formal meaning of signal processing expressions is defined in Fig. 2. In order to make the mathematics right, we assume that $c \circ \perp = \perp \circ c = \perp$ and $c \odot \perp = \perp \odot c = false$ for $c \in \mathbb{R}$, and analogously we assume for aggregate functions. If the value of a signal function at a time point is not defined with these rules, then we define it as $\perp$.

Example 2. The data-driven rules to determine car door functioning as in Eq. (1) from the running example can be expressed with two concepts in *SDRL* as follows:

$$\text{DoorsLocked} = sum\ \text{MainCarDoors} : value(=, LockedValue), \tag{5}$$
$$\text{PressureUp} = \text{CabinPressure} : trend(\text{'}up\text{'}) : duration(>, 33sec) \tag{6}$$

Here, MainCarDoors is the CQ defined in Eq. (4). For brevity we do not introduce a new concept for each expression but we just join them with symbol ":". Constant *LockedValue* is parameters of an analysed door of a train, and they are instantiated from the train configuration when the expressions are evaluated.

Diagnostic Programs and Messages. We now show how to use signal expressions to compose diagnostic programs and to alert messages. In the following we will consider *well formed* sets of signal expressions, that is, sets where each concepts is defined at most once and where definitions of new concepts are assumed to be acyclic: if C_1 is used to define C_2 (directly or indirectly) then C_1 cannot defined (directly or indirectly) using C_2.

A *diagnostic program* (or simply *program*) Π is a tuple $(\mathcal{S}, \mathcal{K}, \mathcal{M})$ where $\mathcal{S}$ a set of basic signals, $\mathcal{K}$ a KB, $\mathcal{M}$ a set of well formed signal processing expressions such that each concept that is defined in $\mathcal{M}$ does not appear in $\mathcal{K}$.

Example 3. The running example program $\Pi = (\mathcal{S}, \mathcal{K}, \mathcal{M})$ has the following components: sensors $\mathcal{S} = \{\mathsf{SKNF\_X01}, \mathsf{SKNF\_X02}, \mathsf{SKNF\_X03}, \mathsf{SKNF\_X04}\}$, KB $\mathcal{K}$ that consists of axioms from Eqs. (2) and (3), and $\mathcal{M}$ that consists of expressions from Eqs. (5) and (6).

On top of diagnostic programs Π SDRL allows to define *message rules* that report the current status of a system. Formally, they are defined as Boolean combinations of signal processing expressions:

$$D := \quad C \quad | \quad not\ D_1 \quad | \quad D_1\ and\ D_2.$$

A *message rule* is a rule of the form, where D is a concept and m is a (text) message:

$$message(m) = D.$$

Example 4. Using Eqs. (5)–(6) we define the message:

$$message(\text{“All car doors OK”}) = \mathsf{DoorsLocked}\ and\ \mathsf{PressureUp}. \tag{7}$$

The message intuitively indicates that the doors are functioning and locked.

Now we are ready to define the semantics of the rules, expression and programs.

Semantics of SDRL. We now define how to determine whether a program Π fires a rule r. To this end, we extend first-order interpretations that are used to define semantics of OWL 2 KBs. In OWL 2 a first class citizen is an object o and interpretation is defining whether $C(o)$ is true or not for particular concept C. In our scenario, domain of objects is a domain of sensor ids (basic or ones defined by expressions). Thus, each object o is also has an assigned function f_o that represents the signal value of that object. Observe that o can also be an id of a train component that does not have signal function. At the moment, (since it is not crucial for this study and it simplifies the formalism) we also assign undefined signal $f_\perp$ to such (non-signal) objects.

Formally, our *interpretation* $\mathcal{I}$ is a pair $(\mathcal{I}_{FOL}, \mathcal{I}_\mathcal{S})$ where $\mathcal{I}_{FOL}$ interprets objects and their relationships (like in OWL 2) and $\mathcal{I}_\mathcal{S}$—signals. First, we define how $\mathcal{I}$ interprets basic signals. Given a set of signals for an interpretation $\mathcal{I}$: $\mathcal{S}^\mathcal{I} = \{s_1^\mathcal{I}, \ldots, s_n^\mathcal{I}\}$ s.t. $\mathcal{I}_{FOL}$ 'returns' the signal id, $s^{\mathcal{I}_{FOL}} = o_s$ and $\mathcal{I}_\mathcal{S}$ 'returns' the signal itself, $s^{\mathcal{I}_\mathcal{S}} = s$.

Now we can define how $\mathcal{I}$ interprets KBs. Interpretation of a KB $\mathcal{K}^\mathcal{I}$ extends the notion of first-order logics interpretation as follows: $\mathcal{K}^{\mathcal{I}_{FOL}}$ is a first-order logics interpretation $\mathcal{K}$ and $\mathcal{K}^{\mathcal{I}_\mathcal{S}}$ is defined for objects, concepts, roles and attributes following $S^\mathcal{I}$. That is, for each object o we define $o^{\mathcal{I}_\mathcal{S}}$ as s if o is the id of s from $\mathcal{S}$; otherwise $(o, f_\perp)$. Then, for a concept A we define $A^{\mathcal{I}_\mathcal{S}} = \{s^{\mathcal{I}_\mathcal{S}} \mid o_s^{\mathcal{I}_{FOL}} \in A^{\mathcal{I}_{FOL}}\}$. Similarly, we define $\cdot^{\mathcal{I}_\mathcal{S}}$ for roles and attributes.

Finally, we are ready to define $\mathcal{I}$ for signal expressions and we do it recursively following the definitions in Fig. 2. We now illustrate some of them. For example, if $C = \{s_1, \ldots, s_m\}$, then $C^\mathcal{I} = \{s_1^\mathcal{I}, \ldots, s_m^\mathcal{I}\}$; if $C = Q$ then $C^{\mathcal{I}_{FOL}} = Q^{\mathcal{I}_{FOL}}$ where $Q^{\mathcal{I}_{FOL}}$ is the evaluation of Q over $\mathcal{I}_{FOL}$ and $C^{\mathcal{I}_\mathcal{S}} = \{s \mid o_s^{\mathcal{I}_{FOL}} \in Q^{\mathcal{I}_{FOL}}\}$, provided that $\mathcal{I}_{FOL}$ is a model of $\mathcal{K}$. Otherwise we define $C^\mathcal{I} = \emptyset$. Similarly, we define interpretation of the other expressions.

Firing a Message. Let Π be a program and '$r : message(m) = C$' a message rule. We say that Π *fires* message r if *for each* interpretation $\mathcal{I} = (\mathcal{I}_{FOL}, \mathcal{I}_\mathcal{S})$ of Π it holds $C^{\mathcal{I}_{FOL}} \neq \emptyset$, that is, the concept that fires r is not empty. Our programs and rules enjoy the *canonical* model property, that is, each program has a unique (Hilbert) interpretation [2] which is minimal and can be constructed starting from basic signals and ontology by following signal expressions. Thus, one can verify $C^{\mathcal{I}_{FOL}} \neq \emptyset$ only on the canonical model. This implies that one can evaluate *SDRL* programs and expressions in a bottom-up fashion. We now illustrate this approach on our running example.

Example 5. Consider our running program Π from Example 3 and its canonical interpretation $\mathcal{I}_\Pi$. First, for each query Q in $\mathcal{M}$ we evaluate Q over KB $\mathcal{K}$ by computing $Q^{\mathcal{I}_\Pi}$. In our case, the only query is MainCarDoors that collects all sensor ids for a particular train. Then, we evaluate the expressions in $\mathcal{M}$ following the dependency graph of definitions. We start by evaluation the expression from Eq. (5), again in a bottom-up fashion. Concept MainCarDoors$^{\mathcal{I}_\Pi}$ contains sensor ids: SKNF_X01, SKNF_X02, SKNF_X03 and SKNF_X04. At the same time, those sensors have signal functions assigned from $\mathcal{S}^{\mathcal{I}_\Pi}$. Let us call them f_1, f_2, f_3 and f_4. Expression sum MainCarDoors computes a new signal, say s_5, by taking sum of f_1, f_2, f_3 and f_4 at each time point. After this, it eliminates all values of s_5 that are $\neq LockedValue$. Similarly, we compute signal transformations for the expression from Eq. (6). Finally, we use those two expressions to evaluate the message rule from Eq. (7). If there exists at least one signal in evaluated expressions corresponding to Eqs. (5) and (6), then the message is fired.

3   Our System and Siemens Deployment

System Implementation. The main functionality of our Semantic Rule-based Diagnostics system is to author *SDRL* diagnostic programs, to deploy them in trains, to execute the programs, and to visualise the results of execution. We now give details of our system by following its architecture in Fig. 3. There are four essential layers in the architecture: *applications, OBDA backend, data-oriented backend,* and *data.* Our system is mostly implemented in Java. We now discuss the system layer by layer.

On the *application* layer, the system offers user-oriented modules that allow engineers to author, store, and load diagnostic programs by formulating sets of SPRs in *SDRL* and sensor retrieving queries. Such formulation is guided by the domain ontology stored in the system. In Fig. 4 (left, top) one can observe a screenshot of the SPR editor which is embedded in the Siemens analytical toolkit. Another module of the layer consists of a monitoring dashboard and a semantic Wiki that allows among other features to visualize signals and messages (triggered by programs), and to track deployment of SPRs in equipment. In Fig. 4 (left, center) one can see visualisation of signals from two components of one train. Diagnostic programs formulated in the application layer are converted into XML-based specifications and sent to the OBDA backend, which returns back the messages and materialised semantic signals, that is, signals over the ontological terms. In Fig. 4 (left, bottom) one can see an excerpt from an XML-based specification.

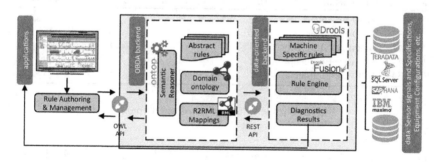

Fig. 3. Architecture of our semantic rule-based diagnostics system.

We rely on OWL API to communicate between the application and OBDA layers and REST API to communicate between the OBDA and data oriented layers.

The *OBDA backend* layer takes care of transforming SPRs written in *SDRL* into either SPRs written in the Siemens data-driven rule language or SQL. This transformation has two steps: rewriting of programs and queries with the help of ontologies (at this step both programs and queries are enriched with the implicit information from the ontology), and then unfolding them with the help

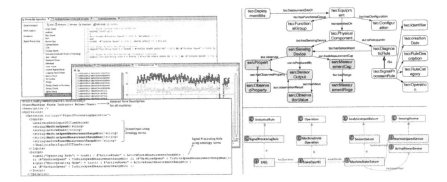

Fig. 4. Left (Screenshots): SPR editor (top), Wiki-based visualisation monitor for semantic signals (centre), and a fragment of an XML-based specification of an SPR (bottom); Right (Ontologies): A fragment of the Siemens ontology that we developed to support diagnostic of equipment with SPRs (top), and an example of how this ontology can be used to specify a concrete SPR related to a machine state operation.

of mappings. For this purpose we extended Ontop, the query transformation module of the Optique platform [9,12] which we were developing earlier within the Optique project [8]. The OBDA layer also transforms signals, query answers, and messages from the data to semantic representation.

#	Age	Occupation	Education	Tech. skills	Similar tools	Sem. Web
P1	34	R&D Engineer	MSc	4	4	yes
P2	32	R&D Engineer	MSc	3	3	yes
P3	47	Diagnostic Engineer	PhD	5	1	yes
P4	45	Software Engineer	MSc	4	3	yes
P5	34	Software Engineer	BSc	3	3	yes

Fig. 5. Profile information of participants.

The *data-oriented backend* layer takes care of planning and executing data-driven rules and queries received from the OBDA layer. If the received rules are in the Siemens SPR language then the rule executor instantiates them with concrete sensors extracted with queries and passes them to Drools Fusion (http://drools.jboss.org/), i.e., the engine used by Siemens. If the received rules are in SQL then it plans the execution order and executes them together with the other queries. Later in Sect. 4 we evaluate the efficiency of our system assuming the SQL case.

Finally, on the *data* layer we store all the relevant data: train design specifications, historical information about services that were performed over the trains, previously detected events, and the raw sensor signals.

	Complexity	# sensor tags	# event codes	# code lines	Monitoring task
T1	Low	23	6	223	Car doors ok
T2	Medium	13	22	453	Start-up normally
T3	Medium	19	23	421	Axle faults
T4	High	21	64	631	Break release

Fig. 6. Diagnostic tasks for Siemens trains that were used in the user study, where complexity is defined using the number of sensor tags, event messages, and lines of code.

Deployment at Siemens. We deployed our Semantic Rule-Based Diagnostics system on the data gathered for 1 year from 100 trains. We rely on Teradata to store signals; MS SQL Server for train manufacturing configurations; SAP HANA for purchase data, material consumption and spare-part information; and IBM Maximo for data about maintenance and repair tasks incident reports, stock information, component history, mileage tracking, defect information etc. For rule processing, we connected our system to the Siemens deployment of Drools Fusion.

An important aspect of the deployment was the development of a diagnostic ontology and mappings. Our ontology was inspired by the *(i)* Siemens Technical System Ontology (TSO) and W3C Semantic Sensor Network Ontology (SSN) and *(ii)* the international standards IEC 81346 and ISO/TS 16952-10. The development of the ontology was a joint effort of domain experts from Siemens businesses units together with the specialist from the Siemens Corporate Technology. Our ontology consists of four modules and it is expressed in OWL 2 QL. In order to connect the ontology to the data, we introduced 376 TriplesMaps using the R2RML language. We present the ontology modules in detail.

The main module of our ontology in partially depicted in Fig. 4 (right, top) where in gray we present SSN and with white TSO terms. In Fig. 4 (right, bottom) we visualise how this ontology can be instantiated with a specific diagnostic rule. The main module of our ontology has 48 classes and 32 object and data properties. The other three modules are about equipment, sensing devices, and diagnostic rules. They provide detailed information about the machines, their deployment profiles, sensor configurations, component hierarchies, functional profiles and logical bindings to the analytical rule definitions. More precisely:

- *The Equipment module* describes the internal structure of an industrial system. The main classes of the module are *DeploymentSite* and *Equipment* and they describe the whole facility of system and machines that have been physically deployed and monitored. It also defines the system boundaries, substantial descriptions of the system environment, set of components it operates on, part-of relations, system configurations and functional grouping of components. For example, it encodes that every *Equipment* should have an *ID*,

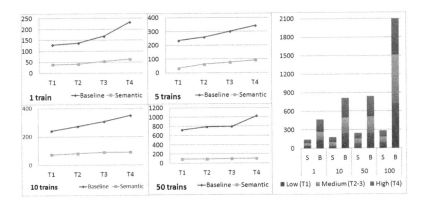

Fig. 7. Results of the user study. Left four figures: the average time in seconds that the users took to express the tasks T1–T4 for 1, 10, 50, and 100 trains using existing Siemens rule language (Baseline or B) and our semantic rule language *SDRL* (Semantic or S). Right figure: the total time in seconds the user took to express the tasks grouped according to their complexity.

Diagnostics Task T_1: "Verify that all car doors ok in locomotive L1?": See Equation (7)

Diagnostic Task T_2: "Does locomotive L1 start-up normally?":

$$StartingTractionEffort = StatorVoltage : trend('up') : duration(>, 10s) : after[5s]$$
$$TractionRotorRPM : value(>, RotorStartMinThreshold) : after[20s]$$
$$TrainSpeed : value(>, MinLineSpeed).$$
$$TractionControlOK = MotorTemperature : value(<, TempMaxThreshold) \text{ and}$$
$$CoolingControlPressure : value(<, PressureMaxThreshold) \text{ and}$$
$$DifferentialCurrent : value(<, CurrentMaxThreshold).$$
$$message("Locomotive Normal Start-up") =$$
$$StartingTractionEffort \text{ and } TractionControlOK \text{ and } NormalBrakeRelease.$$

Diagnostics Task T_3: "Does locomotive L1 have critical axle faults.":

$$HotBearings = avg \ AllBearingsTempSensor : value(>, BearingTemperatureMaxThreshold).$$
$$HotWheelRims = WheelRimsTemperature : trend('up') : duration(>, 10s)$$
$$message("Critical Axle") = (HotBearings \text{ or } HotWheelRims).$$

Diagnostics Task T_4: "Verify that the service breaking is released normally in each car of locomotive L1?":

$$CompressorRestart = CompressorRestartPressure : value(<, BrakeSystemMaxPressure).$$
$$BrakeReleaseOK = BrakeReleaseRate : value(<, BrakeReleaseRateMaxThreshold) \text{ and}$$
$$AllCarBrakePressureValve : value(=, ClosedValue) \text{ and}$$
$$AirBrakesMainResVolume : value(<, AirBrakesMainResVolumeMinThreshold).$$
$$NormalBrakeRelease = CarDoorsOK \ within \ CompressorRestart : after[2s] \ BrakeReleaseOK.$$
$$message("Normal Brake Release") = NormalBrakeRelease.$$

Fig. 8. Signal processing rules that we used for performance evaluation.

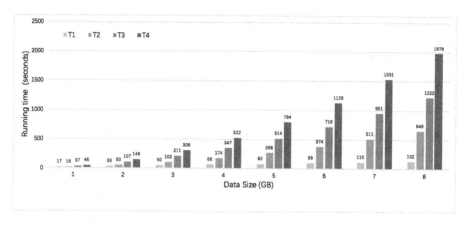

Fig. 9. Performance evaluation results for the Siemens use case.

Configuration and at least one *Component* to operate on, and an optional property *hasProductLine*.

- *The Sensing Device module* is inspired by the SSN ontology. In particular, we reuse and extend the class *SensingDevice*. The module describes sensors, their properties, outputs, and observations. One of our extensions comparing to SSN is that the measurement capabilities can now include measurement property range i.e. maximum and minimum values (which we encode with annotations in order to keep the ontology in OWL 2 QL). For example, *Vibration Sensor* is a sensing device that observes *Vibration* property and measures e.g. *BearingVibrations*.
- *The Diagnostic Rules module* introduces rules and relate them to e.g., *Description*, *Category*, and *Operation* classes. For example, using this module one can say that *SignalProcessingRule* is of a type *DiagnosticRule*, that it has certain *Operation* and it may have different sensor data input associated with its operation.

4   Siemens Experiments

In this section, we present two experiments. The first experiment is to verify whether writing diagnostic programs in *SDRL* offers a considerable time saving comparing to writing the programs in the Siemens data dependent rule language. The second experiment is to evaluate the efficiency of the SQL code generated by our OBDA component (see Sect. 3 for details on our OBDA component).

Preliminary User Study. We conducted a preliminary user study in Siemens with 5 participants, all of them are either engineers or software engineers. In Fig. 5 we summarise relevant information about the participants. Most of them have at least an MSc degree, and all are familiar with the basic concepts of the

Semantic Web. Their technical skills in the domain of diagnostics are from 3 to 5. We use a 5-scale range where '1' means 'no' and '5' means 'definitely yes'. Two out of 5 participants never saw an editor for diagnostic rules, while the other 4 are quite familiar with rule editors.

During brainstorming sessions with Siemens mobility analysts and R&D personnel from Siemens Corporate Technology we selected 4 diagnostic tasks which can be found in Fig. 6. The selection criteria were: diversification on topics and complexity, as well as relevance for Siemens. The tasks have three complexity levels (Low, Medium, and High) and they are defined as a weighted sum of the number of sensor tags, event messages, and lines of code in a task.

Before the study we gave the participants a short introduction with examples about diagnostic programs and message rules in both Siemens and *SDRL* languages. We also explained them the constructs of *SDRL*, presented them our diagnostic ontology, and explained them the data. The data was collected from 100 trains and included sensor measurement, that is, temperature, pressure, train speed, and door control signals, and associated configuration data, that is, types of trains and threshold values. During the study participants were authoring diagnostic programs for the tasks T1 to T4 from Fig. 6 using both existing Siemens rule language (as the baseline) and *SDRL*; while we were recording the authoring time. Note that all participants managed to write the diagnostic tasks correctly and the study was conducted on a standard laptop.

Figure 7 summarises the results of the user study. The four left figures present the average time that the five participants took to formulate the 4 tasks over respectively 1, 10, 50, and 100 trains. We now first discuss how the authoring time changes within each of the four figures, that is, when moving from simple to complex tasks, and then across the four figures, that is, when moving from 1 to 100 trains.

Observe that in each figure one can see that in the baseline case the authoring time is higher than in the semantic case, i.e., when *SDRL* is used. Moreover, in the semantic case the time only slightly increases when moving from simple (T1) to complex (T4) tasks, while in the baseline case it increases significantly: from 2 to 4 times. The reason is that in the baseline case the number of sensor tags makes a significant impact on the authoring time: each of these tags has to be found in the database and included in the rule, while in the semantic case the number of tags does not make any impact since all relevant tags can be specified using queries. The number of event messages and the structure of rules affects both the baseline and the semantic case, and this is the reason why the authoring time grows in the semantic case when going from rules with low to high complexity.

Now consider how the authoring time changes for a given tasks when moving from 1 to 100 trains. In the baseline case, moving to a higher number of trains requires to duplicate and modify the rules by first slightly modifying the rule structure (to adapt the rules to train variations) and then replacing concrete sensors tags, threshold values, etc. In the semantic case, moving to a higher number of train requires only to modify the rule structure. As the result, one can see that in the semantic case all four semantic plots are very similar: the one for 100 trains is only about twice higher than for 1 train. Indeed, to adapt the semantic diagnostic task T4 from 1 to 100 trains the participants in average spent 50 s, while formulating the original task for 1 train took around 30 s.

Finally, let us consider how the total time for all 4 tasks changes when moving from 1 to 100 trains. This information is in Fig. 7 (right). One can see that in the baseline case the time goes from 500 to 2.100 s, while in the semantic case it goes from 90 to 290. Thus, for 4 tasks the semantic approach allows to save about 2.010 s and it is more than 4 times faster than the baseline approach.

Performance Evaluation. In this experiment, we evaluate how well our SQL translation approach scales. For this we prepared 4 diagnostic task, corresponding data, and verified firing of messages using a standard relational database engine PostgreSQL. We conducted experiments on an HP Proliant server with 2 Intel Xeon X5690 Processors (each with 12 logical cores at 3.47 GHz), 106 GB of RAM. We now first describe the diagnostic tasks and the data, and then report the evaluation results.

In Fig. 8 we present three out of four diagnostic tasks, and the task T_4 is the running example. On the data side, we took measurements from 29 sensors as well as the relevant information about the trains where the sensors were installed. Then, we scaled the original data both in number of sensors and time dimensions. Our scaling respect the structure of the original data. The largest data for 232 sensors took 8 GB on disk in a PostgreSQL database engine.

The experiments of our system consisted of two steps: translation of semantic diagnostic programs into SQL queries and then execution of generated queries. During the first step our system generated SQL code that ranging from 113 to 839 lines depending on the diagnostic task and the code is of a relatively complex structure, e.g., for each diagnostic task the corresponding SQL contains at least 10 joins (The most complex one contains 120 joins). The results of the second step are presented in Fig. 9. We observe that query evaluation scales well. Specifically, the running time grows linearly with respect to the data size.

5   Related Work

The authors in [12] introduce temporal streaming language STARQL that extends SPARQL with aim to facilitate data analysis directly in queries. This and other similar semantic streaming languages, e.g., SPARQL$_{stream}$ [7], are different from our work, since we propose *(i)* a rule diagnostic language and *(ii)* focus on temporal properties of signals which are not naturally representable in those languages.

A preliminary idea on how to use semantic technologies in abstracting details of machines was presented in [11,14,15]. There authors use KBs to abstract away details of particular turbines in Siemens. Data about turbines is retrieved using OBDA and send to further analytical analysis (e.g., using KNIME system). This line of work does not aim at using diagnostic rules and does not address the case of trains. Instead they use off-the-shelf software for analytics.

Recent efforts have been made to extend ontologies with analytical and temporal concepts. Authors in [1] allow for temporal operators in queries and ontologies. Still, such approach use temporal logics (e.g., LTL) which in not adequate for our case since sensor data are organized based on intervals, e.g. $[0s, 10s]$.

Works in [10, 12] introduce analytical operations directly into ontological rules in such a way that OBDA scenario is preserved. They define analytical functions on concepts, e.g. avg C, in OBDA setting. However, the authors do not consider temporal dimension of the rules.

Finally, as discussed above, we are related with the work on well-studied Metric Temporal Logic [13]. In particular, we use a non-trivial extension of non-recursive Datalog language $Datalog_{nr}MTL$ which suitable for OBDA scenario. $Datalog_{nr}MTL$ is introduced in [3] where the authors conduct a theoretical and experimental study investigating computational characteristics of the language. They show how query answering over a program in $Datalog_{nr}MTL$ can be rewritten into the problem of query answering in SQL. Following similar principles, we define rewriting of our *SDRL* language into SQL and show that such rewriting performs reasonably well on sensor data.

6   Conclusion

In this paper we showcase an application of semantic technologies to diagnostics of trains. We focused on the advantages and feasibility of the ontology-based solution for diagnostic rule formulation and execution. To this end we studied and described a Siemens diagnostic use-case. Based on the insides gained, we reported limitations of existing Siemens and ontology based solutions to train diagnostics. To address the limitations we proposed a signal processing rule language *SDRL*, studied its formal properties, implemented, and integrated it in an ontology-based system which we deployed at Siemens.

The evaluation shows that diagnostic engineers can save up to 66% of time by employing ontologies. Thus, our semantic solution allows diagnostic engineers to focus more on analyses the diagnostic output rather than on data understanding and gathering that they have to do nowadays for authoring data-driven diagnostic rules. Currently, we are in the process of setting up a deployment of our system into the Siemens remote diagnostic system to further evaluate the usability and impact. Another important lesson we learned is that execution of semantic rules is efficient and scales well to thousands of sensors which corresponds to real-world complex diagnostic tasks.

Acknowledgments. This research is partially supported by the Free University of Bozen-Bolzano projects QUEST, ROBAST and QUADRO.

References

1. Artale, A., Kontchakov, R., Wolter, F., Zakharyaschev, M.: Temporal description logic for ontology-based data access. In: IJCAI 2013, pp. 711–717 (2013)
2. Baader, F., Calvanese, D., McGuinness, D.L., Nardi, D., Patel-Schneider, P.F. (eds.): The Description Logic Handbook: Theory, Implementation, and Applications. Cambridge University Press, New York (2003)
3. Brandt, S., Kalaycı, E.G., Kontchakov, R., Ryzhikov, V., Xiao, G., Zakharyaschev, M.: Ontology-based data access with a horn fragment of metric temporal logic. In: AAAI (2017)
4. Calvanese, D., et al.: Ontop: answering SPARQL queries over relational databases. Semant. Web **8**(3), 471–487 (2017)
5. Calvanese, D., et al.: The MASTRO system for ontology-based data access. Semant. Web **2**(1), 43–53 (2011)
6. Calvanese, D., De Giacomo, G., Lembo, D., Lenzerini, M., Rosati, R.: Tractable reasoning and efficient query answering in description logics: the DL-Lite family. JAR **39**(3), 385–429 (2007)
7. Corcho, O., Calbimonte, J.-P., Jeung, H., Aberer, K.: Enabling query technologies for the semantic sensor web. Int. J. Semant. Web Inf. Syst. **8**(1), 43–63 (2012)
8. Horrocks, I., Giese, M., Kharlamov, E., Waaler, A.: Using semantic technology to tame the data variety challenge. IEEE Int. Comput. **20**(6), 62–66 (2016)
9. Kharlamov, E., et al.: Ontology based access to exploration data at statoil. In: Arenas, M., et al. (eds.) ISWC 2015. LNCS, vol. 9367, pp. 93–112. Springer, Cham (2015). https://doi.org/10.1007/978-3-319-25010-6_6
10. Kharlamov, E., et al.: Optique: towards OBDA systems for industry. In: Cimiano, P., Fernández, M., Lopez, V., Schlobach, S., Völker, J. (eds.) ESWC 2013. LNCS, vol. 7955, pp. 125–140. Springer, Heidelberg (2013). https://doi.org/10.1007/978-3-642-41242-4_11
11. Kharlamov, E., et al.: Semantic rules for machine diagnostics: execution and management. In: CIKM, pp. 2131–2134
12. Kharlamov, E., et al.: How semantic technologies can enhance data access at siemens energy. In: Mika, P., et al. (eds.) ISWC 2014. LNCS, vol. 8796, pp. 601–619. Springer, Cham (2014). https://doi.org/10.1007/978-3-319-11964-9_38
13. Koymans, R.: Specifying real-time properties with metric temporal logic. Real-Time Syst. **2**(4), 255–299 (1990)
14. Mehdi, G., Brandt, S., Roshchin, M., Runkler, T.A.: Semantic framework for industrial analytics and diagnostics. In: IJCAI, pp. 4016–4017 (2016)
15. Mehdi, G., et al.: Semantic rule-based equipment diagnostics. In: d'Amato, C., et al. (eds.) ISWC 2017. LNCS, vol. 10588, pp. 314–333. Springer, Cham (2017). https://doi.org/10.1007/978-3-319-68204-4_29
16. Poggi, A., Lembo, D., Calvanese, D., De Giacomo, G., Lenzerini, M., Rosati, R.: Linking data to ontologies. J. Data Semant. **10**, 133–173 (2008)
17. Rao, B.K.N.: Handbook of Condition Monitoring. Elsevier (1996)
18. Savkovic, O., Calvanese, D.: Introducing datatypes in DL-lite. In: ECAI, pp. 720–725 (2012)

The Game of Bridge: A Challenge for ILP

Swann Legras[1], Céline Rouveirol[2(✉)], and Véronique Ventos[1,3(✉)]

[1] NUKKAI Inc., Paris, France
`vventos@nukk.ai`
[2] L.I.P.N, UMR-CNRS 7030, Univ. Paris 13, Villetaneuse, France
`celine.rouveirol@lipn.univ-paris13.fr`
[3] L.R.I., UMR-CNRS 8623, Univ. Paris-Saclay, Orsay, France

Abstract. Designs of champion-level systems dedicated to a game have been considered as milestones for Artificial Intelligence. Such a success has not yet happened for the game of Bridge because (i) Bridge is a partially observable game (ii) a Bridge player must be able to explain at some point the meaning of his actions to his opponents. This paper presents a simple supervised learning problem in Bridge: given a 'limit hand', should a player bid or not, only considering his hand and the context of his decision. We describe this problem and some of its candidate modelisations. We then experiment state of the art propositional machine learning and ILP systems on this problem. Results of these preliminary experiments show that ILP systems are competitive or even outperform propositional Machine Learning systems. ILP systems are moreover able to build explicit models that have been validated by expert Bridge players.

1 Introduction

Designs of champion-level systems dedicated to a game have long been considered as milestones for Artificial Intelligence; IBM computer Chess Deep Blue beating in 1997 world champion Gary Kasparov was one of these adventures, another more recent one being DeepMind Alphago outperforming in 2017 World Champion Ke Jie at the game of Go [15]. One major challenge still remaining concerns the game of Bridge where the level of robots is far from the best human players. There are two main reasons for that: (i) Bridge is a partially observable game (ii) a Bridge player must be able to explain at some point the meaning of his actions. For example, an opponent can ask for explanations on the inferences related to the choice of an auction rather than another. The need for explainability coupled with the fact that knowledge in Bridge is relational let us think that Bridge is a killer application for ILP. As a proof of concept, this paper[1] presents a simple supervised learning problem in Bridge: given a 'limit hand', should a player bid or not, only considering his hand and the context

---

[1] This research work is conducted as part of the νBridge project (former name AlphaBridge) supported by NukkAI Inc., Paris.

© Springer Nature Switzerland AG 2018
F. Riguzzi et al. (Eds.): ILP 2018, LNAI 11105, pp. 72–87, 2018.
https://doi.org/10.1007/978-3-319-99960-9_5

of his decision. After describing this problem and how it has been modeled, we experiment state of the art propositional machine learning and ILP systems on this problem. Results of these preliminary experiments show that ILP systems are competitive or even outperform propositional Machine Learning systems on this problem. More importantly, ILP systems are flexible enough, given their explicit background knowledge and the fact that they build explicit and expressive models, to support the expert Bridge players in the modelling process.

The goal of the paper is to demonstrate that Bridge displays a certain number of characteristics that would benefit from a relational representation. Building explicit rules or patterns for Bridge indeed requires the expressiveness of ILP: given his thirteen cards (his hand), a player makes decisions according to properties of the hand. These properties can be related to specific cards, sets of cards or other abstractions of the hand. The symbolic approach is quite flexible, and allows experimenting with various abstractions of examples description through the use of background knowledge, in close interactions with the experts. The relational nature of the language used for describing the background knowledge facilitated the task of the experts.

The plan of the paper is as follows: we first describe the target Bridge problem in Sect. 2. We then model this problem as a binary classification one and design a first propositional representation of examples to be handled by a state of the art propositional learning system (Sect. 3). Section 4 describes alternative relational representations of examples as well as settings for the two state of the art ILP systems studied, Aleph and Tilde. Section 5 gives some empirical comparisons of the models learnt in those quite different contexts (accuracy, complexity). Relational models are then discussed and assessed by Bridge experts in Sect. 6. Finally, Sect. 7 draws some conclusions and some perspectives for the νBridge project.

2   Description of the Bridge Problem

In the present section, we give a short overview of the game of Bridge and we present the decision problem handled in this paper. The interested reader can refer for instance to [12] for a more complete presentation.

Bridge is a trick-taking card game opposing four players divided in two partnerships (pairs). A standard 52 card pack is shuffled and each player receives a hand that is only visible to him. Pairs stand across each other. A Bridge deal is divided into two major playing phases using different devices (represented Fig. 1): the bidding phase and the card play. The goal of the bidding is to reach a contract which determines the minimum number of tricks the pair commits to win (between seven and thirteen) during the card play, either with no trump or in a determined suit as trump. The different final contracts are denoted by nS where n is a number between 1 and 7 and S $\in$ (♠, ♡, ♢, ♣, NT). The contract nS determines the minimum number of tricks the pair commits to win (n + 6) and which suit is the trump, NT to expressing the fact that there is no trump. For instance 4♡ is fulfilled if the number of tricks won is at least 10 (4 + 6)

Fig. 1. The two devices used in Bridge: bidding cards (left) and standard cards (right)

with a ♡ trump. The major problem during the bidding phase is to be able to evaluate the trick-taking potential of a pair of hands, each player not knowing what his partner holds. Players use bidding cards to pass information to their partner about their hand. The last bid represents the contract to be played.

During the card play, the goal is to fulfill (or to defeat for the defending side) the contract reached during the first phase. Each player plays a card at his turn. As this paper focuses on a bidding problem we will not go into further detail on this phase.

2.1 Opening Bid Problem

During the bidding phase, the dealer is the first to bid and has to decide between opening (the bidding) or passing. If he passes then the opponent at his left has to decide between opening and passing and so on. It can happen, although rarely, that all 4 players pass: the deal is a 'passout'.

When deciding whether to open or not, the player evaluates his hand by counting the total of 'High-Card Points' (HCP: Ace = 4, King = 3, Queen = 2, Jack = 1). It is a way to rapidly assess the potential of a hand as higher card have more chance to earn a trick during card play. Generally, early bids like opening bids are made according to as set of rules. For instance, in modern Standard American system (SAYC), 1-of-a-suit opening requires at least 12 HCP. In some limit cases, experts allow themselves to deviate slightly from the rules and produce a bid that does not meet with the generally admitted conditions of application of a rule. Thus 11HCP hands are limit cases in which some players may decide to open and some others not. The decision to open or not an 11HCP hand is called in the following the opening bid problem. The opening bid problem is linked to a Bridge situation as that represented in Fig. 2. The example (refered to as Example 1) of this figure will be used in the following to illustrate our explanations.

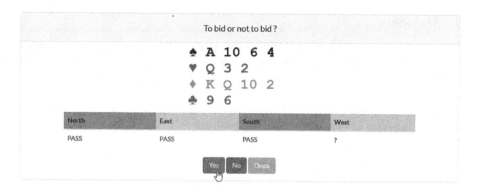

Fig. 2. Example 1: a bidding decision for West (Color figure online)

Parameters: when holding an 11HCP hand, the decision to open or not is based on several parameters: the position (1st if he is the dealer, 2nd after one Pass, 3rd after two Pass or 4th after 3 Pass), the vulnerability measuring the risk/reward score-wise and the evaluation of the hand.

Players are represented by *North, East, South* and *West* (abbreviated to N, E, S, W) the pairs being NS and EW. Here, *North* is the dealer. The vulnerability of the two sides is represented by the color of the players (green is Not vulnerable and red Vulnerable). The decision is related to *West* according to his hand, his position (4th since there are 3 passes from the other players), and his vulnerability (Not Vulnerable since his color is green).

By clicking on 'Yes', *West* decides to open and then he deviates slightly from the 12 HCP rule since his hand has only 11 HCP (4+2+3+2).

The ability to wisely depart from the rule framework does make a difference at an early stage of the bidding phase because the final contract (and therefore the score) depends heavily on initial actions.

Finally, it is said that in these situations, Bridge players exercise their hand judgment without being able to elicit their decision making process: this skill is built on strong and personal experience and is very difficult to get. The decision and evaluation also vary a lot from one player to another, even of similar level.

3 Learning Problem and First Model

The opening bid problem is a binary classification problem where Task T consists in predicting if a given expert opens or passes according to a Bridge situation like that in *Example 1*. The input of the learning problem is a set of n labeled examples $(x_i, class_i)$ where $class_i$ belongs to $\{+, -\}$ (positive or negative examples), the output is a classifier, i.e., a function $h(x)$ that assigns each example x to its class: $+$ (open) or $-$ (pass).

3.1   DataSets

We randomly generated 6 sets of unlabeled samples. Those sets have been labeled by four Bridge experts ($E_1, \ldots, E_4$) who are among the best 100 players of their home country. These experts have similar level but different styles that affect their decision to open or not (with the exact same cards, 2 experts are likely to make different decisions). Table 1 sums up the set features and some statistics about the labeling of examples.

Table 1. Samples sets

Labeled set	S_1	S_2	S_3	S_4	$S_{5,1}$	$S_{5,2}$	S_6
Unlabeled set	R_1	R_2	R_3	R_4	R_5	R_5	R_5
Expert	E_1	E_2	E_2	E_3	E_4	E_4	E_4
Size	1000	1000	970	790	1222	1222	1079
Pos./Neg	768/232	681/319	540/430	603/187	681/541	582/640	560/519
Pos rate (%)	76.80	68.10	55.67	76.33	55.72	47.63	51.90

Sets R_i, $i \in \{1..4\}$ were tagged once and by only one expert. Let us call S_i, $i \in \{1..4\}$ the corresponding sets of labeled examples.

The opening bid decision is a complex issue, being not unusual that the same expert makes different decisions while facing the exact same situation. To get an idea of expert's consistency, expert E_4 was given twice the set R_5 to label, a number of months apart and with the deals arranged in a different order. The 2 labeled sets are called $S_{5,1}$ and $S_{5,2}$. Finally, $S_6 = S_{5,1} \cap S_{5,2}$ represents the set of samples of R_5 which have been 'consistently' labeled by E_4. The consistency rate of expert E_4 when labeling R_5 is only 88.30%.

Bridge players with similar level may have very different features. For instance E_4 is a conservative player who seldom trespasses the limits fixed by the bidding system while E_1 and E_3 are 'aggressive' players. Their ratio of positive examples in the last row of Table 1 is consistent with their presumed aggressiveness.

3.2   Propositional Representation of Examples

We first represent examples using a propositional representation.

Definition 1 (Propositional representation of examples). *A labeled example is represented by: [c_n with $n \in \{1..52\}$, position, vulnerability, class]. We use the following ascending order for cards: ♣, ◇, ♡, ♠ and for each suit : 2, ..., 10, J, Q, K, A.*

$c_i = 1$ if the hand has the corresponding card and 0 otherwise, position $\in \{1..4\}$, vulnerability $\in \{1..4\}$ with 1 = the two pairs are not vulnerable, 2 = not vulnerable opponents vulnerable, 3 = vulnerable opponents not vulnerable and 4 = the two pairs are vulnerable, Class = 1 if the expert opens and 0 if he passes.

3.3 Binary Classification Using SVM

We chose Support Vector Machines among various paradigms that are used for learning binary propositional classifiers (e.g. Decision Trees, Bayesian Classification, Perceptron, etc). Experiments were performed with a SVM learner with linear kernel as implemented in the Scikit-learn[2] toolbox [14].

4 Building Rule Sets with ILP Systems

The ILP systems used in the experiments are Aleph [16] and Tilde [3]. They are both state of the art ILP system, quite different in their learning process. Aleph learns from entailment. Given a set of positive examples E^+ and a set of negative examples E^- and a background theory B, the learning goal is to find a hypothesis H in the form of a Prolog program, such that $\forall e \in E^+ : H \wedge B \models e$ and $\forall e \in E^- : H \wedge B \not\models e$. Examples in this framework are single literals representing the class ($open/1$). Background knowledge is represented as a mixture of facts and rules that can be used to enrich the examples' description.

Aleph's learning proceeds top-down. It learns sets of rules using a covering approach. Aleph selects an example e not covered by the current theory. A learning loop starts by building a bottom clause from e, a most specific clause e given e and B). This bottom clause will be the lower bound of Aleph's search space. Aleph then explores top-down generalizations of bottom clause that satisfy the language bias and mode declarations. Several search strategies have been implemented in Aleph, we have used the default one (best first).

Tilde learns a relational decision tree from interpretations. Given a set of classes C (each class label c is a nullary predicate), a set of examples E (each element of E is of the form (e, c) with e a set of facts (interpretations) and c a class label) and a background theory B, the goal is to find a hypothesis H (a Prolog program), such that $\forall (e, c) \in E, H \wedge e \wedge B \models c$, and $\forall c' \in C - c : H \wedge e \wedge B \not\models c'$. As quoted in [3]:

> Since in learning from interpretations, the class of an example is assumed to be independent of other examples, this setting is less powerful than the standard ILP setting (e.g., for what concerns recursion). With this loss of power comes a gain in efficiency, through local coverage tests. The interesting point is that the full power of standard ILP is not used for most practical applications, and learning from interpretations usually turns out to be sufficient for practical applications.

This is the case for our classification problem.

A first order logical decision tree (FOLDT) is a binary decision tree in which the nodes of the tree contain a conjunction of literals and different nodes may share variables, under the following restriction: a variable that is introduced in a node must not occur in the right branch of that node. In order to refine a node with associated query Q, Tilde computes the refinement of Q given the language

---

[2] http://scikit-learn.org/stable/.

bias and chooses the refinement that results in the best split. The best split is the one that maximizes a certain quality criterion by default the information gain ratio. The conjunction at a given node consists of the literals that have been added to Q in order to produce its refinement.

The ILP systems allow for using a powerful and flexible target representation language through the use of explicit background knowledge, here represented as a set of definite clauses. To cope with the increased size of the hypothesis space, both Aleph and Tilde allow the user to define the search space through sophisticated *language bias*. This language bias can be seen as a grammar-like user defined specification of the search space.

4.1   Relational Representation

In this section, we present the different background knowledges (denoted BK_i in the remainder of the paper) that have been used as an input of the ILP systems as well as modeling assumptions used to obtain them. These BK stem from a joint work with the Bridge experts in order to achieve both an acceptable Bridge-wise representation and an acceptable learning performance. These objectives will be assessed in Sect. 5, the expert validation of the results is given in Sect. 6.

The first BK BK_0 is a simple translation of the propositional representation described in Sect. 3.2.

BK_0: The following predicates form the common background for all BKs (E represents the example primary key).

- $open(E, Class)$ with $Class = pos$ or neg
- $has\_hand(E, H)$ where H is a list of card constants representing the hand's example
- $has\_card(E, C)$ is *true* if C is a card occurring in E's hand
- $position(E, P)$ with P a digit between 1 and 4 representing the position of the expert
- $vuln(E, V1, V2)$ with $V1$ and $V2 = g$ (not vulnerable) or r (vulnerable) representing the vulnerability of the player and of its opponents.

According to BK_0, *Example 1* in Fig. 2 (denoted by $e1$ in the following), is represented by the following facts:
$open(e1, pos)$. $has\_hand(e1, [c6, c9, d2, d10, dq, dk, h2, h3, hq, s4, s6, s10, sa])$.
$position(e1, 4)$. $vuln(e1, g, r)$.
$has\_card(e1, c6)$. $has\_card(e1, c9)$.   ... $has\_card(e1, sa)$.

BK_1: In order to introduce some abstraction and Bridge knowledge in the hand's description, we added some predicates to characterize card properties according to a Bridge expertise such as: the suit, the rank, the suit category (minor/major) and the rank category of the card (*small_card* from 2 to 10 or *honor* from Jack to Ace), represented with the following predicates:

$has\_suit(Card, Suit)$. $has\_rank(Card, Rank)$.
$honor(Card)$. $minor(Card)$. $small\_card(Card)$.

Expert's validation related to the intermediate BK obtained (see Sect. 6), allows us to introduce higher level predicates related to hands' properties:

$nb(E, Suit, Number)$. $plusvalue(E)$.
$lteq(Number, Number)$. $gteq(Number, Number)$.

nb describes the length of a particular suit. nb($h1$, heart, 3) expresses the fact that the hand in *Example 1* has 3 cards in ♡. *plusvalue* allows to rate a hand as 'good'.

One of the difficulties to adequately represent Bridge expertise was to determine at which granularity level the example had to be represented. We illustrate this point with the concept of exact distribution (number of cards per suit) related to a hand, that is an important parameter to evaluate a hand's potential outside the value of HCP. As an illustration, the exact distribution of the hand of *Example 1* is 4-3-4-2 (4♠, 3♡, 4♢ and 2♣). However, a Bridge player will often reason in terms of hand patterns denoting the distribution of the thirteen cards by decreasing order irrespective of the suits in question (e.g. 4-4-3-2 for *Example 1*). The term distribution will further refer to this notion and not to the exact distribution. This notion can be abstracted slightly more by classifying hands into three main classes: *balanced*, *semi_balanced* and *unbalanced* according to their distribution. For example, balanced hands are hands with no short suit (0 or 1 card). The following rules allow to saturate examples with this property:

```
balanced(E)  :- distribution(E,[4,3,3,3]).
balanced(E)  :- distribution(E,[4,4,3,2]).
balanced(E)  :- distribution(E,[5,3,3,2]).
```

Thus, we can change the granularity of the hypothesis language: just give the exact distribution, replace the exact distribution by the distribution, remove both and only use the predicates *balanced*, *semi_balanced* and *unbalanced*, etc.

BK_2: Finally, $BK_2 = BK_1 \cup list\_honor(E, Suit, ListH)$ where $ListH$ is the list of honors of suit $Suit$ in the hand. $list\_honor/3$ introduces an abstraction of the list of cards of a given suit since only the most important cards (honours) are taken into account. We will check in the experiments if this additional predicate impacts and hopefully improves the quality of learned models.

4.2 Aleph and Tilde Settings

In this section, we discuss the different settings used in Aleph and Tilde in the experiments shown in next section. Some of them are inherent to the algorithm used, some are choices to either increase performance, readability of the output or simplicity of implementation. We only detail the most important settings for each system. We refer to the user guides of both systems [2,16].

Target Predicate. The target predicate for Tilde is $open(E, Class)$, and $open(E)$ for Aleph.

Language Bias. After background predicates have been defined, the language bias describes more precisely how these predicates should be used to form rules. The most important information for Aleph is the definition of predicate modes (should constants or variables – input or output[3] – occur in which arguments of the literals. Preliminary tests have shown that the predicate *distribution* better behaves with Aleph than with Tilde.

The lookahead capability of Tilde allows creating nodes labeled with conjunctions of $nb(E, Suit, Value)$ and *gteq* or *lteq* describing length of specific or major/minor suits. Tilde is thus able to generalize the idea of distribution by performing multiple tests on the different length of suits with the predicate. Aleph handles less easily this kind of abstraction, that requires to learn longer clauses, with the counterpart of explosion of search complexity, but behaves well with the *distribution* predicate. We therefore chose to disallow Tilde to use *distribution* predicate in its language bias.

Negative Literals. Aleph does not produce rules that have negative literals in their body (it only builds definite clause programs). We have therefore encoded in the Background Knowledge some predicates representing the negation of another predicate (e.g *notplusvalue*). Tilde as a decision tree learner obviously does not need such explicit negative literals.

Search Options. The goal of this paper being to apply state of the art techniques on a new problem, we chose to use default search options whenever possible in both Aleph and Tilde. Tilde's search options were all default ones (for Aleph: *mincase* = 2, *minacc* = 0; for Tilde: *heuristic* = gainratio, *pruning* = c45 safe pruning, *stopping criterion* = mincase).

When using Aleph, the only options that deviated from default values were *clauselength* (the maximum length of rules generated) that was set to 6, *minpos* (the minimum positive coverage of each rule) set to 2 and *noise* (the maximum number of negative examples a rule can cover) was set to 5. We set this last value empirically, by running the problem with various BKs, datasets and noise values. We observed that a noise of 0 was not appropriate, as even experts may contradict themselves when labeling examples for this problem (see Sect. 3.1). The mean performance curves across datasets do not show any clear trend to help us setting this noise parameter (see Fig. 9 in the Appendix[4]). We have therefore chosen 5 as a good compromise between the performance and specificity of rules obtained. The parameter *minacc* was set to its default value (0) as we observed a loss of accuracy when setting it over 0.5.

---

[3] An input variable already occurs in the left part of the clause under development, while an output variable does not occur in the current clause (and in its head) and is therefore existentially quantified.

[4] http://www.nukk.ai/ILP2018/.

5   Experiments

We have run experiments for all datasets and systems. Because of lack of space, we only comment here on graphs for datasets S_1 et $S_{5.2}$ labeled by experts with different profiles: E_1 which is very structured and concise, and E_4 whose decision making process is driven by special cases. These assumptions will be confirmed in Sect. 6. Graphs for other datasets are provided in the appendix (Fig. 7). Their complete analysis is outside the scope of the paper.

The performance measure to assess all classifiers is accuracy: $\frac{TP+TN}{P+N}$ where TP and TN denote the true positive and true negative examples, whereas P and N denote the number of positive and negative examples.

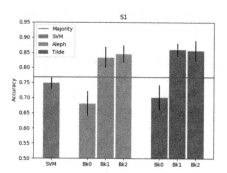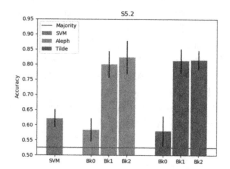

Fig. 3. Accuracy (mean and standard deviation) for all classifiers on S_1 and $S_{5.2}$

5.1   First Experiments

The performance of the classifiers is here evaluated using stratified 10-fold cross-validation. We see on Fig. 3 that:

- SVM together with Aleph and Tilde using BK_0 (refered to in the remainder as propositional learners) behave poorly, whatever dataset is used. The performance of those classifiers seem to depend also on the ratio P/N materialized by the performance of the majority classifier: they better model non-aggressive players. The propositional learners are nevertheless not able to reach a good performance. Some essential (relational) information is missing from the representation;
- Using relational BK (BK_1 and BK_2), ILP systems both significantly outperform the SVM system as well as ILP systems operating on raw propositional examples' representations (Sect. 3.2) on datasets shown, as well as others shown in the appendix. This demonstrates the relational essence of the problem. Their performances are around 82%, which can be considered as quite acceptable, considering E_4's consistency rate (88%), as shown in Sect. 3.1. Again, we evaluate here the relevance of the representation of examples and background knowledge more than the performance of propositional vs. relational learning systems.

– Aleph and Tilde have close performances whatever dataset and BK is used. It is in particular not possible to distinguish from an accuracy point of view models built using BK_1 or BK_2. Tilde may slightly outperform Aleph, although not on all sets.

5.2 Performance in Function of the Training Set Size

To evaluate the sensitivity of the learning systems to the training set size, we proceed as follows. For a given fold i, $1 \leq i \leq 10$, let us denote by $Test_i$ the test set and $Train_i$ the training set of the fold. For each fold i and proportion p, we sampled a stratified sample set $T_{i,p}$ of size $\frac{|Train_i| * p}{100}$ from $Train_i$. Each classifier learned for $T_{i,p}$ was evaluated on $Test_i$. Curves of Fig. 4 show the mean accuracy over 10 folds of the classifier learned with training set $T_{i,p}$ as a function of p for background knowledge BK_1 and BK_2.

As expected, the performance of all classifiers increases with the training set size, although we observe that ILP systems are able to reach a good performance with relatively few examples (only 10% of the training set). Hopefully, we do not observe any loss in performance for the largest training sets, which allows discarding overfitting.

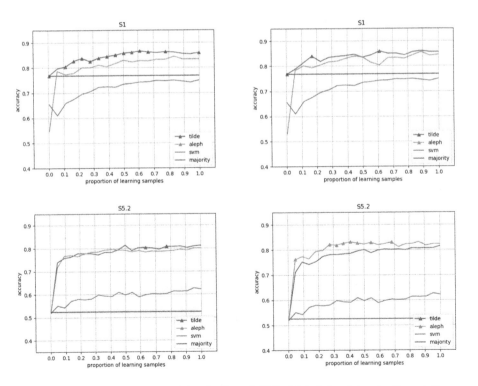

Fig. 4. Accuracy curves for BK_1 (left) and BK_2 (right) for datasets S_1 and $S_{5.2}$

We have again checked whether one ILP system significantly outperforms the other (paired t-test with 95% confidence). Significant differences are reported on the curve with a △. There are very few such differences in the performances of the two ILP systems, however Tilde is almost always the winner in such cases (see Fig. 10 in appendix), except for $S_{5.2}$ on BK_2. In this case, $list\_honor/3$ allows to describe specific rules that Aleph can discover better than Tilde.

The difference w.r.t. the performance between BK_1 and BK_2 is tenuous whereas the differences in the theories and decision trees produced are obvious (see Fig. 5). These curves show the number of rules for Aleph and the number of nodes for Tilde for the same training set size as the previous curves.

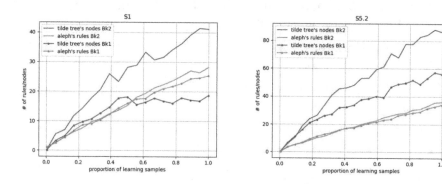

Fig. 5. Model complexity (number of nodes and rules) for S_1 and $S_{5.2}$ datasets and given different background knowledges (BK_1 and BK_2)

The only difference between BK_1 and BK_2 is the $list\_honor/3$ predicate. It is used in about 80% of Aleph's rules and Tilde's nodes for BK_2. Aleph is less resistant to over-fitting (the complexity of the model increases regularly whereas the performance remains relatively stable after seeing about 70% of the training set). This is less true for Tilde, for which the model complexity stabilizes for S_1 and BK_1. Aleph's model complexity does not vary between BK_1 and BK_2 (about 25 rules for S_1 and between 30 and 40 rules for $S_{5.2}$). This is not the case for Tilde : the number of nodes of the learned DT is between 1.3 and 2 times larger for BK_2 than for BK_1.

6   Expert Validation

First of all, expert validations have been used to incrementally update the BK. In order to achieve this task, we made some experiments (not detailed in this paper) on intermediate BKs between BK_0 and BK_1 and we have presented the outputs of the models to the different experts. Their feedback (they validated or not the rules obtained) on the results help us to update at each step the current BK. For instance, seeing that the language used in rules was too poor led experts to advise us to use other features such as the sum of the card numbers in $\heartsuit$ and $\spadesuit$. Experts also provided us with card combinations that make a hand more valuable (for instance King-Queen in a 5+suit) allowing to define and incrementally refine the predicate *plusvalue*. At the end of this process, we obtained BK_1 which is the first BK coupling good performances and positive feedback from experts regarding the learned rules. The experiments presented below are related to BK_1 and BK_2.

All experts noted that this experience had modified their strategy in this part of the game. The difference between the percentages of opened hands by E_4 on the same set (47.63 % the second time vs 55.72% the first time) confirms this point.

The following rule was unanimously validated. It reflects the fact that experts open with at least 6 cards in any suit.

```
r1: (Pos cover = 162 Neg cover = 1)
open(A) :- nb(A,B,C), gteq(C,6).
```

About the 12 rules produced by Aleph, experts gave the following opinion: 3 excellent rules (r1 and r2, r3 below).

```
r2 :  (Pos cover = 68 Neg cover = 3)
open(A) :- plusvalue(A), position(A,3).
```

```
r3 :  (Pos cover = 42 Neg cover = 4)
open(A) :- nb(A,spade,B), gteq(B,4), position(A,4).
```

r2 expresses that a player should open if he is in 3rd position and holds a good hand, whereas r3 means that a player should open if he is in 4th position and has more than 4 spades. When generating r3, Aleph discovered a famous Bridge rule known as 'the rule of 15': a player should open if he is in 4th position and if the number of HCP (11 points for all hands of this problem) plus the number of Spades is greater than or equal to 15. According to Bridge experts, the other rules were non-informative or even ridiculous for 2 of them.

The complexities of the models learned by Aleph are very similar among the experts (about 22 rules, see curves of Figs. 5 and 8 and Table 2 in the appendix). To get rid of the bias of the training set size, Table 2 in the appendix shows an evaluation of the learning model's complexity per expert depending on the background knowledge and the algorithm used for 4 training sets of the same size for each expert (703 training examples randomly selected from each set listed in the table). Set $S3$ that does not appear in the table obtained an average of 37.3 rules, a confirmation that this is a more difficult set (see Sect. 3.1). On the contrary, the complexity of the model learned by Tilde on sets labeled by expert E_1 (S_1) is significantly lower than those of every model related to the other experts.

The size of player's decision tree gives information about the player himself. For instance, E_1 has a scientific background and an analytical mind whereas E_4 has a more intuitive approach of the game. This is confirmed by the fact that

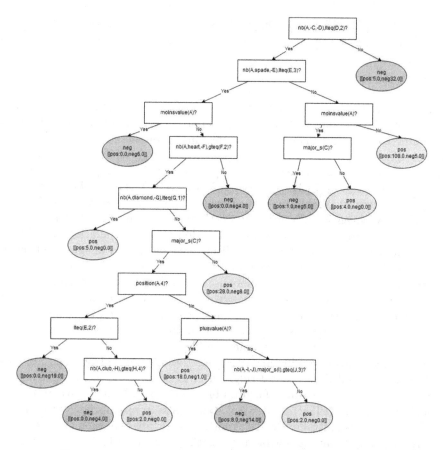

Fig. 6. Decision Tree on S_7 (279 learning samples) with BK_1

E_1's decision tree is two times smaller than E_4's decision tree ($S_{5.2}$ dataset). Moreover, the rules generated from E_4's set are of little interest to other players, being much too specific.

For this reason, we made a new experiment with expert E_1 on a new and smaller set S_7 (310 examples, 279 used for training), with a high level of difficulty since there is no hand in this dataset with more than 5 cards in a suit and the expert's position cannot be 3. The BK used is BK_1. We focus on E_1's validation on the decision tree produced by Tilde given Fig. 6.

Several rules associated with nodes have been described as 'excellent' by E_1. For instance, the rule associated with the root node translated as 'if the distribution of the hand is 4333, I pass' corresponds to one of the first criteria of his decision. The expert validated all the rules related to the nodes except one. Finally, the global vision of the tree appeared to him congruent with his approach of the problem. It is to be noted that before these experiments, the expert was not able to explain clearly his decision-making process on this type of opening.

In other words, Bridge experts make decision using a black-box approach, our methods allowing us to take a look inside the black-box.

7   Conclusions

Bridge has been subject to much research, mostly related to the conception of a Bridge robot. We refer to Paul Bethe's report [1] for extensive state of art on Computer Bridge. Like many programs playing incomplete information games, most current Bridge programs use Monte-Carlo methods which were initiated as early as 1949 by Nicholas Metropolis [13]. This method's adaptation to Bridge has been formalized in [7]. For more than 20 years, best Bridge robots have been competing at official World Computer-Bridge Championships (WCBC). The last 2 WCBC have been won in 2016 and 2017 by a version of AI Wbridge5 that has benefited from an enhancement of its Monte-Carlo simulations (see [17]). Some approaches using symbolic formalisms have been used in sub-problems of Bridge. For instance, in [6] the program Finesse that is coded in Prolog optimizes a card play sub-problem. In [9], authors use Horn clauses to model a bidding rule base. More recently neural approaches (e.g. [8,19]) have been successfully used to automate a limited version of the bidding process. However, these approaches do not provide explanations and do not allow to deviate from the rules as a human does for instance in our opening problem.

The methods displayed in this article for the opening bid problem are currently being extended to other Bridge situations, some of them requiring an upgrade to multi-class learning. Future work related to a Probabilistic Inductive Logic Programming (PILP) framework [4] seems very appropriate since probabilistic reasoning is central in Bridge. Another important extension of the current work is the ability to invent new predicates, using various techniques such as relational pattern mining [5], or more recent approaches in a Statistical Relational Learning context [10,11]. As stated in [18], Bridge is a great challenge for AI and much work related to the definition of a Bridge AI remains to be done. The design of a hybrid architecture including recent numerical, probabilistic, symbolic machine learning modules is currently under process in a project called νBridge (new version of the AlphaBridge project), this work is the prime stone of the ILP-PILP module that will be central in νBridge. In such a framework, ILP systems could be used as a front-end to statistical learning systems in order to generate appropriate representations of examples that take into account some relational traits of the learning problem at hand.

References

1. Bethe, P.: The state of automated bridge play. PDF (2010)
2. Blockeel, H., et al.: The ace data mining system user's manual. https://dtai.cs. kuleuven.be/ACE/doc/ACEuser-1.2.16.pdf
3. Blockeel, H., De Raedt, L., Jacobs, N., Demoen, B.: Scaling up inductive logic programming by learning from interpretations. Data Min. Knowl. Discov. 3(1), 59–93 (1999)

4. De Raedt, L., Kersting, K.: Probabilistic inductive logic programming. In: De Raedt, L., Frasconi, P., Kersting, K., Muggleton, S. (eds.) Probabilistic Inductive Logic Programming. LNCS (LNAI), vol. 4911, pp. 1–27. Springer, Heidelberg (2008). https://doi.org/10.1007/978-3-540-78652-8_1

5. Dehaspe, L., Toivonen, H.: Discovery of frequent datalog patterns. Data Mining Knowl. Discov. **3**(1), 7–36 (1999)

6. Frank, I., Basin, D., Bundy, A.: Combining knowledge and search to solve single-suit bridge. In: Proceedings of AAAI/IAAI, pp. 195–200 (2000)

7. Ginsberg, M.L.: GIB: imperfect information in a computationally challenging game. J. Artif. Intell. Res. **14**, 303–358 (2001)

8. Ho, C.-Y., Lin, H.-T.: Contract bridge bidding by learning. In: Proceedings of Workshop on Computer Poker and Imperfect Information at AAAI Conference on Artificial Intelligence (2015)

9. Jamroga, W.: Modelling artificial intelligence on a case of bridge card play bidding. In: Proceedings of the 8th International Workshop on Intelligent Information Systems, pp. 267–277 (1999)

10. Kazemi, S.M., Poole, D.: RelNN: a deep neural model for relational learning. In: Proceedings of the Thirty-Second AAAI Conference on Artificial Intelligence (2018)

11. Kok, S., Domingos, P.M.: Statistical predicate invention. In: Proceedings of the Twenty-Fourth International Conference on Machine Learning, ICML 2007, pp. 433–440 (2007)

12. Mahmood, Z., Grant, A., Sharif, O.: Bridge for Beginners: A Complete Course. Pavilion Books, London (2014)

13. Metropolis, N., Ulam, S.: The Monte Carlo method. J. Am. Stat. Assoc. **44**(247), 335–341 (1949)

14. Pedregosa, F., Varoquaux, G., Gramfort, A., Michel, V., Thirion, B.: Scikit-learn: machine learning in Python. J. Mach. Learn. Res. **12**, 2825–2830 (2011)

15. Silver, D., Huang, A., Maddison, C.J., Guez, A., Sifre, L., et al.: Mastering the game of go with deep neural networks and tree search. Nature **529**(7587), 484–489 (2016)

16. Srinivasan, A.: The aleph manual (1999). http://www.comlab.ox.ac.uk/oucl/research/areas/machlearn/Aleph/

17. Ventos, V., Costel, Y., Teytaud, O., Ventos, S.T.: Boosting a bridge artificial intelligence. In: Proceedings of International Conference on Tools with Artificial Intelligence (ICTAI), pp. 1280–1287. IEEE (2017)

18. Ventos, V., Teytaud, O.: Le bridge, nouveau défi de l'intelligence artificielle? Revue d'Intelligence Artificielle **31**(3), 249–279 (2017)

19. Yeh, C.-K., Lin, H.-T.: Automatic bridge bidding using deep reinforcement learning. In: Proceedings of the 22nd ECAI, pp. 1362–1369 (2016)

Sampling-Based SAT/ASP Multi-model Optimization as a Framework for Probabilistic Inference

Matthias Nickles[✉]

School of Engineering and Informatics, National University of Ireland, Galway, Galway, Ireland
matthias.nickles@nuigalway.ie

Abstract. This paper proposes multi-model optimization through SAT witness or answer set sampling, with common probabilistic reasoning tasks as primary use cases (including deduction-style probabilistic inference and hypothesis weight learning). Our approach enhances a state-of-the-art SAT/ASP solving algorithm with Gradient Descent as branching literal decision approach, and optionally a cost backtracking mechanism. Sampling of models using these methods minimizes a task-specific, user-provided multi-model cost function while adhering to given logical background knowledge (either a Boolean formula in CNF or a normal logic program under stable model semantics). Features of the framework include its relative simplicity and high degree of expressiveness, since arbitrary differentiable cost functions and background knowledge can be provided.

Keywords: Probabilistic logic programming · SAT
Answer set programming · Projective gradient descent
Numerical optimization · Relational AI

1 Introduction

With this work, we propose multi-model optimization through SAT Boolean assignment (witness) or answer set sampling. The main goal is to provide an expressive and flexible unified framework for performing and experimenting with probabilistic propositional reasoning tasks, but our basic framework is not restricted to probabilistic inference. Multi-model optimization is implemented as an enhancement of an existing SAT/ASP solving algorithm with iterative model sampling capabilities, using a Gradient Descent (GD) approach. Sampled models are added to a multi-model sample until a task-specific cost (objective) function is sufficiently minimized (down to some specified error threshold) while ensuring that all sampled models adhere to the given logical background knowledge (either a Boolean formula in CNF or a non-monotonic logic program). The custom cost function evaluates statistics over an entire multiset of models, as opposed to existing approaches to ASP or SAT-based optimization.

© Springer Nature Switzerland AG 2018
F. Riguzzi et al. (Eds.): ILP 2018, LNAI 11105, pp. 88–104, 2018.
https://doi.org/10.1007/978-3-319-99960-9_6

Using appropriate cost functions, this can solve some common probabilistic inference tasks (in particular deductive probabilistic inference and hypothesis weight determination). A simple counting step over the sample computes approximate probabilistic queries or hypothesis weights. Benefits of the proposed framework include its relative simplicity and high degree of flexibility (in principle, arbitrary differentiable cost functions can be provided), however, the high expressiveness can certainly introduce performance penalties which we seek to reduce by "injecting" our approach directly into the current state-of-the-art approach to SAT/ASP solving, namely Conflict-Driven Nogood Learning (CDNL) [6], a variant of the older Conflict-Driven Clause Learning (CDCL). The extensions of our approach compared to these are (1) a Gradient Descent step in the branching literal heuristics of the partial assignment loop and (2) an optional cost backtracking mechanism, to cover non-deductive probabilistic inference. Over [14], we allow for arbitrary differentiable cost functions, separable measured and parameter atoms, and cost backtracking, besides an optimized prototypical implementation of the algorithm.

2   Related Work

Being based on sampling, our approach is firstly related to existing approaches to SAT or ASP sampling. Such approaches mostly employ near-uniform sampling [9,15] using parity (XOR) constraints [8], a family of approaches devised for Boolean assignment sampling with SAT solvers (made efficient using specialized solvers such as CryptoMiniSat [22]). Uniform sampling is a related but different task. [4] proposes a form of distribution-aware sampling for SAT, considering weight functions over entire models only (which can be seen as an instance of our scenario, albeit technically approached very differently). Also related is the weighted satisfiability problem which aims at maximizing the sum of the given weights of satisfied clauses (e.g., using MaxWalkSAT [10]), which can be used for inference in Bayesian networks. The main difference to existing approaches to optimization in ASP, SAT and related paradigms such as constraint solving is that we aim for optimal multisets of models, not optimal individual models, preference relations among individual models, or individual variables. PSAT (Probabilistic Boolean Satisfiability) [5,19] tackles a closely related but different problem than ours (see Sect. 5.1). The SSAT problem [17] assigns probabilities to random variables to be true, and a solution is an assignment of truth values to existential variables which yields the maximum formula probability of satisfaction. The envisaged main application case for our multi-model sampling approach is probabilistic logic (programming), in particular Probabilistic ASP (of which existing approaches include, e.g., [1,11,13,15]), but we expect other uses cases too, such as working with combinatorial and search problems with uncertain facts and rules. In contrast to the common MC-SAT sampling approach to inference with Markov Logic Networks (MLNs) [18] (a form of slice sampling), our approach is not wrapped around a uniform sampler. We found in earlier experiments with MCMC methods the required amount of uniformly sampled candidate models too large to reach acceptable times and accuracies with our probabilistic logic programming semantics (which is different from MLNs). Also in contrast to MLNs, our algorithm always (consistency provided) allows to specify probabilistic rule or clause weights directly. In contrast to established P(I)LP frameworks from the Distribution Semantics family, probabilistic inference in our framework does not make any assumptions about probabilistic independence of random variables. Existing approaches to the combination of gradient descent/neural network-based techniques or numerical optimization with SAT solving (such as [21]) either aim at an improvement of the SAT solving process itself using machine learning, or enable individual Boolean assignment or answer set optimization. To our best knowledge, the algorithm proposed in this work is the first approach to SAT multi-model optimization and the first approach to SAT and ASP which allows for arbitrary differentiable cost functions for guiding branching decisions.

3   Multi-model Optimization via Gradient Descent-Directed Sampling

3.1   Preliminaries

We consider ground normal logic programs under stable model semantics and SAT problems in form of propositional formulas in Conjunctive Normal Form (CNF). Recall that a normal logic program is a finite set of rules of the form $h :- b_1, ..., b_m, not\ b_{m+1}, ..., not\ b_n$ (with $0 \le m \le n$). h and the b_i are atoms without variables. *not* represents default negation. Rules without body literals are called facts. Most other syntactic constructs supported by contemporary ASP solvers (like constraint rules, choice rules or classical negation) can be translated into (sets of) normal rules. We consider only ground programs in this work. The *answer sets (stable models)* of a normal logic program are as defined in [7]. Throughout the paper, we use the term "answer set program" to mean a ground normal logic program and "model" in the sense of answer set or Boolean assignment (SAT case). Ψ_Υ denotes the set of all models of program or formula Υ. Sometimes we use only logic programming terminology where the translation to SAT terminology is obvious (e.g., "program" instead of set of clauses or CNF formula). The set of all atoms in a program, model or formula f is denoted as $atoms(f)$. We write $\overline{S}$ to denote the set of negative literals $\{\overline{s_i} : s_i \in S\}$. We sometimes refer to individual elements of some set S using notation S_i, assuming some arbitrary but fixed element order.

A model is a set of atoms such that setting these atoms to true and all other atoms to false constitutes a satisfying Boolean assignment for the CNF formula, respectively, in the ASP case, such that the set is a stable model of the answer set program. A *partial assignment* denotes a "model candidate under construction": a set of literals which have been iteratively added to the partial assignment - and sometimes retracted from the assignment in backtracking steps - until the assignment is complete or we abort with UNSAT.

We use a unified approach to SAT and ASP solving based on *nogoods* [6] (a concept originally introduced for constraint solving; nogoods correspond to clauses with all literals negated) which provides a unified approach to both clauses in the CNF and ASP rules, so that we almost never deal with clauses or rules directly: both are translated into nogoods in a straightforward pre-processing step, with additional handling of loops in ASP programs to obtain loop-nogoods in a lazy fashion (a requirement for sampling stable models in the ASP case). This is outlined in Sect. 4, but for details we need to refer the reader to [6].

3.2 Scenario

Our proposed approach aims at allowing to sample models, accumulated in a multiset *sample*, until the value of a user-provided cost function falls under a given threshold. The cost function refers to the optimality of the *entire multiset* (opposed to the optimality of individual models) and can comprise statistics over the models in the sample, such as, informally, "In $\approx$30% of all models, atom a should hold and in $\approx$40% of all models, atom b should hold" or "Atom a should hold more often than the square root of the frequency of atom b minus 10%". The degree of optimality reached can be influenced by the user-provided cost threshold, allowing to trade performance against accuracy. Particular forms of the cost function can be used to model common probabilistic logic programming scenarios, including the assignment of marginal probabilities to arbitrary facts and rules. In that case, once a sample has been generated, probabilities of facts and rules can be computed by treating the sample multiset as a multiset of possible worlds, i.e., by adding up the (approximate) probabilities of those models where the query or hypothesis holds.

3.3 Cost Functions, Parameter and Measured Atoms

The cost functions considered in this work can refer to normalized counts (i.e., frequencies) of uncertain atoms in the current, possibly incomplete, sample (a multiset of sampled models). With each newly sampled model, these counts are updated. This format allows to conveniently express optimization objectives involving given atom weights (example: minimization of $(0.6 - freq(a))^2$) or hypothesis weight learning (example: minimization of $-\prod_i e_i + 1$, using an i.i.d. assumption for the examples e_i).

We distinguish two non-empty, possibly overlapping or identical, subsets of the atoms in the program or CNF term: the set $\theta = \{\theta_i\}$ of *parameter atoms* and the set $\beta = \{\beta_i\}$ of *measured atoms*. We also use the terms parameter and measured literals, for the sets of parameter (measured) atoms and their negations.

The measured atoms are those atoms whose frequencies of models within the current (incomplete) sample where these atoms hold can be used in the evaluation of the cost function. The parameter atoms are those atoms for which the solving algorithm can decided whether to include them positively or negatively in the partial assignment in order to minimize the cost function. For deductive probabilistic inference the two sets are identical. Consider repeated tosses of an (unfair) coin where the known probability of "heads" is 0.6. To approximately model this biased coin, we declare the coin a measured atom as well as a parameter atom: the "measurement" aspect of the coin informs us about the current frequency of "heads" in the multimodel sample under construction. Using $(0.6 - freq(heads))^2$ as cost function, the cost function defines heads' *desired* frequency as 0.6. Finally, the "parameter" aspect of the coin allows us to decide, depending on the latest measurement, whether or not to include "heads" nondeterministically in the next model which is then added to the sample.

If these two atoms sets are not identical, we still require that the truth values of the measured atoms are directly or indirectly influenced by the truth values of the parameter atoms. For example, the parameter atoms (which need to be nondeterministic) might be used as abducibles and the measured atoms might be used for observations (a simple concrete example where the sets of measured and parameter atoms are disjunct is shown in Sect. 5.2).

We write $\beta(sample)$ to denote vector $\langle \frac{|[m_j : m_j \in sample, \beta_1 \in m_j]|}{|sample|}, ...,$ $\frac{|[m_j : m_j \in sample, \beta_n \in m_j]|}{|sample|} \rangle$ of measured atom frequencies in model multiset $sample$. $cost(v)$ evaluates the cost function with measured atoms frequencies $(v_1, ..., v_{|\beta|})$ (for example, $cost(\beta(sample))$). $\beta(sample)_i$ or $\beta(sample)(\beta_i)$ denote the sample frequency of measured atom β_i.

Our framework (being "closer to the metal" than probabilistic logic programming languages) does not impose restrictions on the choice of cost function or parameter atoms, that is, the burden is here on the user. While the selection of measured atoms is determined by the cost function expression, selecting a set of parameter atoms is only required for performance reasons: theoretically, we could appoint all atoms parameter atoms, but this might lead to a costly and unnecessary examination of atoms which have not been assigned by unit propagation even if they are not involved in probabilistic inference. Within the scope of this paper, selecting an appropriate set of parameter atoms is easy: for deduction-style inference, it is identical with the set of measured atoms. For abduction or induction-style weight learning, it is exactly the set of atoms whose weights we want to find given a set of example facts.

Note that it makes sense to allow only atoms in θ whose truth values are not fully fixed by rules or clauses in the input program or CNF. In the ASP case, it is thus sensible to give the program the form of a so-called *spanning program* [11,15] where uncertain atoms a are defined by choice rules or analogous constructs, such as $0\{a\}1$ or (informally) $a \lor not\ a$. If arbitrary rules should be used as "parameter rules" or "measured rules" (e.g., to learn their weight or for assigning weights to them), we need to assign them each a fresh auxiliary atom first which then serves as parameter or measured atom, by adding spanning rules of the form $h :- b_1, ..., b_n, not\ aux$ and $aux :- b_1, ..., b_n, not\ h$ [11]. However, our framework does not require any particular form of input program or formula, provided it is satisfiable.

3.4   Steepest Gradient Descent (with Optional Cost Backtracking) as a Branching Heuristics in SAT Solving

We present the parameter update iterations within our multi-model optimization process as an iterative gradient descent (GD) approach with optional *cost backtracking* (CBT) which minimizes the cost function over the measured atom frequencies in the current sample. More precisely, we use a projected form of the method of steepest gradient descent [3], as outlined in Algorithm 1 for the SAT case. "Projected" means here that the GD parameters - the frequencies of the parameter atoms by which we indirectly change the sample frequencies of the models in which these atoms hold - can take on only values from a specific set of possible values, which is caused by the fact that in our non-standard GD scenario, the only things the GD steps can influence are the truth values of the parameter literals in the partial assignment (leading to the next model which is then added to the sample multiset).

The GD steps are only useful when the parameter atoms are a subset of the measured atoms, as otherwise the derivative of the cost function would not tell us anything about the direction to move.

Algorithm 1 serves only as an explanation tool; the actual implementation of the gradient descent mechanism is much simpler, as explained further below.

Our GD approach is somewhat complicated by the fact that we are constrained by the overall SAT solving process in which we embed the steeped descent steps: (1) although the cost function is typically multidimensional, we can move only into one direction (change the frequency of one parameter atom within the partial sample) at each step, whereas any other literals are either decided deterministically using unit propagation or nondeterministically in other branching decisions (although theoretically we could assign multiple decision literals in each iteration, this would not fit in well with DPLL/CDCL-style solving and possibly generate a large number of conflict-induced backtracks if these literals conflict with each other), and (2) the step-width we take for parameter (i.e., decision) atom a is determined by the fact that we can only decide whether to add a or $\overline{a}$ to the partial assignment at each step, i.e., we cannot arbitrarily update uncertain atom or model frequencies - hence the use of Projected GD.

These constraints make the gradient descent iterations coarse in the beginning when there are only a few models in the sample (like with a non-optimal line search), but with each additional model added to the sample multiset, the impact of adding a parameter literal to the assignment has a smaller effect on the cost function, which means that over time, the step widths with which our algorithm moves into the direction of the steepest gradient get monotonically smaller and smaller (informally: $\lim_{i\to\infty} |\beta(sample^i) - \beta(sample^{i-1})| = \mathbf{0}$), eventually reaching the same granularity as standard GD.

Algorithm 1 conveniently assumes that *all* literals in the CNF formula are parameter literals (which would be inefficient, so in practice we should define a dedicated set of parameter atoms). Also, it assumes that the change of *cost* when assigning a literal (from which *cost* depends) is opposite compared to the negation of that literal.

Algorithm 1. Projective Steepest Gradient Descent as a SAT branching heuristics with custom cost function (algorithm outline)

$L \leftarrow atoms \cup \overline{atoms}$

2:    $as \leftarrow \{\}$ ▷ Partial assignment (the model constructed by the loop below)

   repeat

4:      $as \leftarrow$ UNITPROP   ▷ Enhances as deterministically until fixpoint is reached

     Backtrack if conflict (or abort if UNSAT). Otherwise:

6:      $L' = L \setminus as \setminus \overline{as}$ ▷ We consider only unassigned parameter literals

     Define directional unit vectors $\ell(l_i) \leftarrow e_i, e_i \in \mathbb{R}^{|L|}$ for each unassigned positive literal

8:      l_i and $\ell(\overline{l_i}) \leftarrow -e_i$ for each unassigned negative literal $\overline{l_i}$

     $\nabla_{l_i} = \lim_{h \to 0} \dfrac{cost(\beta(sample \uplus as) + h\ell(l_i)) - cost(\beta(sample \uplus as))}{h}$ per $l_i \in L'$

10:    $\widehat{\ell(l)} \leftarrow \operatorname{argmin}_{\ell(l_i), l_i \in L'}(\nabla_{l_i})$ ▷ Direction of literal resulting in steepest descent

     If $rand_0^1 > \epsilon$ as $\leftarrow as \cup \{l\}$ else $as \leftarrow as \cup L'_{random}$ ▷ $\epsilon \ll 1$ (noise)

12:    $x \leftarrow \beta(sample \uplus atoms(as)) + \alpha\widehat{\ell(l)}$ ▷ α to be found by a line search

     $\beta_{cand} \leftarrow \langle \dfrac{|[m_j \; : \; m_j \in sample \uplus \{atoms(as) \cup a_i\}, a_i \in m_j]|}{|sample| + 1} : a_i \in \beta \rangle$

14:      $\cup \langle \dfrac{|[m_j \; : \; m_j \in sample \uplus \{atoms(as)\}, a_i \in m_j]|}{|sample| + 1} : a_i \in \beta \rangle$

     $\beta(sample \uplus atoms(as)) \leftarrow \operatorname{argmin}_{c \in \beta_{cand}} \|c - x\|$ ▷ Projection

16:      Optional: Cost backtracking if needed (see further below)

   until as complete   ▷ we have found a model and add the set of atoms within as to $sample$

The actual implementation of Algorithm 1 is much simpler than it perhaps looks: We never have to actually update β using line 15 or to actually perform the projection, as we can simply add the literal for which a steepest descent of the cost is expected (line 10) to the partial assignment as and update $\beta(sample)$ later with the current measured atom frequencies, after the assignment is complete and has been added as a model (i.e., as the set of its positive literals) to $sample$. Furthermore, the $\uplus as$ in line 9 is typically negligible. We propose two alternative ways to implement Algorithm 1: using **numerical differentiation** as in line 9, and using **automatic differentiation** (for a suitable cost function form and with measured atoms = parameter atoms). We use automatic differentiation with a somewhat different formula instead of $\widehat{\ell(l)} \leftarrow \operatorname{argmin}_{\ell(l_i), l_i \in L'}(\nabla_{l_i})$, to speed up computation: we demand here that the cost function is defined using $cost(v_1, ..., v_n) = \frac{1}{n}\sum_k innerCost_{atoms_k}(v_k)$ with exactly one (arbitrary) inner cost function per each uncertain atom $atoms_k$. Each v_k gets instantiated with the current frequency of atom $atoms_k$ in the sample.

The derivatives of the inner costs are $innerCost'_{atoms_k} = \dfrac{d \; innerCost_{atoms_k}(v_k)}{dv_k}$. To compute the gradients we use then

$$\widehat{\ell(l)} = \operatorname{argmin}_{\ell(l_i), l_i \in L'} \begin{cases} innerCost'_{l_i}(\beta(sample)(l_i)) & \text{if } l_i \in atoms \text{ (i.e., positive)} \\ -innerCost'_{\overline{l_i}}(\beta(sample)(\overline{l_i})) & \text{else (i.e., } l_i \text{ is a negative literal)} \end{cases}$$

Cost Backtracking (Optional). Using gradient descent is only suitable when evaluating the cost function derivative always allows to directly decide whether or not to add a certain parameter literal to the partial assignment. This is not the case if the set of parameter atoms is disjoint from the set of measured atoms, as only measured atoms can appear in cost functions. To account for this situation, we can *decouple* the nondeterministic decision on whether to add a certain parameter literal to the partial assignment and the evaluation of the cost function. This so-called *cost backtracking* (CBT), which amounts in undoing the latest decisions and the subsequent unit propagations if the cost has not improved after choosing and assigning a parameter literal, is relevant in particular if the inference task is abduction or hypothesis weight learning given observed facts. CBT can be combined with GD or used as exclusive optimization method. CBT can be seen as a coarse sort-of gradient descent approach where the effect of parameter changes on the cost function is observed only with a delay, namely after one or more unit propagation steps (firing of rules in the logic program) or even branching decisions. Technical details are provided in Sect. 4.

4   Differential SAT/ASP

This section presents the full algorithm - named *Differential SAT/ASP* (ΔSAT/ASP for short) - implemented as an extension of CDNL-ASP [6]. In contrast to enumerating any, or individually optimal, models, or providing a witness in case of satisfiability, ΔSAT/ASP is a model sampling algorithm, i.e., it iteratively generates a multiset *sample* of models until the cost function falls below a user-specified error (accuracy) threshold ψ.

At the core of the algorithm are the "pluggable" nondeterministic literal branching heuristics which use differentiation of a user-provided cost function for deciding on unassigned parameter literals, and some standard SAT/ASP branching heuristics such as VSIDS in other cases. We propose two such differentiation-based heuristics in this paper (others certainly exist): DECISION$_{Numdiff}$ and DECISION$_{Autodiff}$, which implement the numerical respectively automatic differentiation approach described in the previous section. For lack of space, we only show in more detail the former (Algorithm 2).

Algorithm 2. Branching decision heuristics DECISION$_{Numdiff}$

---

    procedure DECISION$_{Numdiff}$($sample$, as, L, θ) $\triangleright$ *as* is the partial assignment, L is the set of candidate literals

        $cost_1 \leftarrow cost(\beta(sample \uplus \{as\}))$

3:     $stats \leftarrow \beta(sample \cup \{as\})$ $\triangleright$ Vector of measured atom frequencies in $sample \cup \{as\}$

        $S \leftarrow [stats, ..., stats] \in \mathbb{R}^{|\beta| \times |\beta|}$

        $S' \leftarrow S + hI_{|\beta|}$ $\triangleright$ h is a positive number $\ll 1$ (10^{-6} in our experiments). I is the identity matrix

6:     $S'' \leftarrow (S' | S - hI_{|\beta|})$ $\triangleright$ for negative literals, we move into the negative direction

        $dl \leftarrow \text{argmin}_{p_i \in \beta \cup \overline{\beta}, p_i \in (\theta \cup \overline{\theta}) \cap L} \dfrac{cost(S_i'') - cost_1}{h}$

        if $dl = \{\}$ **then**

9:         $decisionLit \leftarrow$ SELECT(as) $\triangleright$ Choose decision literal using some conventional branching heuristics

        else

         $decisionLit \leftarrow dl_{random}$

12:   **end if**

        return ($decisionLit$, $1 - \epsilon$) $\triangleright$ ϵ being some very small value (artificial noise)

        end procedure

Overall Algorithm. Algorithm 3 shows the full ΔSAT/ASP -CDNL algorithm. The algorithm works with both ASP programs and SAT CNF formulas (input program or formula Υ), the latter using a simple preprocessing step (omitted here for lack of space) which translates clauses into nogoods. For answer set programs, the initial set Ξ of nogoods is obtained as usual from Clark's completion of the original program as described in [6]. To keep the presentation focused on probabilistic and optimization-related aspects, we also omit or simplify in this work some features available in the original CDNL procedure: loop nogoods (required in case the answer set program is not tight) are added on-demand using the simpler approach introduced in [12], as sketched later. The loop in procedure COMPMODELCAND iteratively adds literals to a partial Boolean assignment (a sequence of literals) until all literals are covered positively or negatively and no nogood is violated. The procedure for this is guided by three factors: the nogoods initially obtained from Clark's completion of the answer set program and enhanced during conflict resolution, further nogoods added when a discovered supported model of a non-tight program is not a stable model, and an approach to select nondeterministic decision literals (that is, the aforementioned branching heuristics). The first two points (i.e., the non-probabilistic CDNL algorithm) are very briefly recalled at the end of this section, but for a complete description we refer to [6,12] (for our rather elementary loop handling approach), for lack of space.

The main differences to existing variants of CDNL/CDCL are our "pluggable" decision literal choice policy DECISION$_{heuristics}$ in line 25 in procedure COMPMODELCAND, for which alternative options have been proposed in the previous section (numerical and automatic differentiation), and the optional cost backtracking (CBT) mechanism, which is required for cases where the parameter atoms are disjoint from the measured atoms.

The CBT approach builds directly on the conflict backtracking mechanism of CDNL but instead of jumping back if a violated nogood is encountered, it jumps backs if the cost function did not improve. Jumping back means that all deterministic and nondeterministic literal assignments which occurred on all decision levels $\geq ndl$ are undone, with ndl being the decision level to which we jump back. CBT's cost check (line 43) is by default performed immediately after an assignment is complete. However, performing the backtrack check there can be costly: we might have performed a lot of improper parameter literal decisions until the check shows us that the cost function did not improve. Therefore, it can be sensible to do the cost check earlier or more frequently. Currently, there exists no automatic approach to find the optimal times for the backtrack checks, so we made these times configurable by the user (e.g., "evaluate cost function every 5 decisions and backtrack if no improvement"), with checks at assignment completion as the default.

As for the not directly sampling-related aspects of Algorithm 3: When a conflict (a nogood violation) is encountered, the conflict is analyzed in CON-FLICTANALYSIS (line 36) and the algorithm jumps back to one of the previous decision levels, and adds a new nogood (conflict analysis and nogood learning

---

Algorithm 3. ΔSAT/ASP -CDNL: Multi-Model Optimization in Conflict-Driven Nogood Learning for SAT/ASP

---

    procedure ΔSAT/ASP-CDNL(Υ, Ξ (nogoods, see Sect. 4), θ, ψ (accuracy), *stable_only* (to restrict sampling to answer sets), *heuristics* (for branching on nondeterministic literals))
        $sample \leftarrow [\,]$
3:    **repeat**
        $bounced \leftarrow true$
        repeat
6:            $cand \leftarrow$ COMPMODELCAND($\Upsilon, \Xi, \theta, \psi, heuristics$)
            if $cand = UNSAT$ **then return** $UNSAT$
            if $\neg stable\_only \lor cand \in \Psi_\Upsilon$ **then**   ▷ Stable model check (omit if Υ tight)
9:                $sample \leftarrow sample \uplus \{cand\}$
                $bounced \leftarrow false$
            else
12:              add loop nogoods to Ξ as described in [12]
            end if
        until $\neg bounced$
15:    **until** $cost(\beta(sample)) \leq \psi$ or no further significant changes of $cost(\beta(sample))$
    end procedure
    procedure COMPMODELCAND(Υ, Ξ, θ, ψ, *heuristics*)   ▷ (see algorithm part 1)
18:    $dl \leftarrow 0$, $as \leftarrow \{\}$ ▷ decision level and partial assignment (incomplete model candidate)
    $(as, \varepsilon) \leftarrow$ UNITPROP($\{\}, \Xi$)
    $initialCost \leftarrow cost(\beta(sample))$
21:    **while** as not complete $\lor \varepsilon \neq \{\}$ **do**
        if $\varepsilon = \{\}$ **then**   ▷ Branching...
            $dl \leftarrow dl + 1$
24:            $L' \leftarrow (atoms \cup \overline{atoms}) \setminus as \setminus \overline{as}$
            $(decLit, decLitPr) \leftarrow$ DECISION$_{heuristics}(as, L' \setminus paramsTried(dl))$
            if $rand_0^1 < decLitPr$ **then** $as = as \cup decLit$ **else** $as = as \cup \overline{decLit}$
27:            **if** $decLit \in \theta \lor \overline{decLit} \in \theta$ **then**
                $paramsTried(dl) \leftarrow paramsTried(dl) \cup \{decLit\}$
            end if
30:            **if** $\theta \setminus paramsTried(dl)) = \{\}$ **then** $paramsTried(dl) \leftarrow$ "complete"
            $paramsTried(dl + 1) \leftarrow \{\}$
            $(as, \varepsilon) \leftarrow$ UNITPROP(as, Ξ)
33:        **end if**
        if $\varepsilon \neq \{\}$ **then**   ▷ Conflict handling...
            if $dl = 0$ **then return** $UNSAT$
36:            $(newNogood, unitLit, newLevel) \leftarrow$ CONFLICTANALYSIS($\varepsilon, \Upsilon, \Xi, as$)
            $\Xi \leftarrow \Xi \cup \{newNogood\}$
            ▷ Conflict-triggered backtracking:
39:            $as \leftarrow as \setminus \{lit \in as : newLevel < dl(lit)\}$ ▷ $dl(lit)$ gives the decision level of lit

            $dl \leftarrow newLevel$
            $as \leftarrow as \cup unitLit$
42:        **else if** *costBacktrackCheck* (default: check when as complete) **then**
            if $cost(\beta(sample \uplus \{atoms(as)\})) \geq initialCost$ **then**
                $nl :\Leftrightarrow paramsTried(nl) \neq \{\} \land paramsTried(nl) \neq$ "complete"
45:                      $\land \neg \exists nl', nl' > nl :\Leftrightarrow paramsTried(nl') \neq \{\}$
                      $\land paramsTried(nl') \neq$ "complete"
                $as \leftarrow as \setminus \{lit \in as : nl \leq dl(lit)\}$ ▷ we backtrack to a previous level...
48:                $dl \leftarrow nl - 1$
            end if
        end if
51:    **end while**
    return $as^T \cap atoms(\Upsilon)$ ▷ Model found. as^T represents the positive literals in as
    end procedure

---

sets CDNL apart from the related older DPLL-style approaches to SAT/ASP solving). Every literal that is added to the partial assignment is added on a certain decision level dl (the same level which we also use in the context of CBT); each time we make a decision (i.e., when we add a literal which is not enforced to hold deductively given the nogoods), we increase the decision level. Sub-procedure UNITPROP adds non-decision literals which must hold deductively (forced deterministically by so-called unit-resulting nogoods). CONFLICTANALYSIS and UNITPROP are as in [6] except for loop-handling (see below), and are thus omitted here. $atoms(asp)$ and $bodies(asp)$ denote the atom respectively body literals for answer set program asp (body literals are literals which represent entire rule bodies). Argument Ξ represents the set of all nogoods of the input program or formula. For any answer set m, $\forall \xi \in \Xi : \xi \not\subseteq m$ holds. Loop nogood generation differs in our prototypical implementation from [6] by using the simpler ASSAT [12] approach, just to simplify our experimental implementation.

5   Probabilistic Inference

5.1   Instantiating ΔSAT/ASP for Probabilistic Deduction

To instantiate the ΔSAT/ASP approach for probabilistic deduction, we need a suitable cost function form (we propose the *Mean Squared Error* (MSE)) and a suitable selection of parameter and measured atoms. We use ASP terminology in this section, but everything analogously applies also to the SAT case.

As mentioned before, we assume in this case that the sets of measured and parameter atoms are identical here, so in this section we refer to both as parameter atoms or just uncertain atoms. $\beta(sample)$ thus now denotes the vector of frequencies of the parameter atoms in the incomplete or complete sample. The use case we are targeting is formulated like a PSAT problem in normal form [5], however, we aim at finding a sampled multiset of possible worlds such that the user-provided probabilistic constraints are observed, in addition to the hard constrains in form of the non-probabilistic rules and facts in the logic program. These probabilistic constraints consist of any number of given weights associated with individual parameter atoms. Weights directly represent probabilities. The tuple of the given weights of all uncertain atoms (assuming the same order as in $\theta = \{\theta_i\}$) is written as ϕ, with ϕ_i or $\phi(\theta_i)$ denoting the given weight $\in [0; 1]$ of uncertain atom θ_i. The atom-weights associations are translated into addends in a normalized sum-form cost functions which is then minimized by ΔSAT/ASP . Observe that we do not impose any restrictions on the weight annotations or the choice of uncertain atoms such as independence assumptions, except consistency. Informally, using an appropriate cost function, the sampling process iteratively adds models to the sample until either for each uncertain atom its frequency in the sample is equal to its given weight, or close to the given weight up to the specified cost (or error) threshold (*accuracy*). If, for example, the given weight of atom a is 0.4, the sample should contain ~40% (not necessarily different) answer sets where a holds (equivalently: the frequencies of the individual answer sets in the sample where a holds add up to 0.4).

Note that such given weights do, in general, not directly tell us anything about the probabilities of models or formulas, in contrast to scenarios like *Weighted Model Counting* (WMC) [2].

We define a distribution-aware *sample* of answer sets of answer set program asp as a non-empty multiset $[m_i]$, $Supp([m_i]) = \Psi_{asp}$, such that the probability that a specific answer set m_i is included in this sample (with replacement) is defined by a discrete probability distribution over answer sets with probability mass function $pmf^{asp}(m_i) = Pr(m_i)$, where $m_i \in \Psi_{asp}$ and $Pr(m_i)$ denotes the probability of m_i.

The given atom weights induce a set of probability distributions as follows: We call set $pds = \{pmf_i^{asp}\}$ the set of weight-induced probability distributions (over the set Ψ_{asp} of answer sets of asp) *iff* $\forall pmf_i^{asp} \in pds \ \forall \theta_j \in \theta :$ $\sum_{m_k : m_k \in \Psi_{asp} \wedge \theta_j \in m_k} pmf_i^{asp}(m_k) = \phi_j$.

The condition for pds above defines a system of linear equations which is the typical way of defining possible world probabilities in Nilsson-style [16] probabilistic logics:

Per each uncertain atom θ_k, we obtain equation $v(k, m_1)pmf_i^{asp}(m_1) + ... + v(k, m_n)pmf_i^{asp}(m_n) = \phi(k)$, with $\Psi_{asp} = \{m_i\}$, $n = |\Psi_{asp}|$, and $v(k, m_j) = 1$ if $m_j \models \theta_k$ and $v(k, m_j) = 0$ otherwise.

The solution sets pmf_i^{asp} of this equation system with the two extra conditions $pmf_i^{asp}(m_i) \in [0, 1]$ and $\sum_i pmf_i^{asp}(m_i) = 1$ are precisely the elements of pds. We say that the user-specified atom weights define a set pds of *target distributions*. The program together with the atoms' target weights typically under-specifies the equation system, so typically multiple (even infinitely many) correct solutions (target distributions) exist. However, the algorithm presented in this paper does not guarantee a maximum entropy target distribution. We only consider programs with weight associations for which the above system of equations and extra conditions is solvable, which requires that the program is logically consistent and that the given weights do not imply probabilistic inconsistency. To allow the user to trade off sampling accuracy against speed, our algorithm samples iteratively until the given error threshold (accuracy) ψ is reached for the cost function, namely the Mean Squared Error (MSE) $cost(\beta(sample)) = \frac{1}{n}\sum_{i=1}^{n}(\phi_i - \beta(sample)_i)^2$ (squared Euclidean distance normalized with the number n of uncertain atoms). MSE is a cost function often used in statistics and with linear regression, but other distance or divergence-style cost functions might be usable in this scenario too. The form of MSE also means we can employ the automatic differentiation approach from Sect. 3.4. MSE expresses the acceptable minimum accuracy directly in terms of the maximum acceptable difference between an uncertain atom's given weight and its actual weight in the sample (sum of the frequencies of its possible worlds in the sample). If MSE reaches zero, the model frequencies in the sampled multiset of models are solutions of the equation system above. Further details on using MSE in connection with this sampling scenario can be found in [14], which presents a more restricted form of the sampling approach introduced here.

5.2 Instantiating ΔSAT/ASP for Hypothesis Weight Search

This paper focuses on deduction-style probabilistic inference here, but we can also approach abduction and induction-style determination of fact weights, with the help of cost backtracking (CBT). CBT alone does not allow to generalize from examples to new universally quantified rules, but we can search for the probabilities of hypothesis atoms such that the probabilities of given example atoms are maximized [20]. The example atoms are measured atoms in ΔSAT/ASP terminology, and the hypothesis atoms are parameter atoms θ. Making the i.i.d. assumption, ΔSAT/ASP should find a sample of models such that $\prod_i Pr(\beta_i|\theta)$ is maximized (maximum likelihood estimation). One suitable cost function would thus be $1 - \prod_i \beta(sample)_i$.

As indicated in Sect. 3.4, GD is not helpful here, since varying the parameter atoms in the models does not directly change the frequencies of the measured atoms here, as required for obtaining a meaningful gradient by means of cost function differentiation. Thus, we need to use CBT (unless a better approach is found for use with our basic algorithm). CBT (Sect. 3.4) basically means we vary the assignment of positive and negative parameter literals each time we branch until the cost function improves. A simple example: Let us assume we want to determine the weight of hypothesis fact h from a (positive) example fact e and "hard" background rule $e :- h$. We aim at finding a weight for h which maximizes the probability of e. $(1 - \beta(sample)(e))^2$ would be sufficient here as cost function, since there is only one example atom. To arrive at the correct weight $Pr(h) = \text{argmax}_{wh \in [0;1]} Pr(e|sample) = 1 \wedge Pr(h|sample) = wh$, we need to find a multiset of models st. the cost function evaluates to 0, which involves searching the parameter space $\{h, \neg h\}$ each time we compute a new model. Deciding for one of these two alternatives does not directly influence the value of the cost function, so we need to propagate the effect of the parameter decision first, by considering rule $e :- h$ (or generally: all rules (respectively the nogoods obtained from the rules) affected by our decision until a fixpoint for the partial assignment is reached, which is achieved by UNITPROP) and afterwards measuring the effect on the cost function. If no improvement is observed, we backtrack (line 43f in Algorithm 3) and try some alternative assignment in the space of parameter literals.

6   Experiments

We examine using preliminary experiments how the performance of our current prototype implementation of ΔSAT/ASP -CDNL roughly compares to a popular existing approach, namely Markov Logic Network, using Tuffy 0.4[1]). We believe that these results are useful to give a first ballpark performance estimate from the perspective of a potential user who is mainly interested in short inference times. However, a difficulty in quantitatively comparing probabilistic logic frameworks is their differing semantics (e.g., MLN works with unnormalized weight annotations), expressiveness and achieved accuracies - therefore the results should obviously be taken with a grain of salt.

---

[1] http://i.stanford.edu/hazy/hazy/tuffy/.

We performed two synthetic experiments (Fig. 1): a coin game (adapted from [15]) with background rules and a variant of the well-known "Friends & Smokers" scenario. Durations have been averaged over three trials per experiment on a i7-4810MQ machine (4 cores, 2.8 GHz) with 16 GB RAM. The ΔSAT/ASP tasks have been performed using a preliminary implementation in Scala (running in a Java VM 10). Tuffy was used with default runtime arguments. ΔSAT/ASP experiments have been performed with different accuracy thresholds ψ and with numerical as well as automatic differentiation. Cost backtracking was disabled (since not required here). Cut-off graphs indicate time outs. All times are "end-to-end" durations which include some overhead for starting external processes, I/O, parsing, etc. (for ΔSAT/ASP, the benchmarks provide the (weighted) rules and facts in textual form which is serialized into aspif format and a binary representation of the cost function).

In the coin game, a number of coins are tossed and the game is won if a certain subset of all coins comes up with "heads". The inference task is the approximation of the winning probability. In addition, another random subset of coins are magically dependent from each other and one of the coins is biased (probability of "heads" is 0.6). This scenario covers probabilistically indepen-dent as well as dependent uncertain facts. In pseudo-syntax, such a partially randomly generated program looks, e.g., as follows (the adaptation for MLN is straightforward):

```
coin(1..8).
0.6: coin_out(1,heads).
0.5: coin_out(N,heads) :- coin(N), N != 1.
1{coin_out(N,heads), coin_out(N,tails)}1 :- coin(N).
win :- 2{coin_out(3,heads),coin_out(4,heads)}2.
coin_out(4,heads) :- coin_out(6,heads).
```

Since ΔSAT/ASP cannot cope with non-ground rules, weighted non-ground rules anywhere have been translated into sets of ground rules, each annotated with the given weight. Non-normal ASP rules such as the choice constructs above have been converted using `clingo --trans-ext=all --pre=aspif` .

In the "Friends & Smokers" scenario (which is different from the variant in [14]), a randomly chosen number of persons are friends, a randomly cho-sen subset of all people smoke, there is a certain probability for being stressed (`[0.3] stress(X)`), it is assumed that stress leads to smoking (`smokes(X) :- stress(X)`), and that some friends influence each other with a certain probability (`[0.2] influences(X,Y)`), in particular with regard to their smoking behavior `smokes(X) :- friend(X,Y), influences(Y,X), smokes(Y)`. With a certain probability, smok-ing leads to asthma (`[0.4] h(X). asthma(X) :- smokes(X), h(X)`). The query atoms are `asthma(X)` per each person X. The Tuffy task starts with 10 smokers, as with lower item numbers this task sometimes did not complete for unknown reasons.

What can safely be said from these initial experiments is that for the Smoker-scenario, ΔSAT/ASP task duration depends heavily on the specified threshold ($\psi = 0.05$ vs. 0.001), and that automated differentiation is clearly superior to numerical differentiation, which is likely largely due to the fact that our numeri-cal differentiation approach compares hypothetical cost changes for all currently unassigned parameter literals. For the coins game, the times increase almost linearly using automatic differentiation, possibly reflecting that by each parameter branching decision, only a single value lookup needs to take place (the order of parameters by their derivative values is computed only once per model) and the growth of items is, for the given numbers of coins, almost linear, with a high amount of mutual independence. For the smokers tasks, the exponential increase seems to reflect mainly the exponential growth of relations among the items with increasing numbers of items.

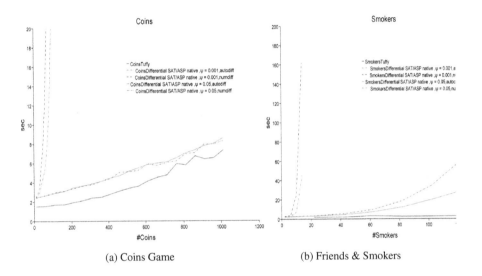

(a) Coins Game   (b) Friends & Smokers

Fig. 1. Performance

7   Conclusion

To our best knowledge, we have presented the first approach to SAT multi-model optimization with user supplied arbitrary differentiable cost functions, and the first approach to SAT and ASP which is able to sample witnesses or stable models using a gradient descent approach which minimizes this cost function, which covers deductive probabilistic inference as a use case. Cost backtracking can be used as an alternative mechanism in case the parameter atoms are not identical with the measured atoms (for example in case the measured atoms are learning examples whose weights should be maximized). Planned work focuses on further performance improvements, in particular of cost backtracking. It is also planned to include (faster) handling of the special case where mutual independence of parameter atoms can be exploited.

References

1. Baral, C., Gelfond, M., Rushton, N.: Probabilistic reasoning with answer sets. Theory Pract. Log. Program. **9**(1), 57–144 (2009)
2. Biere, A., Heule, M., van Maaren, H., Walsh, T. (eds.): Handbook of Satisfiability, Frontiers in Artificial Intelligence and Applications, vol. 185. IOS Press, Amsterdam (2009)
3. Boyd, S., Vandenberghe, L.: Convex Optimization. Cambridge University Press, New York (2004)
4. Chakraborty, S., Fremont, D.J., Meel, K.S., Seshia, S.A., Vardi, M.Y.: Distribution-aware sampling and weighted model counting for SAT. In: Proceedings of 28th AAAI Conference on Artificial Intelligence (AAAI), pp. 1722–1730, July 2014
5. Finger, M., Bona, G.D.: Probabilistic satisfiability: logic-based algorithms and phase transition. In: Proceedings of 22nd International Joint Conference on Artificial Intelligence (2011)
6. Gebser, M., Kaufmann, B., Neumann, A., Schaub, T.: Conflict-driven answer set solving. In: Proceedings of the 20th International Joint Conference on Artificial Intelligence (IJCAI 2007) (2007)
7. Gelfond, M., Lifschitz, V.: The stable model semantics for logic programming. In: Proceedings of the 5th International Conference on Logic Programming, vol. 161 (1988)
8. Gomes, C.P., Sabharwal, A., Selman, B.: Near-uniform sampling of combinatorial spaces using XOR constraints. In: NIPS, pp. 481–488 (2006)
9. Greßler, A., Oetsch, J., Tompits, H.: Harvey: a system for random testing in ASP. In: Balduccini, M., Janhunen, T. (eds.) LPNMR 2017. LNCS, vol. 10377, pp. 229–235. Springer, Cham (2017). https://doi.org/10.1007/978-3-319-61660-5_21
10. Kautz, H., Selman, B., Jiang, Y.: A general stochastic approach to solving problems with hard and soft constraints. In: The Satisfiability Problem: Theory and Applications, pp. 573–586. American Mathematical Society (1996)
11. Lee, J., Wang, Y.: A probabilistic extension of the stable model semantics. In: 2015 AAAI Spring Symposium on Logical Formalizations of Commonsense Reasoning (2015)
12. Lin, F., Zhao, Y.: ASSAT: computing answer sets of a logic program by SAT solvers. Artif. Intell. **157**(1), 115–137 (2004). Nonmonotonic Reasoning
13. Ng, R.T., Subrahmanian, V.S.: Stable semantics for probabilistic deductive databases. Inf. Comput. **110**(1), 42–83 (1994)
14. Nickles, M.: Distribution-aware sampling of answer sets. In: Ciucci, D., Pasi, G., Vantaggi, B. (eds.) Proceedings of 12th International Conference on Scalable Uncertainty Management (SUM 2018). LNAI, vol. 11142. Springer (2018, to appear)
15. Nickles, M., Mileo, A.: A hybrid approach to inference in probabilistic non-monotonic logic programming. In: 2nd International Workshop on Probabilistic Logic Programming (PLP 2015) (2015)
16. Nilsson, N.J.: Probabilistic logic. Artif. Intell. **28**(1), 71–87 (1986)
17. Papadimitriou, C.H.: Games against nature. J. Comput. Syst. Sci. **31**(2), 288–301 (1985)
18. Poon, H., Domingos, P.: Sound and efficient inference with probabilistic and deterministic dependencies. In: Proceedings of the 21st National Conference on Artificial Intelligence, AAAI 2006, vol. 1, pp. 458–463. AAAI Press (2006)

19. Pretolani, D.: Probability logic and optimization SAT: The PSAT and CPA models. Ann. Math. Artif. Intell. **43**(1), 211–221 (2005)
20. De Raedt, L., Kersting, K.: Probabilistic inductive logic programming. In: De Raedt, L., Frasconi, P., Kersting, K., Muggleton, S. (eds.) Probabilistic Inductive Logic Programming. LNCS, vol. 4911, pp. 1–27. Springer, Heidelberg (2008). https://doi.org/10.1007/978-3-540-78652-8_1
21. Selsam, D., Lamm, M., Bünz, B., Liang, P., de Moura, L., Dill, D.L.: Learning a SAT solver from single-bit supervision. CoRR abs/1802.03685 (2018)
22. Soos, M.: CryptoMiniSat – a SAT solver for cryptographic problems (2009)

Explaining Black-Box Classifiers with ILP – Empowering LIME with Aleph to Approximate Non-linear Decisions with Relational Rules

Johannes Rabold[✉], Michael Siebers, and Ute Schmid

Cognitive Systems, University of Bamberg, Bamberg, Germany
{johannes.rabold,michael.siebers,ute.schmid}@uni-bamberg.de

Abstract. We propose an adaption of the explanation-generating system LIME. While LIME relies on sparse linear models, we explore how richer explanations can be generated. As application domain we use images which consist of a coarse representation of ancient graves. The graves are divided into two classes and can be characterised by meaningful features and relations. This domain was generated in analogy to a classic concept acquisition domain researched in psychology. Like LIME, our approach draws samples around a simplified representation of the instance to be explained. The samples are labelled by a generator – simulating a black-box classifier trained on the images. In contrast to LIME, we feed this information to the ILP system Aleph. We customised Aleph's evaluation function to take into account the similarity of instances. We applied our approach to generate explanations for different variants of the ancient graves domain. We show that our explanations can involve richer knowledge thereby going beyond the expressiveness of sparse linear models.

1 Introduction

While during the last 20 years machine learning approaches have been mainly evaluated with respect to their accuracy, recently, the importance of explainability of machine learned classifiers has been recognised. In the context of many application domains, it is crucial that system decisions are transparent and comprehensible and in consequence trustworthy (Guidotti et al. 2018; Muggleton et al. 2018; Pu and Chen 2007). An illustration of how classifier decisions can be made transparent by explanations is given in Fig. 1. Here an aerial view of an ancient site is classified as belonging to the iron age – for instance, in contrast to the Viking age. The user can ask for an explanation for the systems decision. A verbal explanation is given, involving different objects which are part of the site and relations between them. For example, there is a circle of stones *included* into another circle. Current systems typically focus on explanations based on simple features. However, there are many domains where object classification depends on relations between

© Springer Nature Switzerland AG 2018
F. Riguzzi et al. (Eds.): ILP 2018, LNAI 11105, pp. 105–117, 2018.
https://doi.org/10.1007/978-3-319-99960-9_7

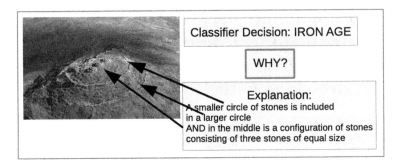

Fig. 1. Image of an ancient site classified to belong to iron age with a textual explanation related to the image. (Aerial View of the Iron Age Site Foel Drygarn Hillfort adapted from http://orapweb.rcahms.gov.uk/coflein/D/DI2006_1293.jpg)

primitive constituents – such as molecular chemistry (King et al. 1996). Furthermore, current approaches to explanation generation either focus on textual or on visual explanations (Guidotti et al. 2018). Typically, images are explained by highlighting pixels which strongly contributed to the classifier decision (Samek et al. 2017). Verbal explanations are used in the context of text classification (Ribeiro et al. 2016) and in the context of learning from symbolic features (Lakkaraju et al. 2016). However, there is evidence that humans can profit from a dual representation relating visual and verbal information (Mayer and Sims 1994).

In principle, there are two possibilities to address explainability: On the one hand, machine learning approaches – such as inductive logic programming (ILP) – can be designed which learn interpretable rules, on the other hand, black-box approaches – such as (deep) neural networks – can be extended by an interface for explanation generation.

The first perspective on explainability can be characterised as knowledge-level learning (Dietterich 1986) which has been also proposed to be a constituent of (human and artificial) cognitive systems (Langley 2016). Typical approaches of this category are decision trees and variants such as decision sets (Lakkaraju et al. 2016). Decision trees generalise over feature vectors and express concepts as disjunction of conjunctions of constraints over features. More expressive approaches are offered by inductive logic programming (Muggleton and De Raedt 1994). In ILP training instances are characterised by relations and induced concepts are represented by Horn clauses, that is, relational and even infinite (recursive) concepts can learned. Common to such symbol-level machine learning approaches is that prediction and description of a concept are addressed within the same representation. Learned hypotheses are represented as rules and therefore can be naturally included in rule-based systems such as decision support or expert systems. Techniques for explanation generation which have been already proposed in the early days of AI can be directly applied (Clancey 1983), for example, the trace of rules which have been applied to reach a conclusion can be shown to the user.

Symbol-level machine learning inherently is explainable AI (Gulwani et al. 2015; Muggleton et al. 2018). However, it often is outperformed by back-box approaches with respect to accuracy since symbolic approaches typically are less suited to highly non-linear decision functions. Therefore, currently there is a lot of research interest addressing the second perspective on explainability, that is to preserve the strong representational power of non-linear classifiers and provide additional methods which can be applied ex-post to make the decisions of a black-box classifier transparent to the user (Guidotti et al. 2018). The motivation here is to be independent of the internals of the classifier and just examining the mapping of input to the classification output. One of the most considered approaches of this type is LIME (Local Interpretable Model-Agnostic Explanations) which generates sparse linear models as local approximations for a (non-linear) classifier decision (Ribeiro et al. 2016). For image classification domains, LIME identifies that group of pixels (called super-pixel) with the strongest contribution to the classifier decision.

Currently LIME is limited to simple linear explanations, such as which set of pixels are responsible for classification decision 'electric guitar' (Ribeiro et al. 2016). Such simple explanations might be not enough for more domains involving relational concepts. Therefore, we propose an extension of LIME with the ILP approach Aleph (Srinivasan 2004) for generation of explanations for more complex domains. We demonstrate the approach for coarse images of ancient graves. In the next section (Sect. 2), we first introduce LIME's explanation generation approach in more detail. Afterwards (Sect. 3) we present our modified approach and specifically how similarity between images in the non-linear decision space can be included in Aleph's evaluation function. We present experiments with two variants of the ancient grave domain in Sect. 4 and conclude in Sect. 5 with a short discussion and pointers to future work.

2   Generating Local Explanations in LIME

LIME addresses the problem of finding an easy to understand explanation for the classification result of a more complex black-box classifier. The original paper describes the work-flow of LIME for two types of input, images and text. For every instance $x \in X$, there exists an interpretable representation $x' \in X'$. For text, x' consists of a binary vector stating if a word occurs in the text or not. For images, x is a tensor containing the pixel values and x' is a binary vector describing whether small parts (super-pixels) of the image are present or not. The words or the super-pixels can be seen as features which can be used to explain the original classifier function $f(x)$. This function typically has a multi-dimensional and non-linear decision surface. LIME aims at finding a linear model which helps to explain classifier decisions for the original instances in X. This model is a local approximation of the original classifier function where the simple features in the vector representations x' are weighted by their relevances w. The model construction is described in Algorithm 1.

Algorithm 1. Linear Model Generation with LIME (adapted from Ribeiro *et al.*, 2016)

1: **Require:** Classifier f, Number of samples N
2: **Require:** Instance x and its interpretable version x'
3: **Require:** Similarity kernel π_x, Length of explanation K
4:     $\mathcal{Z} \leftarrow \{\}$
5:     **for** $i \in \{1, 2, 3, \ldots, N\}$ **do**
6:         $z_i' \leftarrow$ sample_around(x')
7:         $\mathcal{Z} \leftarrow \mathcal{Z} \cup (z_i', f(z_i), \pi_x(z_i))$
8:     **end for**
9: $w \leftarrow$ K-Lasso($\mathcal{Z}, \mathcal{K})\triangleright$ with z_i' as features, $f(z)$ as target
10: **return** w

LIME constructs a sparse linear model by sampling N instances around x' where each sample represents a perturbed version of this instance. Each perturbation z' is sampled uniformly at random drawing non-zero elements of x'. For each sample z', the classifier decision $f(z)$ and the distance $\pi_x(z)$ between the perturbed and the original instance is calculated and stored. The distance measure is highly dependent on the form of input. For text the cosine distance can be used. An assumption-free distance measure for images is the Mean Squared Error (MSE). The distance measure represents the relative importance of an instance with respect to fitting a locally faithful model. The final step of the LIME algorithm is picking the K most important features from the input by fitting a regression model on the data. The weights w are learned via least squares (K-Lasso, see Ribeiro et al. (2016) for details).

The simpler linear model characterises the original input x in terms of weighted attributes of x'. These weights can be exploited to highlight superpixels that the classifier seems to find important. In the text domain, the words with the highest (or lowest) weights can be highlighted to show positive (or negative) importance for the classification result. Such linear models are sufficient for some tasks like showing what the important parts for the classification result of an image are. However, there are more intricate tasks such as explaining why a sepia toned image is considered to be retro (Ribeiro et al. 2016). Also problematic is explaining classifications which rely on combinations of features or relations between objects. LIME in its current version could at best highlight the pixels where the relation is located at, but there is no possibility to describe the constellation further.

3   Model Agnostic Explanation Generation with LIME-Aleph

In the following, we describe our adaptation of the LIME system in order to get richer explanations for the classification of images. In principle our approach can also be extended to deal with other input, given an appropriate method to come up with a logical representation. We will apply the ILP approach Aleph

(Srinivasan 2004) to generate explanations in terms of logic rules. In the context of images, logical rules can capture combinations of features and also relations between objects. For example, to explain why an image is classified as a face does not only depend on the occurrence of eyes, nose and mouth, but also on the relations between these entities.

Currently, we presuppose that for a sample of instances there exists not only the image but additionally a logic description. In a next step, our approach can be extended to an interactive system which presents the super-pixels identified by LIME and asks the user for meaningful labels for single super-pixels as well as pairs or even larger tuples. However, even without such interactive labelling, logical rules defined with anonymous predicate names might be helpful: In a recent empirical study in the context of the family domain, it has been shown that for some classification tasks, logical rules can be comprehensible even if predicate names are not meaningful (Muggleton et al. 2018).

The LIME-Aleph algorithm differs from the original LIME as given in Algorithm 1 in lines 6 and 9: Sampling is done by uniformly picking N instances from the pool of logical representations. Furthermore, instances are picked such that they are distributed over the complete instance space. The distance to x' will however become relevant during learning with Aleph (see Sect. 3.1). The instance to explain is also part of this sample. As in the original LIME, the sample is stored together with the classification calculated by the black-box classifier and the distance to the currently to be explained original instance x. Like in the original, this measure indicates how close two images are. We need this information later in order to decide which examples are more important for the explanation of our image. For the original LIME, an L2 distance which is the Mean Squared Error between the two images has been used.

The images considered in Ribeiro et al. (2016) are photographic images. For more sparse image representations such as black and white line drawings, the L2 measure would over-estimate the distance of two equal sketches that are just shifted by one pixel. Consequently, for the coarse images of ancient graves which we will investigate (see Sect. 4) we need to take care of this issue. In order to gain translation invariance, we first down-sample the images, which creates a compact summary of the important parts. We then also calculate the L2 distance of these small images.

Line 9 of Algorithm 1 is replaced by Aleph. That is, now a model in form of logical rules is learned instead of a set of weights for a linear classifier. In the following we give a short description of Aleph followed by a proposition for a new evaluation function to guide Aleph's refinement search.

3.1   The Aleph System

The inductive logic programming system Aleph is based on a specific-to-general refinement search. The induction algorithm can be described as follows (Srinivasan 2004):

1. Take one example from the example set. If none exists stop.
2. Build the most-specific clause that entails the example selected.

3. Search for a clause that is more general than the current clause.
   - A more general clause is defined as a subset of the current set of literals.
   - Search is guided by an evaluation function.
4. Remove the redundant examples (all examples covered by the current clause).
5. Repeat from the step 1.

3.2 Adapted Evaluation Function

By default, the search in Aleph is guided by a coverage measure that takes into account how many positive (p) and negative (n) examples a clause covers. The evaluation score is simply calculated by $score = p - n$. The clause with the highest $score$ is selected. However, in our implementation of LIME, the distance measure plays an important role in defining the locality of an image to the image we want to explain. Consequently, we adapted Aleph's evaluation function to take into account distances between examples. Having a clause covering many positive examples with a small distance needs to be preferred over having a clause covering many negative examples with a small distance. We can state this in a cost measure $cost(Clause)$ of a clause $Clause$ with respect to positive and negative examples:

$$cost(Clause) =$$

$$\sum_{e \in E^+} \begin{cases} -c(e), & \text{if e gets covered by the clause} \\ 0, & \text{otherwise} \end{cases}$$

$$+$$

$$\sum_{e \in E^-} \begin{cases} 0, & \text{if e does not get covered by the clause} \\ c(e), & \text{otherwise} \end{cases}$$

where $c(e)$ is defined as $\frac{1}{(1+d(e))^2}$ with $d(e)$ being the distance assigned to e as described above (L2 distance of down-sampled images). E^+ is the set of all positive examples and E^- the set of all negative examples.

4 Experiments

To investigate how LIME can profit from explanation generation with ILP, we used a concept learning domain introduced by Medin and Schaffer (1978) which has been investigated extensively in cognitive psychology (Goodman et al. 2008). The concepts are typically depicted graphically, mostly by simple line drawings. The concept to be learned for the original domain can be represented by a decision tree (Lafond et al. 2009) or three rules with a conjunction of two feature attributes each. The representation of this type of concept goes already beyond the simple single feature approximation of LIME. In a next step, we extended the concept learning problem to include a conjunction of binary relations, structurally similar to the grandparent rule which has been extensively studied in ILP (Muggleton et al. 2018). Bitmaps of training examples for both variants were produced by a generator program. The images together with the classification decision were input for the LIME-Aleph algorithm.

4.1   The Medin and Schaffer Concept Acquisition Task

The classical domain introduced by Medin and Schaffer (1978) is characterised by four binary features. A concept A has to be learned from five positive examples and four negative examples (concept B). The remaining seven instances are used as transfer items to explore how humans generalise under different experimental conditions. The abstract learning problem is given in Table 1. It has been instantiated with different graphical domains. The most basic domain investigated are geometrical forms with figure as triangle or circle, colour as red or green, size as small or large, position as left or right. A more natural domain is Brunswick faces where metric information is given in two discrete instantiations for eye height, eye distance, nose length, mouth height (Medin and Schaffer 1978; Nosofsky et al. 1994).

Table 1. Abstract structure of the concept learning domain introduced by Medin and Schaffer (1978)

Category A	Category B	Transfer
A1 0001	B1 0011	T1 0110
A2 0101	B2 1001	T2 0111
A3 0100	B3 1110	T3 0000
A4 0010	B4 1111	T4 1101
A5 1000		T5 1010
		T6 1100
		T7 1011

We instantiate the domain with fictitious patterns of ancient graves which are either from iron age or from Viking age. The four features are not given by two specific instantiations but by decision boundaries (Goodman et al. 2008):

- form: narrow/round (axis ratio < 0.5),
- number of stones: many/few (number of stones > 10),
- corner stones: think/normal (circumference > 2× of average size),
- orientation: north/west (angle between −45 and +45 from vertical).

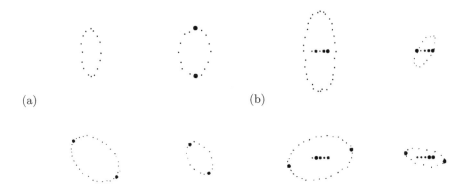

Fig. 2. Examples for the ancient grave domain based on the Medin and Schaffer (1978) structure (a) and extended for learning concepts involving relations (b), top row shows positive and bottom row negative examples.

Examples for the training instances are given in Fig. 2. Using decision boundaries rather than Boolean features, the 16 distinct patterns can be instantiated with arbitrarily many images. Nevertheless, linguistic labels can be used to characterise membership to a category.

Given the pattern in Table 1, the classification rules which correctly discriminate iron age graves from Viking age graves are

```
iron(X) :- narrow(X), north(X).
iron(X) :- narrow(X), thick(X).
iron(X) :- thick(X), north(X).
```

That is, one feature (the number of stones) is irrelevant and a grave can be classified as belonging to iron age by a combination of a specific value of either two of the remaining features. For Aleph, training examples are represented in the usual way as

```
iron(iron93).        not iron(viking87).
narrow(iron93).      many(viking87).
thick(iron93).       north(viking87).
many(iron93).
```

4.2 Complex Relational Concepts

To extend the classification problem such that relational information has to be taken into account, we modified the ancient graves domain such that there is an additional pattern of stones within the stone circle. A grave now shall be of iron age, if the included stones contain a sequence of exactly three stones growing in size. Examples are given in Fig. 2. The target predicate $iron(X)$ still is defined for individual graves, that is, it is not itself relational, such as for instance $grandparent(A,B)$. However, relations have to be used in the rule body to model a sequence of stones growing in size. For a grave belonging to the iron age, the following rules have to hold:

```
iron(X) :- outer(X,A), next(A,B), next(B,C), larger(A,B), larger(B,C).
iron(X) :- outer(X,A), next(A,B), next(B,C), next(C,D), larger(B,C),
           larger(C,D).
iron(X) :- outer(X,A), next(A,B), next(B,C), next(C,D), next(D,E),
           larger(C,D), larger(D,E).
```

Examples are described in the following way:

```
iron(iron79).                              not iron(viking9).
thick(iron79).                             thick(viking9).
north(iron79).                             outer(viking9, stone_a_viking9).
outer(iron79, stone_a_iron79).             smallest(stone_a_viking9).
medium(stone_a_iron79).                    largest(stone_b_viking9).
smallest(stone_b_iron79).                  next(stone_a_viking9, stone_b_viking9).
next(stone_a_iron79, stone_b_iron79).      medium(stone_c_viking9).
small(stone_c_iron79).                     next(stone_b_viking9, stone_c_viking9).
next(stone_b_iron79, stone_c_iron79).      largest(stone_d_viking9).
largest(stone_d_iron79).                   next(stone_c_viking9, stone_d_viking9).
next(stone_c_iron79, stone_d_iron79).      largest(stone_e_viking9).
small(stone_e_iron79).                     next(stone_d_viking9, stone_e_viking9).
next(stone_d_iron79, stone_e_iron79).
```

The binary relation *larger/2* is given as background knowledge for the five sizes *smallest/1, small/1, medium/1, large/1, largest/1* – for example, *larger(X, Y) :- smallest(X), small(Y)*.

4.3   A Generator for Coarse Images

For the construction of training examples we let the graves be created by a generator. By using a generator instead of real images we are able to derive the classification result right away since the attributes for the graves are known by construction. Instead of using a black-box classifier, we can simulate such a classifier by the generator. Using a generator has also the advantage that one can have an almost infinitely large variety in the examples. Furthermore, different classification rules can be created.

For the original ancient graves domain we only need the predicates *narrow(X), thick(X), many(X)* and *north(X)*. The generator first produces random truth values for the four predicates and then draws images corresponding to the predicates. By allowing small random variations we get a large variety of images of grave sites. Next, the generated examples are filtered according to the pre-defined classifier rules for *iron(X)*. That way we obtain the classification result and can simulate a black-box classifier. For the relational graves domain we use a similar approach. In addition to generating the boundary of a grave, the generator now sets stones of different sizes in the middle. First, sizes are assigned randomly to the stones and then images are filtered according to the classification rules.

4.4   Results for the Original Ancient Graves Domain

To test LIME-Aleph for the original ancient graves domain we generated 100 images together with their corresponding logic representations. To simulate the intended application of explanation generation for a classifier decision, we can pick one of the images as new image x_1 as input to a black-box classifier which returns a classification decision, for instance, that x_1 belongs to iron age. Image x_1 is associated with a logic representation x_1'. An illustration is given in Fig. 3: A narrow grave with thick corner stones and oriented towards north is presented to a classifier which labels it as belonging to the iron age. That it does not hold that the predicate has *many* stones is inferred due to closed world assumption.

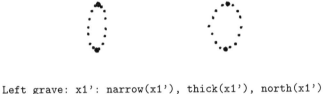

Left grave: x1': narrow(x1'), thick(x1'), north(x1')

Fig. 3. The left grave is the query image, the right image the closest neighbour according to our distance measure.

LIME-Aleph now samples 20 images – 10 positives, including the to be explained image, and 10 negatives. The distances from all images to x_1 are calculated and Aleph generates the rule which classifies x_1' from this sample. For the given example, only one, very simple rule has been learned:

iron(X) :- north(X).

Although not the original rule *iron(X) :- thick(X), north(X).* has been induced but a more general one, the result is a reasonable approximation. Which rule is generated for an explanation depends on the sample from which is learned.

In a second trial, an image labelled as belonging to iron age had the following attributes:

narrow(x2).
many(x2).
thick(x2).
north(x2).

and Aleph induced the hypothesis

iron(X) :- north(X).
iron(X) :- narrow(X), thick(X).

which covers all relevant features of the image for the class *iron*.

LIME-Aleph is also capable of showing why an instance is not part of the target class *iron*. We picked an instance with the features

```
narrow(x3).
many(x3).
```

without thick corner stones and not oriented towards north (which Aleph infers due to closed world assumption). Aleph learned the rules

```
iron(X) :- north(X).
iron(X) :- narrow(X), thick(X).
```

which are the same rules as above. Here LIME-Aleph explains why the example does not belong to iron age because it is not north or not simultaneously narrow and with thick corner stones. So in order to describe what indicator there is that the example does not belong to the target class, LIME-Aleph gives a contrast and shows which rules must hold for the true target class.

The three examples give a proof-of-concept that LIME-Aleph can induce explanatory rules from small samples and with the modified evaluation function which takes into account distances of examples to the to be explained instance.

4.5   Results for the Relational Ancient Graves Domain

We also explored LIME-Aleph's ability to generate helpful explanations for the relational variant of the graves domain. For an instance, which can be characterised in the following way:

```
many(x4).     medium(a).
thick(x4).    smallest(b).
north(x4).    smallest(c).
outer(x4,a).  small(d).
next(a,b).    largest(e).
next(b,c).
next(c,d).
next(d,e).
```

LIME-Aleph induced the following rules to explain the current instance in contrast to a sample of other instances:

```
iron(X) :- outer(X,A), next(A,B), next(B,C), next(C,D), larger(C,D),
           next(D,E), larger(C,E).
iron(X) :- outer(X,A), next(A,B), next(B,C), larger(B,C), next(C,D),
           larger(C,D).
```

While the first rule did not quite get the correct relation (it includes a *larger* relation between C and D but not the corresponding *larger* relation between D and E), the second rule matches exactly one of the correct rules. The example can be explained to belong to the iron age because the line of stones in its centre contains a sequence of three stones with ascending size from west to east.

5   Conclusions and Further Work

We presented an extension to the model agnostic explanation generation app-roach LIME. This extension allows to generate explanations which take into account combinations of features and relations between parts of an to be classi-fied object. As illustrated in Fig. 1, there exist domains, where relations between constituents are crucial for a concept. This is obviously true for molecules, but has also been demonstrated in early days of AI by Winston (1970) who showed how the relational concept of an arc can be learned from near misses. We pre-sented ancient grave sites as an example domain and explored it in a classic feature based variant and in a relational variant.

The goal of this paper was to present a first proof-of-concept of how explana-tion generating approaches which have been developed in the context of end-to-end learning of images could profit from more sophisticated, logic based learning mechanisms such as ILP. We could demonstrate, that combining LIME with Aleph can indeed help to generate more complex explanations. However, cur-rently, LIME-Aleph needs not only the images but also their logic descriptions as input. In the context of ILP, it is quite usual to generate logical descriptions from images (Farid and Sammut 2014). Nevertheless, automatic or at least semi-automatic extraction of features and relations from images would be a large step towards more general applicability. We plan to investigate whether information represented in convolution layers of a deep network can be used for generating meaningful features and (spatial) relations. Thereby, we can build on ongoing research in computer visions (Rohrbach et al. 2013).

Acknowledgements. The research reported is funded by the German Research Soci-ety (DFG) within the Priority Research Program on 'Intentional Forgetting in Organi-sations' (DFG-SPP 1921), project Dare2Del (SCHM1239/10-1). The authors cordially thank Laura Henning who proposed the ancient grave domain as an instantiation of the Medin and Schaffer concept learning task. We also want to thank three anonymous reviewers for their very helpful comments.

References

Clancey, W.J.: The epistemology of a rule-based expert system-a framework for explanation. Artif. Intell. **20**(3), 215–251 (1983)

Dieterich, T.G.: Learning at the knowledge level. Mach. Learn. **1**(3), 287–315 (1986)

Farid, R., Sammut, C.: Plane-based object categorisation using relational learn-ing. Mach. Learn. **94**(1), 3–23 (2014)

Goodman, N.D., Tenenbaum, J.B., Feldman, J., Griffiths, T.L.: A rational anal-ysis of rule-based concept learning. Cognit. Sci. **32**(1), 108–154 (2008)

Guidotti, R., Monreale, A., Turini, F., Pedreschi, D., Giannotti, F.: A survey of methods for explaining black box models. arXiv preprint arXiv:1802.01933 (2018)

Gulwani, S., Hernandez-Orallo, J., Kitzelmann, E., Muggleton, S.H., Schmid, U., Zorn, B.: Inductive programming meets the real world. Commun. ACM **58**(11), 90–99 (2015)

King, R.D., Muggleton, S.H., Srinivasan, A., Sternberg, M.: Structure-activity relationships derived by machine learning: the use of atoms and their bond connectivities to predict mutagenicity by inductive logic programming. In: Proceedings of the National Academy of Sciences, vol. 93, pp. 438–442. National Acad Sciences (1996)

Lafond, D., Lacouture, Y., Cohen, A.L.: Decision-tree models of categorization response times, choice proportions, and typicality judgments. Psychol. Rev. **116**(4), 833 (2009)

Lakkaraju, H., Bach, S.H., Leskovec, J.: Interpretable decision sets: a joint framework for description and prediction. In: Proceedings of the 22nd ACM SIGKDD International Conference on Knowledge Discovery and Data Mining, pp. 1675–1684. ACM (2016)

Langley, P.: The central role of cognition in learning. Adv. Cognit. Syst. **4**, 3–12 (2016)

Mayer, R.E., Sims, V.K.: For whom is a picture worth a thousand words? extensions of a dual-coding theory of multimedia learning. J. Educ. Psychol. **86**(3), 389 (1994)

Medin, D.L., Schaffer, M.M.: Context theory of classification learning. Psychol. Rev. **85**(3), 207 (1978)

Muggleton, S., De Raedt, L.: Inductive logic programming: theory and methods. J. Logic Program. **19–20**, 629–679 (1994). Special Issue on 10 Years of Logic Programming

Muggleton, S.H., Schmid, U., Zeller, C., Tamaddoni-Nezhad, A., Besold, T.: Ultra-strong machine learning: comprehensibility of programs learned with ILP. Mach. Learn., 1–22 (2018)

Nosofsky, R.M., Palmeri, T.J., McKinley, S.C.: Rule-plus-exception model of classification learning. Psychol. Rev. **101**(1), 53 (1994)

Pu, P., Chen, L.: Trust-inspiring explanation interfaces for recommender systems. Knowl. Based Syst. **20**(6), 542–556 (2007)

Ribeiro, M.T., Singh, S., Guestrin, C.: Why should I trust you?: Explaining the predictions of any classifier. In: Proceedings of the 22nd ACM SIGKDD International Conference on Knowledge Discovery and Data Mining, pp. 1135–1144. ACM (2016)

Rohrbach, M., Qiu, W., Titov, I., Thater, S., Pinkal, M., Schiele, B.: Translating video content to natural language descriptions. In: International Conference on Computer Vision (ICCV), pp. 433–440. IEEE (2013)

Samek, W., Binder, A., Montavon, G., Lapuschkin, S., Müller, K.-R.: Evaluating the visualization of what a deep neural network has learned. IEEE Trans. Neural Netw. Learn. Syst. **28**(11), 2660–2673 (2017)

Srinivasan, A.: The Aleph Manual (2004). http://www.cs.ox.ac.uk/activities/machinelearning/Aleph/

Winston, P.H.: Learning structural descriptions from examples. Technical report MIT/LCS/TR-76. MIT (1970)

Learning Dynamics with Synchronous, Asynchronous and General Semantics

Tony Ribeiro[1,2,4(✉)], Maxime Folschette[3], Morgan Magnin[1,4], Olivier Roux[1], and Katsumi Inoue[4]

[1] Laboratoire des Sciences du Numérique de Nantes, 1 rue de la Noë, Nantes, France
tony.ribeiro@ls2n.fr
[2] Pôle-Emploi, Saumur, France
[3] Univ Rennes, Inria, CNRS, IRISA, IRSET, Rennes, France
[4] National Institute of Informatics, Tokyo, Japan

Abstract. Learning from interpretation transition *(LFIT)* automatically constructs a model of the dynamics of a system from the observation of its state transitions. So far, the systems that *LFIT* handles are restricted to synchronous deterministic dynamics, i.e., all variables update their values at the same time and, for each state of the system, there is only one possible next state. However, other dynamics exist in the field of logical modeling, in particular the asynchronous semantics which is widely used to model biological systems. In this paper, we focus on a method that learns the dynamics of the system independently of its semantics. For this purpose, we propose a modeling of multi-valued systems as logic programs in which a rule represents *what can occur rather than what will occur*. This modeling allows us to represent non-determinism and to propose an extension of *LFIT* in the form of a semantics free algorithm to learn from discrete multi-valued transitions, regardless of their update schemes. We show through theoretical results that synchronous, asynchronous and general semantics are all captured by this method. Practical evaluation is performed on randomly generated systems and benchmarks from biological literature to study the scalability of this new algorithm regarding the three aforementioned semantics.

Keywords: Dynamical semantics
Learning from interpretation transition
Dynamical systems · Inductive logic programming

1 Introduction

Learning the dynamics of systems with many interacting components becomes more and more important due to many applications, e.g., multi-agent systems, robotics and bioinformatics. Knowledge of a system dynamics can be used by agents and robots for planning and scheduling. In bioinformatics, learning the dynamics of biological systems can correspond to the identification of the mutual

© Springer Nature Switzerland AG 2018
F. Riguzzi et al. (Eds.): ILP 2018, LNAI 11105, pp. 118–140, 2018.
https://doi.org/10.1007/978-3-319-99960-9_8

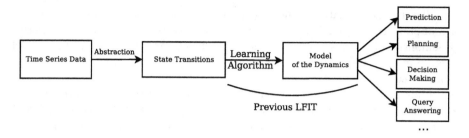

Fig. 1. Assuming a discretization of time series data of a system as state transitions, we propose a method to automatically model the system dynamics.

influence of genes and can help to understand their interactions. While building a model, the choice of a relevant semantics associated to the studied system, that is, how the dynamics is generated from the system's description, represents a major issue with regards to the kind of dynamical properties to analyze. The differences and common features of different semantics w.r.t. properties of interest (attractors, oscillators, ...) constitutes an area of research per itself, especially in the field of Boolean networks. The most common semantics are the synchronous semantics, where all variables update their values at each time step, and the asynchronous semantics, where a single variable updates its value at each time step. In this paper, we also tackle the general semantics, where any subset of variables update their values at each time step, thus especially encompassing the synchronous and asynchronous ones.

Several works have focused on exploring and comparing properties on these semantics. In [8], the author exhibits the translation from Boolean networks into logic programs and discusses the point attractors in both synchronous and asynchronous semantics. In [6], Garg et al. address the differences and complementarity of synchronous and asynchronous semantics to model biological networks and identify attractors. The benefits of the synchronous model are to be computationally tractable, while classical state space exploration algorithms fail on asynchronous ones. However, for some applications, like the biological ones, the asynchronous semantics is said to capture more realistic behaviors, despite a potential combinatorial explosion of the number of states. To illustrate this issue, the authors of [6] compare the time needed to compute the attractors of various models (mammalian cell, T-helper, dendritic cell, ...) and compare the results with synchronous and asynchronous semantics. More recently, in [3], the authors question the kind of properties that may be preserved, whatever the semantics, while discussing the merits of the usual ones including synchronous, asynchronous and general semantics. As a good choice of semantics is key to a sound analysis of a system, it is critical to be adaptive and embrace a wide range of them.

So far, learning from interpretation transition *(LFIT)* [9] has been proposed to automatically construct a model of the dynamics of a system from the observation of its state transitions. Figure 1 shows this learning process. Given some raw data, like time-series data of gene expression, a discretization of those data in the form of state transitions is assumed. From those state transitions, according to the semantics of the system dynamics, different inference algorithms that model the system as a logic program have been proposed. The semantics of system dynamics can indeed differ with regard to the synchronism of its variables, the determinism of its evolution and the influence of its history. The *LFIT* framework proposes several modeling and learning algorithms to tackle those different semantics. To date, the following systems have been tackled: memory-less consistent systems [9], systems with memory [14], non-consistent systems [12] and their multi-valued extensions [11,15]. Although all those methods are dedicated to discrete systems or assume an abstraction of time series data as discrete transitions, [16] proposes a method that allows to deal with continuous time series data, the abstraction itself being learned by the algorithm. However, the systems that *LFIT* handles so far are restricted to synchronous deterministic dynamics implying that for each state of the system, there is only one possible next state. Yet, as stated previously, other dynamics exist in the field of logical modeling, in particular the asynchronous and generalized semantics which are of deep interest to model biological systems, and even the synchronous semantics can be non-deterministic in the general (multi-valued) case.

In this paper, we focus on a method that learns the dynamics of the system independently of its underlying semantics. For this purpose, we propose a modeling of discrete multi-valued systems as logic programs in which each rule represents that a variable possibly takes some value in the next state, extending the formalism introduced in [11,12,15]. Research in multi-valued logic programming has proceeded along three different directions [10]: bilattice-based logics [5,7], quantitative rule sets [17] and annotated logics [1,2]. The multi-valued logic representation used in our new algorithm is based on annotated logics. Here, to each variable corresponds a domain of discrete values. Intuitively, a variable models a biological component (gene, protein, ...) and each associated discrete value models a level of activity or an internal state (active, inactive, phosphorylated, ...). In a rule, a literal is an atom consisting of a variable annotated with one of these values. It allows us to represent annotated atoms simply as classical atoms and thus to remain in the normal logic program semantics. This modeling allows us to represent non-determinism and to propose an extension of *LFIT* in the form of a semantics free algorithm to learn from discrete multi-valued transitions, regardless of their update schemes. We show from theoretical results and experimental evaluation that our new algorithm can learn systems dynamics from both synchronous (deterministic or not), asynchronous and general semantics transitions.

The organization of the paper is as follows. Section 2 provides a formalization of multi-valued logic program, dynamics semantics under logic programs, the learning operations and their properties. Section 3 presents the **GULA** learning algorithm and Sect. 4 its experimental evaluation. Section 5 concludes the paper and provides possible outlooks about applications and improvements of the method. All proofs of theorems and propositions are given in Appendix.

2   Formalization

In this section, the concepts necessary to understand the learning algorithm are formalized. In Sect. 2.1 the basic notions of *multi-valued logic* ($\mathcal{M}$VL) and a number of important properties that the learned programs must have are presented. Then in Sect. 2.2 the operations that are performed during the learning, as well as results about the preservation of the properties introduced in Sect. 2.1 throughout the learning are exposed. Finally, Sect. 2.3 introduces the formalization of several dynamical semantics of multi-valued logic and show that the learning process of Sect. 2.2 is independent of the chosen semantics.

In the following, we denote by $\mathbb{N} := \{0, 1, 2, ...\}$ the set of natural numbers, and for all $k, n \in \mathbb{N}$, $[\![k; n]\!] := \{i \in \mathbb{N} \mid k \leq i \leq n\}$ is the set of natural numbers between k and n included. For any set S, the cardinal of S is denoted $|S|$.

2.1   Multi-valued Logic Program

Let $\mathcal{V} = \{v_1, \ldots, v_n\}$ be a finite set of $n \in \mathbb{N}$ variables, and $\mathsf{dom} : \mathcal{V} \to \mathbb{N}$ a function associating a maximum value (and thus a domain) to each variable. The atoms of $\mathcal{M}$VL are of the form v^{val} where $v \in \mathcal{V}$ and $val \in [\![0; \mathsf{dom}(v)]\!]$. The set of such atoms is denoted by $\mathcal{A}_{\mathsf{dom}}^{\mathcal{V}}$ for a given set of variables $\mathcal{V}$ and a given domain function dom. In the following, we work on specific $\mathcal{V}$ and dom that we omit to mention when the context makes no ambiguity, thus simply writing $\mathcal{A}$.

A $\mathcal{M}$VL rule R is defined by:

$$R \;=\; v_0^{val_0} \leftarrow v_1^{val_1} \wedge \cdots \wedge v_m^{val_m} \tag{1}$$

where $\forall i \in [\![0; m]\!]$, $v_i^{val_i} \in \mathcal{A}$ are atoms in $\mathcal{M}$VL so that every variable is mentioned at most once in the right-hand part: $\forall j, k \in [\![1; m]\!], j \neq k \Rightarrow v_j \neq v_k$. Intuitively, the rule R has the following meaning: the variable v_0 can take the value val_0 in the next dynamical step if for each $i \in [\![1; m]\!]$, variable v_i has value val_i in the current step.

The atom on the left-hand side of the arrow is called the *head* of R and is denoted $h(R) := v_0^{val_0}$. The notation $\mathrm{var}(h(R)) := v_0$ denotes the variable that occurs in $h(R)$. The conjunction on the right-hand side of the arrow is called the *body* of R, written $b(R)$ and can be assimilated to the set $\{v_1^{val_1}, \ldots, v_m^{val_m}\}$; we thus use set operations such as $\in$ and $\cap$ on it. A *multi-valued logic program* ($\mathcal{M}$VLP) is a set of $\mathcal{M}$VL rules.

In the following, we define several notions on $\mathcal{M}$VL rules and programs that will be used for dynamics learning. Definition 1 introduces a domination relation between rules that defines a partial anti-symmetric ordering, as stated by Proposition 1.

Definition 1 (Rule Domination). *Let R_1, R_2 be two $\mathcal{M}$VL rules. The rule R_1 dominates R_2, written $R_2 \leq R_1$ if $h(R_1) = h(R_2)$ and $b(R_1) \subseteq b(R_2)$.*

Proposition 1. *Let R_1, R_2 be two $\mathcal{M}$VL rules. If $R_1 \leq R_2$ and $R_2 \leq R_1$ then $R_1 = R_2$.*

Rules with the most general bodies dominate the other rules. In practice, these are the rules we are interested in since they cover the most general cases.

The dynamical system for which we want to learn the rules is represented by a succession of *states* as formally given by Definition 2. We also define the "compatibility" of a rule with a state in Definition 3 and with another rule in Definition 4, and give a property on this last notion in Proposition 2.

Definition 2 (Discrete State). *A discrete state s is a function from $\mathcal{V}$ to $\mathbb{N}$, i.e., it associates an integer value to each variable in $\mathcal{V}$. It can be equivalently represented by the set of atoms $\{v^{s(v)} \mid v \in \mathcal{V}\}$ and thus we can use classical set operations on it. We write $\mathcal{S}$ to denote the set of all discrete states, and a couple of states $(s, s') \in \mathcal{S}^2$ is called a* transition.

Definition 3 (Rule-State matching). *Let $s \in \mathcal{S}$. The $\mathcal{M}$VL rule R matches s, written $R \sqcap s$, if $b(R) \subseteq s$.*

Definition 4 (Cross-Matching). *Let R and R' be two $\mathcal{M}$VL rules. These rules* cross-match, *written $R \sqcap R'$, when there exists $s \in \mathcal{S}$ such that $R \sqcap s$ and $R' \sqcap s$.*

Proposition 2. *Let R and R' be two $\mathcal{M}$VL rules.*

$$R \sqcap R' \text{ iff } \forall v \in \mathcal{V}, \forall val, val' \in \mathbb{N}, (v^{val}, v^{val'}) \in b(R) \times b(R') \implies val = val'.$$

The final program we want to learn should be complete and consistent within itself and with the observed transitions. The following definitions formalize these desired properties. In Definition 5 we characterize the fact that a rule of a program is useful to describe the dynamics of one variable in a transition; this notion is then extended to a program and a set of transitions, under the condition that there exists such a rule for each variable and each transition. A conflict (Definition 6) arises when a rule describes a change that is not featured in the considered set of transitions. Two rules are concurrent (Definition 7) if they cross-match but have a different head on the same variable. Finally, Definitions 8 and 9 give the characteristics of a complete (the whole dynamics is covered) and consistent (without conflict) program.

Definition 5 (Rule and Program Realization). *Let R be a $\mathcal{M}$VL rule and $(s, s') \in \mathcal{S}^2$. The rule R realizes the transition (s, s'), written $s \xrightarrow{R} s'$, if $R \sqcap s \wedge h(R) \in s'$.*

A $\mathcal{M}$VLP P realizes $(s, s') \in \mathcal{S}^2$, written $s \xrightarrow{P} s'$, if $\forall v \in \mathcal{V}, \exists R \in P, \text{var}(h(R)) = v \wedge s \xrightarrow{R} s'$. It realizes $T \subseteq \mathcal{S}^2$, written $\xrightarrow{P} T$, if $\forall (s, s') \in T, s \xrightarrow{P} s'$.

In the following, for all sets of transitions $T \subseteq \mathcal{S}^2$, we denote: $\text{fst}(T) := \{s \in \mathcal{S} \mid \exists (s_1, s_2) \in T, s_1 = s\}$. We note that $\text{fst}(T) = \emptyset \implies T = \emptyset$.

Definition 6 (Conflicts). *A $\mathcal{M}$VL rule R conflicts with a set of transitions $T \subseteq \mathcal{S}^2$ when $\exists s \in \text{fst}(T), \big(R \sqcap s \wedge \forall (s, s') \in T, h(R) \notin s'\big).$*

Definition 7 (Concurrent Rules). *Two $\mathcal{MVL}$ rules R and R' are* concurrent *when $R \sqcap R' \wedge \mathrm{var}(h(R)) = \mathrm{var}(h(R')) \wedge h(R) \neq h(R')$.*

Definition 8 (Complete Program). *A $\mathcal{MVLP}$ P is* complete *if $\forall s \in \mathcal{S}, \forall \mathrm{v} \in \mathcal{V}, \exists R \in P, R \sqcap s \wedge \mathrm{var}(h(R)) = \mathrm{v}$.*

Definition 9 (Consistent Program). *A $\mathcal{MVLP}$ P is* consistent *with a set of transitions T if P does not contains any rule R conflicting with T.*

2.2   Learning Operations

This section focuses on the manipulation of programs for the learning process. Definitons 10 and 11 formalize the main atomic operations performed on a rule or a program by the learning algorithm, whose objective is to make minimal modifications to a given $\mathcal{MVLP}$ in order to be consistent with a new set of transitions.

Definition 10 (Rule Least Specialization). *Let R be a $\mathcal{MVL}$ rule and $s \in \mathcal{S}$ such that $R \sqcap s$. The* least specialization *of R by s is:*

$$L_{\mathrm{spe}}(R,s) := \{h(R) \leftarrow b(R) \cup \{\mathrm{v}^{val}\} \mid \mathrm{v}^{val} \in \mathcal{A} \wedge \mathrm{v}^{val} \notin s \wedge \forall val' \in \mathbb{N}, \mathrm{v}^{val'} \notin b(R)\}.$$

Definition 11 (Program Least Revision). *Let P be a $\mathcal{MVLP}$, $s \in \mathcal{S}$ and $T \subseteq \mathcal{S}^2$ such that $\mathrm{fst}(T) = \{s\}$. Let $R_P := \{R \in P \mid R$ conflicts with $T\}$. The* least revision *of P by T is $L_{\mathrm{rev}}(P,T) := (P \setminus R_P) \cup \bigcup\limits_{R \in R_P} L_{\mathrm{spe}}(R,s)$.*

Theorem 1 states properties on the least revision, in order to prove it suitable to be used in the learning algorithm. We recall that the notation $\overset{P}{\hookrightarrow} T$ was introduced in Definiton 5.

Theorem 1. *Let R be a $\mathcal{MVL}$ rule and $s \in \mathcal{S}$ such that $R \sqcap s$. Let $S_R := \{s' \in \mathcal{S} \mid R \sqcap s'\}$ and $S_{\mathrm{spe}} := \{s' \in \mathcal{S} \mid \exists R' \in L_{\mathrm{spe}}(R,s), R' \sqcap s'\}$.*
Let P be a $\mathcal{MVLP}$ and $T, T' \subseteq \mathcal{S}^2$ such that $|\mathrm{fst}(T)| = 1 \wedge \mathrm{fst}(T) \cap \mathrm{fst}(T') = \emptyset$. The following results hold:

1. *$S_{\mathrm{spe}} = S_R \setminus \{s\}$,*
2. *$L_{\mathrm{rev}}(P,T)$ is consistent with T,*
3. *$\overset{P}{\hookrightarrow} T' \implies \xrightarrow{L_{\mathrm{rev}}(P,T)} T'$,*
4. *$\overset{P}{\hookrightarrow} T \implies \xrightarrow{L_{\mathrm{rev}}(P,T)} T$,*
5. *P is complete $\implies L_{\mathrm{rev}}(P,T)$ is complete.*

Proof Sketch. The first two points follow from Definitons 10 and 11. The third point follows from Definiton 5 and the first point. The fourth point follows from Definitons 5 and 11. The last point follows from Definiton 8 and the first point. □

Definiton 12 groups all the properties that we want the learned program to have: suitability and optimality, and Proposition 3 states that the optimal program of a set of transitions is unique.

Definition 12 (Suitable and Optimal Program). *Let $T \subseteq \mathcal{S}^2$. A $\mathcal{M}VLP$ P is suitable for T when:*

- *P is consistent with T,*
- *P realizes T,*
- *P is complete*
- *for all $\mathcal{M}VL$ rules R not conflicting with T, there exists $R' \in P$ such that $R \leq R'$.*

If in addition, for all $R \in P$, all the $\mathcal{M}VL$ rules R' belonging to $\mathcal{M}VLP$ suitable for T are such that $R \leq R'$ implies $R' \leq R$ then P is called optimal.

Proposition 3. *Let $T \subseteq \mathcal{S}^2$. The $\mathcal{M}VLP$ optimal for T is unique and denoted $P_{\mathcal{O}}(T)$.*

Proof Sketch. Reasoning by contradiction, a rule that should occur in only one $\mathcal{M}VLP$ optimal for T necessarily occurs in another one.   □

The next properties are directly used in the learning algorithm. Proposition 4 gives an explicit definition of the optimal program for an empty set of transitions, which is the starting point of the algorithm. Proposition 5 gives a method to obtain the optimal program from any suitable program by simply removing the dominated rules; this means that the $\mathcal{M}VLP$ optimal for a set of transitions can be obtained from any $\mathcal{M}VLP$ suitable for the same set of transitions by removing all the dominated rules. Finally, in association with these two results, Theorem 2 gives a method to iteratively compute $P_{\mathcal{O}}(T)$ for any $T \subseteq \mathcal{S}^2$, starting from $P_{\mathcal{O}}(\emptyset)$.

Proposition 4. $P_{\mathcal{O}}(\emptyset) = \{v^{val} \leftarrow \emptyset \mid v^{val} \in \mathcal{A}\}$.

Proposition 5. *Let $T \subseteq \mathcal{S}^2$. If P is a $\mathcal{M}VLP$ suitable for T, then $P_{\mathcal{O}}(T) = \{R \in P \mid \forall R' \in P, R \leq R' \implies R' \leq R\}$.*

Theorem 2. *Let $s \in \mathcal{S}$ and $T, T' \subseteq \mathcal{S}^2$ such that $|\mathrm{fst}(T')| = 1 \wedge \mathrm{fst}(T) \cap \mathrm{fst}(T') = \emptyset$. $L_{\mathrm{rev}}(P_{\mathcal{O}}(T), T')$ is a $\mathcal{M}VLP$ suitable for $T \cup T'$.*

Proof Sketch. Consistency is proved by contradiction. Completeness and realization stem from Theorem 1. The final point is proved by exhibiting for each R not conflicting with $T' \cup T$ the rule in $L_{\mathrm{spe}}(P_{\mathcal{O}}(T'), T)$ that dominates it.   □

2.3   Dynamical Semantics

In this section, the notion of semantics is formalized in Definiton 13 as a function that, to a complete program, associates a set of transitions where each state has at least one outgoing transition. Such a set of transitions can also be seen as a function that maps any state to a non-empty set of states, regarded as possible dynamical branchings. Several examples of semantics are given afterwards.

Definition 13 (Semantics). *Let $\mathcal{A}_{dom}^{\mathcal{V}}$ be a set of atoms and $\mathcal{S}$ the correspond-ing set of states. A* semantics *(on $\mathcal{A}_{dom}^{\mathcal{V}}$) is a function that associates, to each complete $\mathcal{M}$VLP P, a set of transitions $T \subseteq \mathcal{S}^2$ so that: $\mathrm{fst}(T) = \mathcal{S}$. Equiva-lently, a semantics can be seen as a function of $\left(\text{c-}\mathcal{M}\text{VLP} \to (\mathcal{S} \to \wp(\mathcal{S}) \setminus \emptyset)\right)$ where c-$\mathcal{M}$VLP is the set of complete $\mathcal{M}$VLPs and $\wp$ is the power set operator.*

In the following, we present a formal definition and a characterization of three particular semantics that are widespread in the field of complex dynamical systems: synchronous, asynchronous and general, and we also treat the partic-ular case of the deterministic synchronous semantics. Note that some points in these definitions are arbitrary and could be discussed depending on the modeling paradigm. For instance, the policy about rules R so that $\exists s \in \mathcal{S}, s \sqcap R \wedge h(R) \in s$, which model stability in the dynamics, could be to consider them (such as in the synchronous and general semantics) or exclude them (such as in the asyn-chronous semantics) from the possible dynamics. The learning method of this paper, however, is independent to the chosen semantics as long as it respects Definiton 13, which includes the three aforementioned semantics.

Definiton 14 introduces the synchronous semantics, consisting in updating each variable in order to compute the next state, according to the heads of rules matching the current state. Note that this is taken in a loose sense: as stated above, rules that make a variable change its value are not prioritized over rules that don't. Furthermore, if several rules on a same variable match the current state, then several transitions are possible, depending on which rule is applied. Thus, for a self-transition (s, s) to occur, there needs to be, for each atom $\mathrm{v}^{val} \in s$, a rule that matches s and whose head is v^{val}. Note however that such a loop is not necessarily a point attractor; it is only the case if all rules of the program that match s have their head in s.

Definition 14 (Synchronous Semantics). *The synchronous semantics $\mathcal{T}_{syn}$ is defined by:*

$$\mathcal{T}_{syn} : P \mapsto \{(s, s') \in \mathcal{S}^2 \mid s' \subseteq \{h(R) \in \mathcal{A} \mid R \in P, R \sqcap s\}\}$$

We note that if two different transitions are observed from the same state s, all states that are combinations of those two states are also successors of s. This is used in Proposition 6 as a characterization of the synchronous semantics.

In the following, if $s \in \mathcal{S}$ is a state and $X \subseteq \mathcal{A}$ is a set of atoms such that $\forall \mathrm{v}_1^{val_1}, \mathrm{v}_2^{val_2} \in X, \mathrm{v}_1 = \mathrm{v}_2 \implies val_1 = val_2$, we denote: $s \backslash\!\backslash X := \{\mathrm{v}^{val} \in s \mid \mathrm{v} \notin \{\mathrm{w} \mid \mathrm{w}^{val'} \in X\}\} \cup X$. In other words, $s \backslash\!\backslash X$ is the discrete state s where all variables mentioned in X have their value replaced by the value in X.

Proposition 6 (Synchronous Transitions). *Let $T \subseteq \mathcal{S}^2$ so that $\mathrm{fst}(T) = \mathcal{S}$. The transitions of T are synchronous, i.e., $\exists P$ a $\mathcal{M}$VLP such that $\mathcal{T}_{syn}(P) = T$, if and only if $\forall (s, s_1), (s, s_2) \in T, \forall s_3 \in \mathcal{S}, s_3 \subseteq s_1 \cup s_2 \implies (s, s_3) \in T$.*

Proof Sketch. ($\Rightarrow$) By definition of $\mathcal{T}_{syn}$. ($\Leftarrow$) Consider the most naive program P realizing T; the characterization applied iteratively allows to conclude that $\mathcal{T}_{syn}(P) \subseteq T$ while $T \subseteq \mathcal{T}_{syn}(P)$ comes by definition of P and $\mathcal{T}_{syn}$. $\qquad\square$

In Definiton 15, we formalize the asynchronous semantics that imposes that no more than one variable can change its value in each transition. Contrary to the previous one, this semantics prioritizes the changes. Thus, for a self-transition (s, s) to occur, it is required that all rules of P that match s have their head in s, i.e., this only happens when (s, s) is a point attractor. Proposition 7 characterizes the asynchronous semantics by stating that from a state s, either the only successor is s, or all successors differ from s by exactly one atom.

Definition 15 (Asynchronous Semantics).   *The* asynchronous semantics $\mathcal{T}_{asyn}$ *is defined by:*

$$\mathcal{T}_{asyn} : P \mapsto \{(s, s \backslash\backslash\{h(R)\}) \in \mathcal{S}^2 \mid R \in P \wedge R \sqcap s \wedge h(R) \notin s\}$$
$$\cup \{(s, s) \in \mathcal{S}^2 \mid \forall R \in P, R \sqcap s \implies h(R) \in s\}.$$

Proposition 7 (Asynchronous Transitions). *Let* $T \subseteq \mathcal{S}^2$ *so that* $\mathrm{fst}(T) = \mathcal{S}$. *The transitions of* T *are asynchronous, i.e.,* $\exists P$ *a* $\mathcal{MVLP}$ *such that* $\mathcal{T}_{asyn}(P) = T$, *if and only if* $\forall s, s' \in \mathcal{S}, s \neq s', ((s, s) \in T \implies (s, s') \notin T) \wedge ((s, s') \in T \implies |s \setminus s'| = 1)$.

Proof Sketch. ($\Rightarrow$) By contradiction. ($\Leftarrow$) Consider the most naive program P realizing T; from the characterization, it comes: $\mathcal{T}_{syn}(P) = T$.   □

Finally, Definiton 16 formalizes the general semantics as a more permissive version of the synchronous one: any subset of the variables can change their value in a transition. A self-transition (s, s) thus occurs for each state s because the empty set of variables can always be selected for update. However, as for the synchronous semantics, such a self-transition is a point attractor only if all rules of P that match s have their head in s. The general semantics encompasses more than the union of both synchronous and asynchronous semantics. Its characterization, given in Proposition 8, is similar to the synchronous characterization but the combination of the two successor states is also combined with the origin state.

Definition 16 (General Semantics).   *The* general semantics $\mathcal{T}_{gen}$ *is defined by:*

$$\mathcal{T}_{gen} : P \mapsto \{(s, s \backslash\backslash r) \in \mathcal{S}^2 \mid r \subseteq \{h(R) \in \mathcal{A} \mid R \in P \wedge R \sqcap s\} \wedge$$
$$\forall \mathrm{v}_1^{val_1}, \mathrm{v}_2^{val_2} \in r, \mathrm{v}_1 = \mathrm{v}_2 \implies val_1 = val_2\}.$$

Proposition 8 (General Transitions).   *Let* $T \subseteq \mathcal{S}^2$ *so that* $\mathrm{fst}(T) = \mathcal{S}$. *The transitions of* T *are general, i.e.,* $\exists P$ *a* $\mathcal{MVLP}$ *such that* $\mathcal{T}_{gen}(P) = T$, *if and only if:* $\forall (s, s_1), (s, s_2) \in T, \forall s_3 \in \mathcal{S}, s_3 \subseteq s \cup s_1 \cup s_2 \implies (s, s_3) \in T$.

Proof Sketch. Similar to the synchronous case.   □

In addition, in Definiton 17, we define the notion of deterministic dynamics, that is, a set of transitions with no "branching", and give a particular characterization of deterministic dynamics in the synchronous case in Proposition 9.

Definition 17 (Deterministic Transitions). *A set of transitions* $T \subseteq S^2$ *is* deterministic *if* $\forall (s, s') \in T, \nexists (s, s'') \in T, s'' \neq s'$. *A* $\mathcal{MVLP}$ P *is* deterministic regarding a semantics *if the set of all transitions* T_P *obtained by applying the semantics on* P *is deterministic.*

Proposition 9 (Synchronous Deterministic Program). *A* $\mathcal{MVLP}$ P *produces* deterministic *transitions with synchronous semantics if it does not contain concurrent rules, i.e.,* $\forall R, R' \in P, \big(\text{var}(h(R)) = \text{var}(h(R')) \wedge R \sqcap R'\big) \implies h(R) = h(R')$.

Until now, the *LFIT* algorithm only tackled the learning of synchronous deterministic program, as given by Definiton 17. Using the formalism introduced in the previous sections, it can now be extended to learn systems from transitions produced from the three semantics defined above. Furthermore, both deterministic and non-deterministic systems can now be learned.

Finally, with Theorem 3, we state that the definitions and method developed in the previous section are independent of the chosen semantics.

Theorem 3 (Semantics-Free Correctness). *Let* P *be a* $\mathcal{MVLP}$ *such that* P *is complete.*

- $T_{syn}(P) = T_{syn}(P_{\mathcal{O}}(T_{syn}(P)))$,
- $T_{asyn}(P) = T_{asyn}(P_{\mathcal{O}}(T_{asyn}(P)))$,
- $T_{gen}(P) = T_{gen}(P_{\mathcal{O}}(T_{gen}(P)))$.

Proof Sketch. Using the properties of an optimal program (Definiton 12) and by contradiction.   □

3 GULA

In this section we present **GULA**: the General Usage *LFIT* Algorithm, an extension of the **LF1T** algorithm to capture both synchronous, asynchronous and general semantics dynamics. **GULA** learns a logic program from the observations of its state transitions. Given as input a set of transitions T, **GULA** iteratively constructs a model of the system by applying the method formalized in the previous section as follows:

GULA:

- **INPUT:** a set of atoms $\mathcal{A}$ and a set and of transitions $T \subseteq \mathcal{S}^2$.
- For each atom $\mathrm{v}^{val} \in \mathcal{A}$
  - Extract all states from which no transition to v^{val} exist:
    $Neg_{\mathrm{v}^{val}} := \{s \mid \nexists(s, s') \in T, \mathrm{v}^{val} \in s'\}$
  - Initialize $P_{\mathrm{v}^{val}} := \{\mathrm{v}^{val} \leftarrow \emptyset\}$
  - For each state $s \in Neg_{\mathrm{v}^{val}}$
    - ∗ Extract each rule R of $P_{\mathrm{v}^{val}}$ that matches s:
      $M_{\mathrm{v}^{val}} := \{R \in P \mid b(R) \subseteq s\}, P_{\mathrm{v}^{val}} := P_{\mathrm{v}^{val}} \setminus M_{\mathrm{v}^{val}}.$
    - ∗ For each rule $R \in M_{\mathrm{v}^{val}}$
      - · Compute its least specialization $P' = L_{\mathrm{spe}}(R, s)$.
      - · Remove all the rules in P' dominated by a rule in $P_{\mathrm{v}^{val}}$.
      - · Remove all the rules in $P_{\mathrm{v}^{val}}$ dominated by a rule in P'.
      - · Add all remaining rules in P' to $P_{\mathrm{v}^{val}}$.
  - $P := P \cup P_{\mathrm{v}^{val}}$
- **OUTPUT:** $P_{\mathcal{O}}(T) := P$.

Algorithms 1 and 2 provide the detailed pseudocode of the algorithm. Algorithm 1 learns from a set of transitions T the conditions under which each value val of each variable v may appear in the next state. Here, the learning is performed iteratively for each value of variable to keep the pseudo-code simple. But the process could easily be parallelized by running each loop in an independent thread, bounding the run time to the variable for which the learning is the longest. The algorithm starts by the pre-processing of the input transitions. Lines 4–13 of Algorithm 1 correspond to the extraction of $Neg_{\mathrm{v}^{val}}$, the set of all negative examples of the appearance of v^{val} in next state: all states such that v never takes the value val in the next state of a transition of T. Those negative examples are then used during the following learning phase (Lines 14–32) to iteratively learn the set of rules $P_{\mathcal{O}}(T)$. The learning phase starts by initializing a set of rules $P_{\mathrm{v}^{val}}$ to $\{R \in P_{\mathcal{O}}(\emptyset) \mid h(R) = \mathrm{v}^{val}\} = \{\mathrm{v}^{val} \leftarrow \emptyset\}$ (see Definiton 12). $P_{\mathrm{v}^{val}}$ is iteratively revised against each negative example neg in $Neg_{\mathrm{v}^{val}}$. All rules R_m of $P_{\mathrm{v}^{val}}$ that match neg have to be revised. In order for $P_{\mathrm{v}^{val}}$ to remain optimal, the revision of each R_m must not match neg but still matches every other state that R_m matches. To ensure that, the least specialization (see Definiton 10) is used to revise each conflicting rule R_m. Algorithm 2 shows the pseudo code of this operation. For each variable of $\mathcal{V}$ so that $b(R_m)$ has no condition over it, a condition over another value than the one observed in state neg can be added (Lines 3–8). None of those revision match neg and all states matched by R_m are still matched by at least one of its revision. The revised rules are then added to $P_{\mathrm{v}^{val}}$ after discarding the dominated rules. Once $P_{\mathrm{v}^{val}}$ has been revised against all negatives example of $Neg_{\mathrm{v}^{val}}$, $P = \{R \in P_{\mathcal{O}}(T) \mid h(R) = \mathrm{v}^{val}\}$ and $P_{\mathrm{v}^{val}}$ is added to P. Once all values of each variable have been treated, the algorithm outputs P which becomes $P_{\mathcal{O}}(T)$.

Algorithm 1. GULA($\mathcal{A}$,T)

1: INPUT: A set of atoms $\mathcal{A}$ and a set of transitions $T \subseteq \mathcal{S}^2$
2: OUTPUT: $P = P_{\mathcal{O}}(T)$

3: **for each** $v^{val} \in \mathcal{A}$ **do**
4:    // 1) Extraction of negative examples
5:    $Neg_{v^{val}} := \emptyset$
6:    **for each** $(s_1, s_1') \in T$ **do**
7:       $negative\_example := true$
8:       **for each** $(s_2, s_2') \in T$ **do**
9:          **if** $s_1 == s_2$ and $v^{val} \in s_2'$ **then**
10:             $negative\_example := false$
11:             **Break**
12:       **if** $negative\_example == true$ **then**
13:          $Neg_{v^{val}} := Neg_{v^{val}} \cup \{s_1\}$

14:    // 2) Revision of the rules of v^{val} to avoid matching of negative examples
15:    $P_{v^{val}} := \{v^{val} \leftarrow \emptyset\}$
16:    **for each** $neg \in Neg_{v^{val}}$ **do**
17:       $M := \emptyset$
18:       **for each** $R \in P_{v^{val}}$ **do** // Extract all rules that conflict
19:          **if** $b(R) \subseteq neg$ **then**
20:             $M := M \cup \{R\}; P := P \setminus \{R\}$
21:       **for each** $R_m \in M$ **do** // Revise each conflicting rule
22:          $LS := least\_specialization(R_m, neg, \mathcal{A})$
23:          **for each** $R_{ls} \in LS$ **do**
24:             **for each** $R_p \in P_{v^{val}}$ **do** // Check if the revision is dominated
25:                **if** $b(R_p) \subseteq b(R_{ls})$ **then**
26:                   $dominated := true$
27:                   **break**
28:             **if** $dominated == false$ **then** // Remove old rules that are now dominated
29:                **for each** $R_p \in P$ **do**
30:                   **if** $b(R_{ls}) \subseteq b(R_p)$ **then**
31:                      $P_{v^{val}} := P_{v^{val}} \setminus \{R_p\}$
32:                $P_{v^{val}} := P_{v^{val}} \cup \{R_{ls}\}$ // Add the revision
33:    $P := P \cup P_{v^{val}}$
34: **return** P

Algorithm 2. least_specialization(R, s, $\mathcal{A}$) : specialize R to avoid matching of s

---

1: INPUT: a rule R, a state s and a set of atoms $\mathcal{A}$
2: OUTPUT: a set of rules LS which is the least specialization of R by s according to $\mathcal{A}$.

3: $LS := \emptyset$
   // Revise the rules by least specialization
4: **for each** $v^{val} \in s$ **do**
5:    **if** $\nexists v^{val'} \in b(R)$ **then** // Add condition for all values not appearing in s
6:       **for each** $v^{val''} \in \mathcal{A}, val'' \neq val$ **do**
7:          $R' := h(R) \leftarrow (b(R) \cup \{v^{val''}\})$
8:          $LS := LS \cup \{R'\}$
9: **return** LS

Theorem 4 gives good properties of the algorithm, Theorem 5 states that **GULA** can learn from both synchronous, asynchronous and general semantics transitions and Theorem 6 characterizes its time and memory complexity.

Theorem 4 (GULA Termination, Soundness, Completeness, Optimality). *Let $T \subseteq \mathcal{S}^2$. The call **GULA**$(\mathcal{A}, T)$ terminates and **GULA**$(\mathcal{A}, T) = P_{\mathcal{O}}(T)$.*

Theorem 5 (Semantic-Freeness).   *Let P be a $\mathcal{MVLP}$ such that P is complete. From Theorems 3 and 4, the following holds:*

- $\textbf{\textit{GULA}}(\mathcal{A}, \mathcal{T}_{syn}(P)) = P_{\mathcal{O}}(\mathcal{T}_{syn}(P))$
- $\textbf{\textit{GULA}}(\mathcal{A}, \mathcal{T}_{asyn}(P)) = P_{\mathcal{O}}(\mathcal{T}_{asyn}(P))$
- $\textbf{\textit{GULA}}(\mathcal{A}, \mathcal{T}_{gen}(P)) = P_{\mathcal{O}}(\mathcal{T}_{gen}(P))$

Theorem 6 (GULA's Complexity).   *Let $T \subseteq \mathcal{S}^2$ be a set of transitions, $n := |\mathcal{V}|$ be the number of variables of the system and $d := \max(\mathrm{dom}(\mathcal{V}))$ be the maximal number of values of its variables. The worst-case time complexity of $\textbf{GULA}$ when learning from T belongs to $\mathcal{O}(|T|^2 + 2n^3 d^{2n+1} + 2n^2 d^n)$ and its worst-case memory use belongs to $\mathcal{O}(d^{2n} + 2d^n + nd^{n+2})$.*

4   Evaluation

In this section, the benefits from **GULA** are demonstrated on a case study and its scalability is assessed w.r.t. system size and input size, i.e., the number of variables and transitions. All experiments[1] were conducted on an Intel Core I7 (6700, 3.4 GHz) with 32 Gb of RAM. Figure 2 shows results of the evaluations of **GULA** scalability w.r.t. the number of variables of system, the domains size of the variables and the number of transitions in the input of the algorithm.

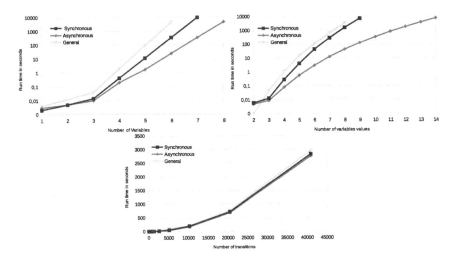

Fig. 2. Evaluation of **GULA**'s scalability w.r.t. number of variables (top left), number of variables values (top right) and number of input transitions (bottom).

For the first experiment, each variable domain is fixed to 3 values and the size of the system evolves from 1 to 8 variables. Run time performances are evaluated on synchronous, asynchronous and general semantics. Given a number of

---

[1] Available at: http://tonyribeiro.fr/data/experiments/ILP_2018.zip.

variables and a semantics, the transitions of a random system are directly generated as follows. First all possible states of the system are generated, i.e., S. For each state, a set $S \subseteq A$ is randomly generated by adding each $v^{val} \in A$ with 50% chance, simulating the matching of rules of each variable value. All possible transitions w.r.t. the considered semantics are then generated according to Proposition 6, 7 or 8. A total of 10 such instances are generated and successively given as input to the algorithm. The average run time in seconds (log scale) is given in Fig. 2 (top left) w.r.t. to the number of variables of the system learned. In those experiments, the algorithm succeeds to handle systems of at most 6 variables for both semantics before reaching the time-out of 10,000 s.

For the second experiment, the number of variables is fixed to 3 and the domain of each variable evolves from 2 to 14 values. Run time performances are once again evaluated on the three semantics. The instances are generated in the same manner as in previous experiment. The average run time in seconds (log scale) is given in Fig. 2 (top right) w.r.t. to the size of the domains of variables in the system. In those experiment the algorithm succeeds to handle systems with variable of at most 8 values for both semantics before reaching the time-out of 10,000 s.

Finally, for the third experiment, the system size is fixed to 13 variables and we change the number of transitions given as input to the algorithm from 10 to 50,000. Given a number N and a semantics, a set of transitions T is generated in the same manner as previous experiments except that the generation stops when $|T| = N$. Again, a total of 10 such instances are generated and successively given as input to the algorithm, the average run time in second is given in Fig. 2 (bottom) w.r.t. the number of input transitions. In those experiment the algorithm succeeds to handle at most 40,000 transitions for both semantics before reaching the time-out of 10,000 s.

The results of the experiments confirm the complexity analysis. The first and second experiment confirm the exponential impact of the system size on the learning time. The third experiment shows that the run time of the algorithm is rather polynomial w.r.t. to the number of input transitions. The exponential shape of the first results is explained by the fact that the number of input transitions is exponentially higher when we increase either the number of variables or the variables domains. General semantics instances are longer to learn than the two others, and synchronous semantics instances are longer to learn than asynchronous ones. The same reasoning w.r.t. the number of input transitions holds here too: from the same logic program there are more transitions generated using general semantics than synchronous (non-deterministic) than asynchronous semantics. The learning time is rather similar for all semantics when the number of transitions is the same. This was quite expected since it only impacts the pre-processing phase of the algorithm when searching for negative examples of each variable values.

Table 1 shows the run time of **GULA** when learning Boolean networks from [4]. Here we reproduced the experiments held in [13]: all transitions of each benchmark are generated and the algorithm has to learn the original rules.

Table 1. Run time of **GULA** (run time in seconds/number of transitions as input) for Boolean network benchmarks up to 15 nodes for the three semantics.

Semantics	Mammalian (10)	Fission (10)	Budding (12)	Arabidopsis (15)
Synchronous	1.84 s/1, 024	1.55 s/1, 024	34.48 s/4, 096	2, 066 s/32, 768
Asynchronous	19.88 s/4, 273	19.18s/4, 217	523 s/19, 876	T.O./213, 127
General	928 s/34, 487	1, 220 s/29, 753	T.O./261, 366	T.O./>500,000

But here the experiment is held for the three considered semantics. The table also provides the number of transitions generated by the semantics for each benchmark. It is important to note that those systems are all synchronous deterministic, meaning that in the synchronous case, the input transitions of **GULA** are the same as the input transitions of **LF1T** in [13]. Here the number of transitions in the synchronous case is much lower than for the random experiment, which explains the difference in terms of run-time. Furthermore the rules to be learned are quite simpler in the sense that the number of conditions (i.e., the size of the body of all rules) never exceeds 6 and the total number of rules is always below 124. Nevertheless, the new algorithm is slower than **LF1T** [13] in the synchronous deterministic Boolean case, which is expected since it is not specifically dedicated to learning such networks: **GULA** learns both values (0 and 1) of each variable and pre-processes the transitions before learning rules, while **LF1T** is optimized to only learn rules that make a variable take the value 1 in the next state. On the other hand, asynchronous and general semantics transitions can only be handled by our new algorithm.

GULA succeeds to learn the two smaller benchmarks for all semantics in less than an hour. The 12 variables benchmark could be learned for both the synchronous and asynchronous semantics. For the general semantics, however, it took more than the 10 h time-out (T.O. in the table), which is due to the very high number of transitions generated by those semantics: more than 200,000. The 15 variables benchmark could only be learned in synchronous case, both asynchronous and general semantics cases having reached the time-out. The current implementation of the algorithm is rather naive and better performances are expected from future optimizations. In particular, the algorithm can be parallelized into as many threads as there are different rule heads (one thread per variable value). We are also developing an approximated version of the algorithm based on local search which could greatly reduce the combinatorial explosion.

5   Conclusions

While modeling a dynamic system, the choice of a proper semantics is critical for the relevance of the subsequent analysis of the dynamics. The works presented in this paper aims to widen the possibilities offered to a system designer in the learning phase. We proposed a modeling of multi-valued systems in the form of annotated logic programs which applies not only for synchronous or asynchronous semantics, but also general semantics. After having defined the theoretical context, we introduce an extension of the **LF1T** algorithm of [13] which was so far restricted to learning synchronous deterministic Boolean systems. **GULA**, presented in this paper, can capture multi-valued deterministic or non-deterministic systems from transitions produced by synchronous, asynchronous and general semantics. The current implementation of the algorithm is rather naive which can explain the quite poor performances compared to previous algorithms on the same ground.

This work opens the way to several theoretical extensions, among them: taking into account dead-ends, memory or update delays; tackling incomplete or incoherent dynamics; formally characterizing the semantics that can, or cannot, be learned; learning the semantics alongside the dynamical rules. Once answered, each of these subjects can greatly extend the expressive power of the *LFIT* framework. A long-term objective is to fully automate the learning of models directly from time series, e.g., gene expression measurements along time (whose intrinsic semantics is unknown or even changeable).

Other possible practical or technical extensions include optimization additions, such as a massive parallelization of the learning of each head of rules, the inclusion of heuristics to guide the learning or the development of approximations methods when exact solutions require too much computation.

A   Appendix: Proofs of Sect. 2.1

Proof 1 (Proposition 1). *Let R_1, R_2 be two $\mathcal{MVL}$ rules. If $R_1 \leq R_2$ and $R_2 \leq R_1$ then $R_1 = R_2$.*

Proof. Let R_1, R_2 be two $\mathcal{MVL}$ rules such that $R_1 \leq R_2$ and $R_2 \leq R_1$. Then $h(R_1) = h(R_2)$ and $b(R_1) \subseteq b(R_2)$ and $b(R_2) \subseteq b(R_1)$, hence $b(R_1) \subseteq b(R_2) \subseteq b(R_1)$ thus $b(R_1) = b(R_2)$ and $R_1 = R_2$.   □

Proof 2 (Proposition 2). *Let R and R' be two $\mathcal{MVL}$ rules.*

$$R \sqcap R' \ \textit{iff} \ \forall v \in \mathcal{V}, \forall val, val' \in \mathbb{N}, (v^{val}, v^{val'}) \in b(R) \times b(R') \implies val = val'.$$

Proof. For the direct implication, assume given two $\mathcal{MVL}$ rules R and R' such that $R \sqcap R'$. By definition, there exists $s \in \mathcal{S}$ such that $R \sqcap s$ and $R' \sqcap s$. Also by definition, for all $(v^{val}, v^{val'}) \in b(R) \times b(R')$, there exists $v^{val}, v^{val'} \in s$. Moreover, by the definition of a state, $v^{val} = v^{val'}$, thus $val = val'$.

For the reverse implication, consider a state s so that $b(R) \cup b(R') \subseteq s$. This is compatible with the definition of a state because if a variable $v \in \mathcal{V}$ is featured in both $b(R)$ and $b(R')$, that is, if there exists $val, val' \in \mathbb{N}$ so that $(v^{val}, v^{val'}) \in b(R) \times b(R')$, then $val = val'$ and $v^{val} = v^{val'}$. For variables not featured in both $b(R)$ and $b(R')$, we can chose any value in the domain of the variable. As a consequence, we have: $b(R) \subseteq s$ and $b(R') \subseteq s$, which gives: $R \sqcap s$ and $R' \sqcap s$, meaning: $R \sqcap R'$.   □

B   Appendix: Proofs of Sect. 2.2

Proof 3 (Theorem 1). *Let R be a $\mathcal{MVL}$ rule and $s \in \mathcal{S}$ such that $R \sqcap s$. Let $S_R := \{s' \in \mathcal{S} \mid R \sqcap s'\}$ and $S_{\mathrm{spe}} := \{s' \in \mathcal{S} \mid \exists R' \in L_{\mathrm{spe}}(R, s), R' \sqcap s'\}$.*
Let P be a $\mathcal{MVLP}$ and $T, T' \subseteq \mathcal{S}^2$ such that $|\mathrm{fst}(T)| = 1 \wedge \mathrm{fst}(T) \cap \mathrm{fst}(T') = \emptyset$. The following results hold:

1. *$S_{\mathrm{spe}} = S_R \setminus \{s\}$,*
2. *$L_{\mathrm{rev}}(P, T)$ is consistent with T,*
3. *$\overset{P}{\hookrightarrow} T' \implies \xrightarrow{L_{\mathrm{rev}}(P,T)} T'$,*
4. *$\overset{P}{\hookrightarrow} T \implies \xrightarrow{L_{\mathrm{rev}}(P,T)} T$,*
5. *P is complete $\implies L_{\mathrm{rev}}(P, T)$ is complete.*

Proof

1. First, let us suppose that $\exists s'' \notin S_R \setminus \{s\}$ such that $\exists R' \in L_{\mathrm{spe}}(R, s), R' \sqcap s''$. By definition of matching $R' \sqcap s'' \implies b(R') \subseteq s''$. By definition of least specialization, $b(R') = b(R) \cup \{v^{val}\}, v^{val'} \in s, v^{val'} \notin b(R), val \neq val'$. Let us suppose that $s'' = s$, then $b(R') \not\subseteq s''$ since $v^{val} \in b(R')$ and $v^{val} \notin s$, this is a contradiction. Let us suppose that $s'' \neq s$ then $\neg(R \sqcap s'')$, thus $b(R) \not\subseteq s''$ and $b(R') \not\subseteq s''$, this is a contradiction.

   Second, let us assume that $\exists s'' \in S_R \setminus \{s\}$ such that $\forall R' \in L_{\mathrm{spe}}(R, s), \neg(R' \sqcap s'')$. By definition of S_R, $R \sqcap s''$. By definition of matching $\neg(R' \sqcap s'') \implies b(R') \not\subseteq s''$. By definition of least specialization, $b(R') = b(R) \cup \{v^{val}\}, v^{val'} \in s, val \neq val'$. By definition of matching $R \sqcap s'' \implies b(R) \subseteq s'' \implies s'' = b(R) \cup I, b(R) \cap I = \emptyset$ and thus $b(R') \not\subseteq s'' \implies v^{val} \notin I$. The assumption implies that $\forall v^{val'} \in I, \forall R' \in L_{\mathrm{spe}}(R, s), v^{val} \in b(R'), val \neq val'$. By definition of least specialization, it implies that $v^{val'} \in s$ and thus $I = s \setminus b(R)$ making $s'' = s$, which is a contradiction.

   Conclusion: $S_{\mathrm{spe}} = S_R \setminus \{s\}$

2. By definition of a consistent program, if two sets of $\mathcal{MVL}$ rules SR_1, SR_2 are consistent with T then $SR_1 \cup SR_2$ is consistent with T. Let $R_P = \{R \in P \mid R \sqcap s, \forall (s, s') \in T, h(R) \notin s'\}$ be the set of rules of P that conflict with T. By definition of least revision $L_{\mathrm{rev}}(P, T) = (P \setminus R_P) \cup \bigcup_{R \in R_P} L_{\mathrm{spe}}(R, s)$. The first part of the expression $P \setminus R_P$ is consistent with T since $\nexists R' \in P \setminus R_P$ such that R' conflicts with T. The second part of the expression $\bigcup_{R \in R_P} L_{\mathrm{spe}}(R, s)$ is also consistent with T: $\nexists R' \in L_{\mathrm{spe}}(R, s), R' \sqcap s$ thus $\nexists R' \in L_{\mathrm{spe}}(R, s)$ that conflict with T and $\bigcup_{R \in R_P} L_{\mathrm{spe}}(R, s)$ is consistent with T. Conclusion: $L_{\mathrm{rev}}(P, T)$ is consistent with T.

3. Let $(s_1, s_2) \in T'$ thus $s_1 \neq s$. From definition of realization, $v^{val} \in s_2 \implies \exists R \in P, h(R) = v^{val}, R \sqcap s_1$. If $\neg R \sqcap s$ then $R \in L_{\mathrm{rev}}(P, T)$ and $\xrightarrow{L_{\mathrm{rev}}(P,T)} (s_1, s_2)$. If $R \sqcap s$, from the first point $\exists R' \in L_{\mathrm{spe}}(R, s), R' \sqcap s_1$ and since $h(R') = h(R) = v^{val}, \xrightarrow{L_{\mathrm{rev}}(P,T)} (s_1, s_2)$. Applying this reasoning on all elements of T' implies that $\overset{P}{\hookrightarrow} T' \implies \xrightarrow{L_{\mathrm{rev}}(P,T)} T'$.

4. Let $(s_1, s_2) \in T$, since $\xrightarrow{P} T$ by definition of realization $\forall v^{val} \in s_2, \exists R \in P, R \sqcap s_1, h(R) = v^{val}$. By definition of conflict, R is not in conflict with T thus $R \in L_{\mathrm{rev}}(P, T)$ and $\xrightarrow{L_{\mathrm{rev}}(P,T)} T$.

5. Let $(s_1, s_2) \in \mathcal{S}^2$, if P is complete, then by definition of a complete program $\forall v \in \mathcal{V}, \exists R \in P, R \sqcap s_1, \mathrm{var}(h(R)) = v$. If $\neg(R \sqcap s)$ then $R \in L_{\mathrm{rev}}(P, T)$. If $R \sqcap s$, from the first point $\exists R' \in L_{\mathrm{spe}}(R, s), R' \sqcap s_1$ and thus $R' \in L_{\mathrm{rev}}(P, T)$ and since $\mathrm{var}(h(R')) = \mathrm{var}(h(R)) = v$, $L_{\mathrm{rev}}(P, T)$ is complete.   □

Proof 4 (Proposition 3). *Let $T \subseteq \mathcal{S}^2$. The $\mathcal{MVLP}$ optimal for T is unique and denoted $P_{\mathcal{O}}(T)$.*

Proof. Let $T \subseteq \mathcal{S}^2$. Assume the existence of two distinct $\mathcal{MVLP}$s optimal for T, denoted by $P_{\mathcal{O}_1}(T)$ and $P_{\mathcal{O}_2}(T)$ respectively. Then w.l.o.g. we consider that there exists a $\mathcal{MVL}$ rule R such that $R \in P_{\mathcal{O}_1}(T)$ and $R \notin P_{\mathcal{O}_2}(T)$. By the definition of a suitable program, R is not conflicting with T and there exists a $\mathcal{MVL}$ rule $R_2 \in P_{\mathcal{O}_2}(T)$, such that $R \leq R_2$. Using the same definition, there exists $R_1 \in P_{\mathcal{O}_1}(T)$ such that $R_2 \leq R_1$ since R_2 is not conflicting with T. Thus $R \leq R_1$ and by the definition of an optimal program $R_1 \leq R$. By Proposition 1, $R_1 = R$ and thus $R \leq R_2 \leq R$ hence $R_2 = R$, a contradiction.   □

Proof 5 (Proposition 4). $P_{\mathcal{O}}(\emptyset) = \{v^{val} \leftarrow \emptyset \mid v^{val} \in \mathcal{A}\}$.

Proof. Let $P = \{v^{val} \leftarrow \emptyset \mid v^{val} \in \mathcal{A}\}$. The $\mathcal{MVLP}$ P is consistent and complete by construction. Like all $\mathcal{MVLP}$s, $\xrightarrow{P} \emptyset$ and there is no transition in $\emptyset$ to match with the rules in P. In addition, by construction, the rules of P dominate all $\mathcal{MVL}$ rules.   □

Proof 6 (Theorem 2). *Let $s \in \mathcal{S}$ and $T, T' \subseteq \mathcal{S}^2$ such that $|\mathrm{fst}(T')| = 1 \wedge \mathrm{fst}(T) \cap \mathrm{fst}(T') = \emptyset$. $L_{\mathrm{rev}}(P_{\mathcal{O}}(T), T')$ is a $\mathcal{MVLP}$ suitable for $T \cup T'$.*

Proof. Let $P = L_{\mathrm{rev}}(P_{\mathcal{O}}(T), T')$. Since $P_{\mathcal{O}}(T)$ is consistent with T, by Theorem 1, P is also consistent with T and thus consistent with $T' \cup T$. Since $P_{\mathcal{O}}(T)$ realize T by Theorem 1, $\xrightarrow{P} T$. Since $s \notin \mathrm{fst}(T)$, a $\mathcal{MVL}$ rule R such that $b(R) = s$ does not conflict with T. By definition of suitable program $\exists R' \in P_{\mathcal{O}}(T), R \leq R'$, thus $\xrightarrow{P_{\mathcal{O}}(T)} T'$. Since $\xrightarrow{P_{\mathcal{O}}(T)} T'$ by Theorem 1 $\xrightarrow{P} T'$ and thus $\xrightarrow{P} T \cup T'$. Since $P_{\mathcal{O}}(T)$ is complete, by Theorem 1, P is also complete. To prove that P verifies the last point of the definition of a suitable $\mathcal{MVLP}$, let R be a $\mathcal{MVL}$ rule not conflicting with $T \cup T'$. Since R is also not conflicting with T, there exists $R' \in P_{\mathcal{O}}(T)$ such that $R \leq R'$. If R' is not conflicting with T', then R' will not be revised and $R' \in P$, thus R is dominated by a rule of P. Otherwise, R' is in conflict with T', thus $R' \sqcap s$ and $\forall (s, s') \in T', h(R') \not\subseteq s'$. Since R is not in conflict with T' and $h(R) = h(R')$, since $R \leq R'$ then $b(R) = b(R') \cup I, \exists v^{val} \in I, v^{val} \not\subseteq s$. By definition of least revision and least specialization, there is a rule $R'' \in L_{\mathrm{spe}}(R', s)$ such that $v^{val} \in b(R'')$ and since $R'' = h(R') \leftarrow b(R') \cup v^{val}$ thus $R \leq R''$. Thus R is dominated by a rule of P.   □

C   Appendix: Proofs of Sect. 2.3

Proof 7 (Proposition 6: Synchronous transitions). *Let $T \subseteq \mathcal{S}^2$ so that* $\mathrm{fst}(T) = \mathcal{S}$. *The transitions of T are* synchronous, *i.e., $\exists P$ a $\mathcal{MVLP}$ such that* $\mathcal{T}_{syn}(P) = T$, *if and only if $\forall(s, s_1), (s, s_2) \in T, \forall s_3 \in \mathcal{S}, s_3 \subseteq s_1 \cup s_2 \implies (s, s_3) \in T$.*

Proof. ($\Rightarrow$) Let (s, s_1) and (s, s_2) in T and $s_3 \in \mathcal{S}$ so that $s_3 \subseteq s_1 \cup s_2$. Let $A := \{h(R) \mid R \in P, R \sqcap s_a\}$. Then it comes: $s_1, s_2 \subseteq A$, thus: $s_3 \subseteq (s_1 \cup s_2) \subseteq A$. By construction of $\mathcal{T}_{syn}$, it comes: $(s, s_3) \in T$.

($\Leftarrow$) Consider $P := \{\mathrm{v}^{val} \leftarrow s \mid (s, s') \in T \wedge \mathrm{v}^{val} \in s'\}$ the program made of the most specific rules that realize T.

($\subseteq$) Let $(s, s') \in \mathcal{T}_{syn}(P)$ and let $x \in s'$. By construction of P, there is a rule R such that $h(R) = x$. Therefore, there exists a state $s^x \in \mathcal{S}$ such that $x \in s^x$ and $(s, s^x) \in T$. This reasoning can be carried for all atoms x in s', and in the end: $s' \subseteq \bigcup_{x \in s'} s^x$. By applying the proposition for each x, it comes: $(s, s') \in T$.

($\supseteq$) Let $(s, s') \in T$. By construction of P, we have $s' \subseteq \{h(R) \mid R \in P, R \sqcap s\}$. Thus, $(s, s') \in \mathcal{T}_{syn}(P)$.   □

Proof 8 (Proposition 7: Asynchronous transitions). *Let $T \subseteq \mathcal{S}^2$ so that* $\mathrm{fst}(T) = \mathcal{S}$. *The transitions of T are* asynchronous, *i.e., $\exists P$ a $\mathcal{MVLP}$ such that $\mathcal{T}_{asyn}(P) = T$, if and only if $\forall s, s' \in \mathcal{S}, s \neq s', \big((s, s) \in T \implies (s, s') \notin T\big) \wedge \big((s, s') \in T \implies |s \setminus s'| = 1\big)$.*

Proof. ($\Rightarrow$) Let $s, s' \in \mathcal{S}$ so that $s \neq s'$. • First suppose that $(s, s) \in T$. Then, by construction of $\mathcal{T}_{asyn}(P)$, $\forall R \in P, R \sqcap s \implies h(R) \in s$. If $(s, s') \in T$, then $\exists R \in P, R \sqcap s \wedge h(R) \notin s$, which is a contradiction. • Now suppose that $(s, s') \in T$. Then, still by construction of $\mathcal{T}_{asyn}(P)$, there exists $R \in P$ so that $s' = s \backslash\!\backslash \{h(R)\}$ and $h(R) \notin s$. Thus, $|s \setminus s'| = 1$.

($\Leftarrow$) Consider $P := \{\mathrm{v}^{val} \leftarrow s \mid (s, s') \in T \wedge \mathrm{v}^{val} \in s'\}$ the program made of the most specific rules that realize T.

($\subseteq$) Let $(s, s') \in \mathcal{T}_{asyn}(P)$. • First suppose that $s = s'$. By construction of $\mathcal{T}_{asyn}$, it means that $\forall R \in P, R \sqcap s \implies h(R) \in s$ which, by construction of P, means that $(s, s) \in T$. • Now suppose that $s \neq s'$. By construction of $\mathcal{T}_{asyn}$, it means that there exists $R \in P$ so that $h(R) \notin s$ and $s' = s \backslash\!\backslash \{h(R)\}$. By construction of P, this means that there exists $(s, s'') \in T$ so that $h(R) \in s''$ (and thus $s'' \neq s$). Moreover, from the right-hand part of the property, it comes that $|s \setminus s''| = 1$, that is, there exists a unique $x \in \mathcal{A}$ such that $x \notin s$ and $s'' = s \backslash\!\backslash \{x\}$. Necessarily, $x = h(R)$, thus $s'' = s'$ and $(s, s') \in T$.

($\supseteq$) Let $(s, s') \in T$. • First suppose that $s = s'$. From the left-hand side of the property, there exists no transition $(s, s'') \in T$ such that $s'' \neq s$. By construction, it comes: $(s, s) \in \mathcal{T}_{asyn}(P)$. • Now suppose that $s \neq s'$. From the right-hand side of the property, $|s \setminus s''| = 1$, meaning that there exists $x \in \mathcal{A}$ such that $s' = s \backslash\!\backslash x$ and $x \notin s$. Thus there exists a rule $R \in P$ such that $b(R) = s$ and $h(R) \in (s' \setminus s)$. As $(s' \setminus s) = \{x\}$, and by construction, we have: $(s, s') \in \mathcal{T}_{asyn}(P)$.   □

Proof 9 (Proposition 8: General transitions). *Let $T \subseteq S^2$ so that* $\text{fst}(T) = S$. *The transitions of T are* general, *i.e.,* $\exists P$ *a $\mathcal{MVLP}$ such that $\mathcal{T}_{gen}(P) = T$, if and only if:* $\forall (s, s_1), (s, s_2) \in T, \forall s_3 \in S, s_3 \subseteq s \cup s_1 \cup s_2 \implies (s, s_3) \in T$.

Proof. ($\Rightarrow$) Let (s, s_1) and (s, s_2) in T and $s_3 \in S$ so that $s_3 \subseteq s \cup s_1 \cup s_2$. Let $A := \{h(R) \mid R \in P, R \sqcap s_a\}$. Then it comes: $s_1, s_2 \subseteq A$, thus: $(s_3 \setminus s) \subseteq (s_1 \cup s_2) \subseteq A$. By construction of $\mathcal{T}_{gen}$, it comes: $(s, s\backslash\backslash(s_3 \setminus s)) = (s, s_3) \in T$.

($\Leftarrow$) Consider $P := \{v^{val} \leftarrow s \mid (s, s') \in T \wedge v^{val} \in s'\}$ the program made of the most specific rules that realize T.

($\subseteq$) Let $(s, s') \in \mathcal{T}_{gen}(P)$ and let $x \in s'$. By definition of $\mathcal{T}_{gen}$, either $x \in s$ or there exists $R \in P$ so that $x = h(R)$. In the first case, let $s^x = s$; in the second case, by construction of P, there exists a state $s^x \in T$ so that $(s, s^x) \in T$ and $x \in s^x$. By carrying this reasoning for all atoms x in s', we have: $s' \subseteq \bigcup_{x \in s'} s^x$ where for some x, we have $s^x = s$. By applying the proposition for each x, it comes: $(s, s') \in T$.

($\subseteq$) Let $(s, s') \in T$. By construction of P, $s' \subseteq \{h(R) \mid R \in P \wedge R \sqcap s\}$. Thus, $(s, s\backslash\backslash s') = (s, s') \in \mathcal{T}_{gen}(P)$. □

Proof 10 (Theorem 3: Semantics-Free Correctness). *Let P be a $\mathcal{MVLP}$ such that P is complete.s*

- $\mathcal{T}_{syn}(P) = \mathcal{T}_{syn}(P_{\mathcal{O}}(\mathcal{T}_{syn}(P)))$,
- $\mathcal{T}_{asyn}(P) = \mathcal{T}_{asyn}(P_{\mathcal{O}}(\mathcal{T}_{asyn}(P)))$,
- $\mathcal{T}_{gen}(P) = \mathcal{T}_{gen}(P_{\mathcal{O}}(\mathcal{T}_{gen}(P)))$.

Proof. Let us first consider the case of $\mathcal{T}_{syn}$. Let $T \subseteq S^2$ so that $\text{fst}(T) = S$ and let $M(P, s)$ be the set of heads of rules of P that match the state s: $M(P, s) := \{h(R) \mid R \in P \wedge R \sqcap s\}$.

We first expose two properties about $M(P_{\mathcal{O}}(T), s)$.

According to Definiton 12, $P_{\mathcal{O}}(T)$ realizes T, thus: (a) $\forall (s, s') \in T, s' \subseteq M(P_{\mathcal{O}}(T), s)$.

According to the same definition, $P_{\mathcal{O}}(T)$ is consistent with T, thus: (b) $\forall s \in S, \forall v^{val} \in M(P_{\mathcal{O}}(T), s), \exists (s, s') \in T, v^{val} \in s'$.

Now we prove by contradiction that $\mathcal{T}_{syn}(P) = \mathcal{T}_{syn}(P_{\mathcal{O}}(\mathcal{T}_{syn}(P)))$. Thus, suppose $\mathcal{T}_{syn}(P) \neq \mathcal{T}_{syn}(P_{\mathcal{O}}(\mathcal{T}_{syn}(P)))$ and let

$T := \mathcal{T}_{syn}(P)$. Therefore, there exists $s \in S$ so that $M(P, s) \neq M(P_{\mathcal{O}}(T), s)$. Thus:

- Either $\exists v^{val} \in M(P, s), v^{val} \notin M(P_{\mathcal{O}}(T), s)$ and thus $\exists (s, s') \in T, s' \not\subseteq M(P_{\mathcal{O}}(T), s)$ which is a contradiction with (a).
- Or $\exists v^{val} \in M(P_{\mathcal{O}}(T), s), v^{val} \notin M(P, s)$ and thus $\not\exists (s, s') \in T, v^{val} \in s'$ which is a contradiction with (b).

Then $\forall s \in S, M(P, s) = M(P_{\mathcal{O}}(T), s)$ and according to Definiton 14, $\mathcal{T}_{syn}(P) = \mathcal{T}_{syn}(P_{\mathcal{O}}(\mathcal{T}_{syn}(P)))$.

The case of $\mathcal{T}_{gen}$ is similar with $M(P, s) := s \cup \{h(R) \mid R \in P \wedge R \sqcap s\}$ and noting that $\mathcal{T}_{gen}(P) = \{(s, s') \in S^2 \mid s' \subseteq M(P, s)\}$. The case of $\mathcal{T}_{asyn}$ is also similar with $M(P, s) := \{h(R) \mid R \in P \wedge R \sqcap s\} \setminus s$ and noting that $\mathcal{T}_{asyn}(P) = \{(s, s\backslash\backslash x) \in S^2 \mid x \in M(P, s)\} \cup \{(s, s) \in S^2 \mid M(P, s) = \emptyset\}$. □

D   Appendix: Proofs of Sect. 3

Proof 11 (Theorem 4: *GULA* Termination, Soundness, Completeness, Optimality). *Let $T \subseteq S^2$. The call $GULA(\mathcal{A}, T)$ terminates and $GULA(\mathcal{A}, T) = P_{\mathcal{O}}(T)$.*

Proof. Let $T \subseteq S^2$. The call $GULA(T)$ terminates because all loops iterate on finite sets.

The algorithm iterates over each atom $v^{val} \in \mathcal{A}$ iteratively to extract all state s such that $(s, s') \in T \implies v^{val} \notin s'$. This is equivalent to generate the set $TT = \{T' \subseteq T \mid \forall t, t' \in T \implies t = (s, s'), t' = (s, s'')\}$.

To prove that $GULA(T) = P_{\mathcal{O}}(T)$, and is thus sound, complete and optimal, it suffices to prove that the main loop (Algorithm 1, Lines 16–32) preserves the invariant $P = P_{\mathcal{O}}(T_i)$ after the ith iteration where T_i is the union of all set of transitions already selected line 16 after the ith iteration for all i from 0 to $|TT|$.

Line 15 initializes P to $\{v^{val} \leftarrow \emptyset\}$. Thus by Proposition 4, after line 15, $P = \{R \in P_{\mathcal{O}}(\emptyset) \mid h(R) = v^{val}\}$.

Let us assume that before the $(i + 1)^{\text{th}}$ iteration of the main loop, $P = \{R \in P_{\mathcal{O}}(T_i) \mid h(R) = v^{val}\}$. Through the loop of Lines 18–20, $P' = \{R \in P_{\mathcal{O}}(T_i) \mid R \text{ does not conflict with } T_{i+1}, h(R) = v^{val}\}$ is computed. Then the set $P'' = \bigcup_{R \in P_{\mathcal{O}}(T_i) \setminus P', h(R) = v^{val}} L_{spe}(R, s)$ is iteratively build through the calls to **least_specialization** at line 22 and the dominated rules are pruned as they are detected by the loop of Lines 23–32. Thus by Theorem 2 and Proposition 5, $P = \{R \in P_{\mathcal{O}}(T_{i+1}) \mid h(R) = v^{val}\}$ after the $(i + 1)^{\text{th}}$ iteration of the main loop. Since the same operation is hold for each $v^{val} \in \mathcal{A}$, $P = \bigcup_{R \in P_{\mathcal{O}}(\bigcup_{T' \in TT} T' = T), h(R) = v^{val}} R = P_{\mathcal{O}}(T)$ after all iterations of the loop of line line 3. $\square$

Proof 12 (Theorem 6: *GULA*'s Complexity). *Let $T \subseteq S^2$ be a set of transitions, $n := |\mathcal{V}|$ be the number of variables of the system and $d := \max(\text{dom}(\mathcal{V}))$ be the maximal number of values of its variables. The worst-case time complexity of *GULA* when learning from T belongs to $\mathcal{O}(|T|^2 + 2n^3 d^{2n+1} + 2n^2 d^n)$ and its worst-case memory use belongs to $\mathcal{O}(d^{2n} + 2d^n + nd^{n+2})$.*

Proof. The algorithm takes as input a set of transition $T \subseteq S^2$ bounding the memory use to $O(|S^2|) = O(d^n \times d^n) = O(d^{2n})$ at start. The learning is performed iteratively for each possible rule head $v^{val} \in \mathcal{A}$. The extraction of negative example requires to compare each transition of T one to one and thus has a complexity of $op_1 = O(|T|^2)$. Those transitions are stored in $Neg_{v^{val}}$ which size is at most $|S|$ extending the memory use to $O(d^{2n} + d^n)$.

The learning phase revises a set of rule $P_{v^{val}}$ where each rule has the same head v^{val}. There are at most d^n possible rule bodies and thus $|P_{v^{val}}| \leq d^n$, the memory use of $|P_{v^{val}}|$ is then $O(d^n)$ extending the memory bound to $O(d^{2n} + d^n + d^n) = O(d^{2n} + 2d^n)$.

For each state s of $Neg_{v^{val}}$, each rule of $P_{v^{val}}$ that matches s are extracted into a set of rules R_m. This operation has a complexity of $op_2 = O(d^n \times n^2)$. Each rule of R_m are then revised using least specialization, this operation has a complexity of $O(n^2)$. $|R_m| \leq d^n$ thus the revision of all matching rules is $op_3 = O(d^n \times n^2)$. All revisions are stored in LS and there are at most dn revisions for each rule, thus $|LS| \leq d^n \times dn$ extending the memory bound to $O(d^{2n} + 2d^n + nd^{n+1}) = O(d^{2n} + 2d^n + n \times d^{n+2})$.

The memory usage of **GULA** is therefore $O(d^{2n} + 2d^n + n \times d^{n+2})$.

All rules of LS are compared to the rule of $P_{v^{val}}$ for domination check, this operation has a complexity of $op_4 = O(2 \times |LS| \times |P_{v^{val}}| \times n^2) = O(2 \times d^n \times d \times n \times d^n \times n^2) = O(2 \times n^3 \times d^{2n+1})$. The complexity is bound by $O(op_1 + op_2 + op_3 + op_4) = O(|T|^2 + d^n \times n^2 + d^n \times n^2 + 2 \times n^3 \times d^{2n+1}) = O(|T|^2 + 2 \times n^3 \times d^{2n+1} + 2 \times n^2 d^n)$

The computational complexity of **GULA** is thus $O(|T|^2 + 2n^3 d^{2n+1} + 2n^2 d^n)$. $\qquad\square$

References

1. Blair, H.A., Subrahmanian, V.: Paraconsistent foundations for logic programming. J. Non-classical Logic **5**(2), 45–73 (1988)
2. Blair, H.A., Subrahmanian, V.: Paraconsistent logic programming. Theor. Comput. Sci. **68**(2), 135–154 (1989)
3. Chatain, T., Haar, S., Paulevé, L.: Boolean networks: beyond generalized asynchronicity. In: Baetens, J.M., Kutrib, M. (eds.) AUTOMATA 2018. LNCS, vol. 10875, pp. 29–42. Springer, Cham (2018). https://doi.org/10.1007/978-3-319-92675-9_3
4. Dubrova, E., Teslenko, M.: A SAT-based algorithm for finding attractors in synchronous boolean networks. IEEE/ACM Trans. Comput. Biol. Bioinform. (TCBB) **8**(5), 1393–1399 (2011)
5. Fitting, M.: Bilattices and the semantics of logic programming. J. Logic Program. **11**(2), 91–116 (1991)
6. Garg, A., Di Cara, A., Xenarios, I., Mendoza, L., De Micheli, G.: Synchronous versus asynchronous modeling of gene regulatory networks. Bioinformatics **24**(17), 1917–1925 (2008)
7. Ginsberg, M.L.: Multivalued logics: a uniform approach to reasoning in artificial intelligence. Comput. Intell. **4**(3), 265–316 (1988)
8. Inoue, K.: Logic programming for Boolean networks. In: IJCAI Proceedings-International Joint Conference on Artificial Intelligence, vol. 22, p. 924 (2011)
9. Inoue, K., Ribeiro, T., Sakama, C.: Learning from interpretation transition. Mach. Learn. **94**(1), 51–79 (2014)
10. Kifer, M., Subrahmanian, V.: Theory of generalized annotated logic programming and its applications. J. Logic Programm. **12**(4), 335–367 (1992)
11. Martınez, D., Alenya, G., Torras, C., Ribeiro, T., Inoue, K.: Learning relational dynamics of stochastic domains for planning. In: Proceedings of the 26th International Conference on Automated Planning and Scheduling (2016)
12. Martínez, D.M., Ribeiro, T., Inoue, K., Ribas, G.A., Torras, C.: Learning probabilistic action models from interpretation transitions. In: Proceedings of the Technical Communications of the 31st International Conference on Logic Programming (ICLP 2015), pp. 1–14 (2015)
13. Ribeiro, T., Inoue, K.: Learning prime implicant conditions from interpretation transition. In: Davis, J., Ramon, J. (eds.) ILP 2014. LNCS (LNAI), vol. 9046, pp. 108–125. Springer, Cham (2015). https://doi.org/10.1007/978-3-319-23708-4_8

14. Ribeiro, T., Magnin, M., Inoue, K., Sakama, C.: Learning delayed influences of biological systems. Front. Bioeng. Biotechnol. **2**, 81 (2015)
15. Ribeiro, T., Magnin, M., Inoue, K., Sakama, C.: Learning multi-valued biological models with delayed influence from time-series observations. In: 2015 IEEE 14th International Conference on Machine Learning and Applications (ICMLA), pp. 25–31, December 2015
16. Ribeiro, T., et al.: Inductive learning from state transitions over continuous domains. In: Lachiche, N., Vrain, C. (eds.) ILP 2017. LNCS (LNAI), vol. 10759, pp. 124–139. Springer, Cham (2018). https://doi.org/10.1007/978-3-319-78090-0_9
17. Van Emden, M.H.: Quantitative deduction and its fixpoint theory. J. Logic Program. **3**(1), 37–53 (1986)

Was the Year 2000 a Leap Year?
Step-Wise Narrowing Theories
with Metagol

Michael Siebers[(✉)] and Ute Schmid

Cognitive Systems, University of Bamberg, Bamberg, Germany
{michael.siebers,ute.schmid}@uni-bamberg.de

Abstract. Many people believe that every fourth year is a leap year. However, this rule is too general: year X is a leap year if X is divisible by 4 *except* if X is divisible by 100 *except* if X is divisible by 400. We call such a theory with alternating generalisation and specialisation a step-wise narrowed theory. We present and evaluate an extension to the ILP system Metagol which facilitates learning such theories. We enabled Metagol to learn over-general theories by allowing a limited number of false positives during learning. This variant is iteratively applied on a learning task. For each iteration after the first, positive examples are the false positives from the previous iteration and negative examples are the true positives from the previous iteration. Iteration continues until no more false positives are present. Then, the theories are combined to a single step-wise narrowed theory. We evaluate the usefulness of our approach in the leap year domain. We can show that our approach finds solutions with fewer clauses, higher accuracy, and in shorter time.

Keywords: Step-wise narrowed theory · Metagol · Over-generalization

1 Introduction

Most people assume that every fourth year, that is every year divisible by four, is a leap year. Though this is correct in most cases, on average 3% of years identified as leap years by this rule are no leap years. The rule is slightly too general when compared to the true leap year rule:

> Every year that is exactly divisible by 4 is a leap year, *except* for years that are exactly divisible by 100, *but* these centurial years are leap years if they are exactly divisible by 400. [1, p. 599; emphasis by the authors]

The exact leap year rule follows a not uncommon structure: A holds if B holds *but not* if C holds. Rules of this structure can be used to explain, for example family relations: person X is Person Y's half brother if X is male and both have the same mother *but not* if they also have the same father (or vice versa). In Quinlan's famous Saturday example ([2], EnjoySport in [3], also known as play-golf or

© Springer Nature Switzerland AG 2018
F. Riguzzi et al. (Eds.): ILP 2018, LNAI 11105, pp. 141–156, 2018.
https://doi.org/10.1007/978-3-319-99960-9_9

play-tennis) a Saturday is a positive day if the outlook is overcast or if there is no wind *unless* the outlook is sunny. These examples are characterized using one exception rule from a general rule. This schema can be applied cascadingly to constrain an exception rule by another exception rule. For example, a company might have the policy that business trips must be made by train unless the trip by air plane saves at least 30% travel time. However, the train must be used if it is at least 25% cheaper.

There are several ILP systems which are able to learn rules similar to the ones presented above. The classical system CIGOL [4, 5] induces rules in interactive sessions. The user presents examples to the system which in turn generalizes rules from theses. Then, the user must specify whether a presented rule is always correct. Exceptions are handled by adding a new auxiliary predicate to the original rule which holds for all counterexamples. No rules can be learned for the auxiliary predicate. ATRE [6, 7] is especially suited to learn (mutual) recursive rules. The rules to be learned are organised in layers such that rules in higher layers only depend on rules in lower layers. When adding a new rule would lead to inconsistencies in lower layers involved predicates are renamed to new auxiliary predicates. XHAIL [8] combines abduction, deduction, and induction to learn rules incorporating negation. Predicates which may be negated must be explicitly named, as no auxiliary predicates can be invented.

Inventing auxiliary predicates, known as predicate invention [9], is a key concept to the state-of-the-art ILP system Metagol. In recent years, Metagol has been successfully applied in different domains such as learning grammar rules [10], functional string transformations [11], and higher-order theories [12]. This use of predicate invention has been shown to be beneficial regarding theory size, learning time, and predictive accuracy [13]. However, Metagol cannot use negation in learned theories.[1] We will extend Metagol to incorporate exceptions.

Our Contributions. In this paper, we define the concept of step-wise narrowed theories and introduce Metagol$_{SN}$ which can induce a subset of such theories. In detail,

- we define step-wise narrowed theories,
- we relax Metagol's prohibition to cover negative examples,
- we define Metagol$_{SN}$ by using this relaxed Metagol recursively, and
- we show that Metagol$_{SN}$ may yield smaller theories, in number of clauses, may require less background knowledge, and may run faster than Metagol.

In the next section, we introduce the meta-inductive learning framework and its realization in Metagol. Then, we will present our modifications and extensions to meta-inductive learning and Metagol which allow learning step-wise narrowed theories. Metagol$_{SN}$ will be evaluated in Sect. 4. We concluding the paper with a short discussion and further ideas.

---

[1] Of course, predicates with a "negative" semantic, like *not_father/2*, can be supplied in the background knowledge. Nevertheless, no syntactic negation can be induced.

2   Meta-interpretative Learning and Metagol

Metagol is the realization of the meta-interpretative learning (MIL) framework in Prolog. In MIL a higher-order datalog program is learned from examples using abduction. First, we introduce some logic notation.

2.1   Logic Notation

A variable is represented by a single upper case letter followed by a string of letters and digits. A function or predicate symbol is a lower case letter followed by a string of letters and digits. The arity of a function or predicate symbol is the number of arguments it takes. A constant is a function symbol with arity zero. The set of all constants is referred to as the constant signature and denoted $\mathcal{C}$. The set of all predicate symbols is denoted $\mathcal{P}$.

Variables and constants are terms, and a function symbol immediately followed by a bracketed n-tuple of terms is a term. An atom, or positive literal, is a predicate symbol (of arity n) or a variable immediately followed by a bracketed n-tuple of terms. The negation of an atom $\neg A$ is called negative literal. A variable is higher-order if it can be substituted for by a predicate symbol.

A finite set of literals is called a clause. A clause represents the disjunction of its literals. A clause is unit if and only if it contains exactly one literal. A Horn clause is a clause which contains at most one positive literal which is then called the head of the clause. The negative literals are collectively called the body of the clause. If a Horn clause contains exactly one positive literal it is called definite.

A clausal theory is a set of clauses and represents the conjunction of its clauses. A clausal theory in which each clause is a definite Horn clause is called a definite program. Literals, clauses, and clausal theories are well-formed formulas (wffs) in which all variables are assumed to be universally quantified. Let E be a wff and σ, τ be sets of variables. $\exists \sigma E$ and $\forall \tau E$ are wffs. E is said to be ground whenever it contains no variables. E is said to be datalog if it contains no function symbols other than constants. A clausal theory which contains only datalog Horn clauses is called a datalog program. The set of all ground atoms constructable from $\mathcal{P}, \mathcal{C}$ is called the datalog Herbrand base.

2.2   Meta-inductive Learning

In MIL a datalog program is abduced from examples where only clauses conforming to one of the user-supplied templates, called meta-rules, may be abduced. Every meta-rule is a uniquely named wff

$$\exists \sigma \forall \tau P(s_1, \ldots, s_m) \leftarrow Q_1(t_1^1, \ldots, t_{n_1}^1), \ldots, Q_r(t_1^r, \ldots, t_{n_r}^r)$$

```
metagol(Pos,Neg,Prog) :-
  between(MinClauses,MaxClauses,ClauseLimit),
  prove_all(Pos,[],Prog),
  length(Prog,NProg),
  NProg =< ClauseLimit,
  prove_none(Neg,Prog).

prove_all([],Prog,Prog).
prove_all([Atom|Atoms],Prog1,Prog2) :-
  prove_one(Atom,Prog1,Prog3),
  prove_all(Atoms,Prog3,Prog2).

prove_one(Atom,Prog,Prog) :- call(Atom). % use background knowledge
prove_one(Atom,Prog1,Prog2) :- % use or create abduction
  metarule(Name,MetaSub,(Atom :- Body)),
  store(sub(Name,MetaSub),Prog1,Prog3),
  prove_all(Body,Prog3,Prog2).

prove_none([],Prog).
prove_none([Atom|Atoms],Prog) :-
  not(prove_one(Atom,Prog,Prog)),
  prove_none(Atoms,Prog).
```

Fig. 1. Metagol in pseudo Prolog code. *Pos* are positive, *Neg* negative examples. *Prog* is a program. Only the last argument of every predicates is an output argument. Clause limit is modulated from *MinClauses* to *MaxClauses*, which can be set by the user. *metarule*/3 gets a meta-rule with existentially quantified variables *MetaSub* from the database, *store*/3 tests if this abduction is already known or adds it otherwise.

where σ and τ are disjoint sets of variables, $P, Q_1, \ldots, Q_r \in \sigma \cup \tau \cup \mathcal{P}$, and $s_1, \ldots, s_m, t_1^1, \ldots, t_{n_r}^r \in \sigma \cup \tau \cup \mathcal{C}$ [13, definition 1]. Table 1 shows some example meta-rules. Muggleton *et al.* define the MIL learning setting as follows [13, Definition 2]:

> Given [a set of] meta-rules M, definite program background knowledge B and ground positive and negative unit examples E^+, E^-, MIL returns a higher-order datalog program hypothesis H if one exists such that $M, B, H \models E^+$ and M, B, H, E^- is consistent.

2.3   Metagol

Metagol is a Prolog meta-interpreter which realizes a limited MIL setting. There are different Metagol variants for special use cases or incorporating different features, for example Metagol$_{DF}$ [11] for function induction or Metagol$_{CF}$ [10] for learning context free grammars. We focus on the most recent version, Metagol$_{AI}$ [12,14]. If the version is clear from the context we omit the subscript. In the following, we present Metagol's features and restrictions relevant to this work.

Metagol is a two step approach. First, a candidate program is abduced by successively proving all positive examples. The number of clauses in the candidate program is limited. Second, Metagol verifies that no negative examples can be proven using this program. Prolog's backtracking ensures that a solution is found if it exists. If no solution can be found within the given clause limit, it is step-by-step increased using an iterative deepening strategy. Thus, the smallest program (in number of clauses) will be found first. Figure 1 shows the Metagol algorithm in pseudo-code.

In the first step (*prove_all* in Fig. 1), each example is proven either

- using only background knowledge,
- using clauses from the already induced program, or
- by matching it against the head of one meta-rule, adding the resulting clause to the program, and proving the meta-rule body recursively.

In the second step (*prove_none* in Fig. 1), Metagol verifies that no negative example can be proven using only background knowledge and already abduced clause, that is without changing the program.

Technically, background knowledge is provided by indicating eligible predicate symbols and their arity. Clauses for these predicates, possibly including predefined predicates, are provided in the Prolog database. Meta-rules with their name and a list of variables to be existentially quantified are given as clauses with an appropriate head in the Prolog database. Positive and negative examples are presented as lists of positive ground atoms. Metagol assumes that all positive examples share the same predicate symbol and arity. However, this is not strictly required.[2]

3   Step-Wise Narrowed Theories

In the following, we present a modification to the MIL framework and Metagol to deal with domains such as leap year. That is, we propose a framework for learning over-general theories and their step-wise narrowing to characterize exceptions. First, we define step-wise narrowed theories (SNTs), then we present an induction framework for such theories, and finally, an implementation as Metagol$_{SN}$.

Let $\Phi : \mathcal{P} \to \mathcal{P}$ be a mapping between predicate symbols. Then, $\mathcal{M}_{\Phi}$ is a mapping between atoms such that $\mathcal{M}_{\Phi} : p(t_1, \ldots, t_n) \mapsto \Phi(p)(t_1, \ldots, t_n)$.

Definition 1 (Step-wise Narrowed Theory). *Every higher-order datalog program is a* step-wise narrowed theory *(SNT). Let H be a higher-order datalog program, Φ a mapping between predicate symbols and S a SNT. Then, $\langle H, \Phi, S \rangle$ is also a SNT.*

---

[2] Nevertheless, Metagol can only abduce clauses for the predicate symbol of the first positive example and invented predicate symbols derived thereof.

Definition 2 (SNT Depth). *The depth of a SNT is the number of "unpacking" steps required to access the innermost datalog program:*

$$d(S) = \begin{cases} d(S') + 1 & \text{if } S = \langle H, \Phi, S' \rangle \\ 0 & \text{otherwise} \end{cases}.$$

Definition 3 (SNT Size). *The size of a SNT is the number of clauses it contains. If H has n_H and S has n_S clauses we say $\langle H, \Phi, S \rangle$ has $n_H + n_S$ clauses. If SNT S_1 has less clauses than SNT S_2 we say that S_1 is smaller than S_2.*

Given meta-rules M and some definite program background knowledge B the SNT $\langle H, \Phi, S \rangle$ models the positive ground literal A if A is modelled by H but $\mathcal{M}_\Phi(A)$ is not modelled by H and S, that is

$$M, B, \langle H, \Phi, S \rangle \models A \quad \equiv \quad M, B, H \models A \wedge M, B, H, S \not\models \mathcal{M}_\Phi(A).$$

3.1 Inducing Step-Wise Narrowed Theories

Inducing a SNT from positive and negative examples is called a *step-wise narrowing learning (SNL) task* or *SNL setting*.

Definition 4 (SNL setting). *Given a set of meta-rules M, definite program background knowledge B, and ground positive and negative unit examples E^+, E^-, SNL returns a SNT S if one exists such that $M, B, S \models E^+$ and M, B, S, E^- is consistent.*

We propose a general solution to the SNL setting based on MIL. For this purpose, we abolish the constraint that M, B, H, E^- must be consistent. We call this the *relaxed MIL setting* (rMIL).

Definition 5 (Relaxed MIL setting). *Given a set of meta-rules M, definite program background knowledge B, a non-negative integer l, and ground positive and negative unit examples E^+, E^- relaxed MIL returns a higher-order datalog program hypothesis H if one exists along with a partitioning of E^- in true negative examples $E_\ominus^-$ and false positive examples $E_\oplus^-$ such that $E_\oplus^-$ has at most l elements, $M, B, H \models E^+, E_\oplus^-$, and M, B, H, $E_\ominus^-$ is consistent. We call l the false positive limit.*

Proposition 1 (rMIL decidable). *The rMIL setting is decidable in the case M, B, E^+, E^- are datalog and $\mathcal{P}$, $\mathcal{C}$ are finite.*

Proof. Follows from the fact that the Herbrand base is finite.

Our general solution realizes SNL by recursively applying rMIL. Given a set of meta-rules M, definite program background knowledge B, and ground positive and negative unit examples E^+, E^- we use rMIL to get a datalog program H and false positives $E_\oplus^-$. If there are no false positives, H is a solution in the SNL setting. Otherwise, we define Φ such that every predicate symbol used in E^+ and

---

Algorithm 1. Pseudo-code algorithm for the general solution to the SNL setting. `rMIL` denotes the relaxed MIL setting.

Function $SNL(M, B, l, E^+, E^-)$ **is**

> **Input**: meta-rules M, background knowledge B, false positive limit l,
> positive examples E^+, and negative examples E^-
>
> **Result**: a SNT
>
> $H, E_\ominus^-, E_\oplus^- \leftarrow \texttt{rMIL}(M, B, l, E^+, E^-)$;
>
> **if** $E_\oplus^- = \emptyset$ **then**
>> **return** H;
>
> **else**
>> Let Φ map every predicate symbol from $E^+ \cup E^-$ to a new symbol;
>> $E'^+ \leftarrow \{\mathcal{M}_\Phi(A) \mid \neg A \in E_\oplus^-\}$;
>> $E'^- \leftarrow \{\neg \mathcal{M}_\Phi(A) \mid A \in E^+\}$;
>> **return** $\langle H, \Phi, \texttt{SNL}(M, B \cup H, E'^+, E'^-) \rangle$;
>
> **end**

end

E^- is mapped to a new predicate symbol. The solution is then $\langle H, \Phi, S \rangle$ where S is the solution to the SNL setting with background knowledge $B \cup H$, the mapped false positive examples as positive examples, and the negated mapped positive examples as negative examples. A pseudo-code algorithm for the general solution is provided in Algorithm 1.

3.2   Metagol$_{SN}$

Based on Cropper & Muggleton's Metagol$_{AI}$ implementation[3] we implemented a Prolog realisation of SNL, Metagol$_{SN}$.[4] As first step, we relaxed Metagol to conform to rMIL. The structure of relaxed Metagol is similar to Metagol. First, a program is abduced from all positive examples as in Metagol. Then, false positives are collected by checking which negative examples can be proven without adding clauses (see Fig. 2). We did not change the presentation of meta-rules, background knowledge, or examples.

As second step, we realize Metagol$_{SN}$ using relaxed Metagol. As mentioned above, Metagol assumes that all positive examples share the same predicate symbol and arity. We extend that assumption to all examples: Metagol$_{SN}$ assumes that all examples share the same predicate symbol and arity. Thus, constructing Φ degenerates to inventing one new predicate symbol. We prefix the original predicate symbol with an underscore. Implementing the steps of the general SNL solution is straight forward (cf. Fig. 3):

---

[3] We forked from commit 1524600225a65237de9578e46127049f6f95d1a4 in the GitHub Metagol repository [14].

[4] Metagol$_{SN}$ is available at https://github.com/michael-siebers/metagol/tree/ilp2018.

1. We use rMIL to induce a program and collect false positives.
2. If there are no false positives, we return the induced program.
3. Otherwise, we rename predicates in false positives and positive examples, add the program to the Prolog database, and recurse on the new examples.

```
metagol_relaxed(Pos,Neg,MaxClauses,Prog,FalsePos) :-
    between(1,MaxClauses,ClauseLimit),
    prove_all(Pos,[],Prog),
    length(Prog,NProg),
    NProg =< ClauseLimit,
    prove_some(Neg,Prog,FalsePos).

prove_some([],Prog,[]).
prove_some([Atom|Atoms],Prog,[Atom|Proven]) :-
    prove_some(Atoms,Prog,Proven),
    prove_one(Atom,Prog,Prog).
prove_some([Atom|Atoms],Prog,Proven) :-
    prove_some(Atoms,Prog,Proven),
    not(prove_one(Atom,Prog,Prog)).
```

Fig. 2. Relaxed MIL in pseudo Prolog code. *Pos* are positive, *Neg* negative examples. *Prog* is a program and and *FalsePos* are false positive examples. For *prove_some/3* the last, for *metagol_relaxed/5* the last two arguments are output arguments. The maximally allowed number of clauses *MaxClauses* is a user-given parameter. For *prove_all* and *prove_one* see Fig. 1.

Parameters. For every rMIL run, the *false positive limit* is calculated as the size of the negative examples times the parameter *maximal false positive fraction*, rounded down. As rMIL may result in a program H such that there are no true negatives, SNL is in general undecidable. For Metagol$_{SN}$, we require that there are strictly less false positives than negative examples, that is *maximal false positive fraction* must be lower than 1. Then, the number of positive and negative examples reduces at every second recursion step and Metagol$_{SN}$ is decidable.

To further guide the search, we impose an iterative deepening schema on the size and the depth of the induced SNT. An upper limit for both may be set as a parameter. The depth is deepened within the size of the SNT. That is, size n with depth $m + 1$ is explores before size $n + 1$ with depth m. This assures that Metagol$_{SN}$ finds the smallest theory.

SNT Flattening. As Metagol$_{SN}$ only induces theories for single predicate symbol arity pairs, any induced SNT can easily be flattened into a single clausal theory. If the induced SNT is a datalog program, thus a clausal theory, no flattening is required. Otherwise, given any SNT $\langle H, \Phi, S \rangle$ induced for predicate symbol p and any atom $A = p(t_1, \ldots, t_n)$, let H' be a copy of H where $not(\mathcal{M}_\Phi(A))$ is appended to every clause with head A. Then the flattening of $\langle H, \Phi, S \rangle$ is the union of the flattening of S and H' (see Fig. 4).

4   Evaluation

To evaluate the usefulness of our approach, we compared Metagol$_{SN}$ and Metagol$_{AI}$ on the leap year domain. As introduced above, years must be separated in leap years and not leap years. That is, the target predicate *leapyear(X)* shall hold if and only if X is a leap year. We defined two predicates describing numbers:

divisible/2 where *divisible(X, Y)* holds if and only if the integer Y divides the integer X exactly and

not_divisible/2 where *not_divisible(X, Y)* holds if and only if X and Y are integers and *divisible(X, Y)* does not hold.

Using these two predicates as background knowledge, two clauses suffice to solve the leap year problem (Fig. 5).

To explore the effect of narrowing, first, we focus on a single induction episode on a very small set of examples. As a proof of concept we want to show that extending Metagol with narrowing will result in smaller theories, which can be

```
metagol_sn(Pos,Neg,MaxClauses,SNT) :-
  let P be the predicate symbol used in Pos,
  between(1,MaxClauses,ClauseLimit),
  metagol_relaxed(Pos,Neg,MaxClauses,Prog1,FalsePos),
  if FalsePos=[]
    SNT = Prog1
  else
    let PPrime be P prefixed with '_',
    let PosNext be FalsePos with P renamed to PPrime,
    let NegNext be Pos with P renamed to PPrime,
    assert_prog(Prog1),
    metagol_sn(PosNext,NegNext,MaxClauses - length of Prog1,Prog2),
    SNT=snt(Prog1,PPrime,Prog2)
  end if.
```

Fig. 3. Metagol$_{SN}$ in pseudo Prolog code. *Pos* are positive, *Neg* negative examples. *assert_prog/1* adds its argument to the Prolog database and removes it on backtracking. Maximal theory size *MaxClauses* is configurable by the user.

```
flatten_snt(P,snt(Prog1,PPrime,Prog2),Prog3) :-
  flatten_snt(PPrime,Prog2,Prog4),
  for each P(T1,...,TN) :- Body in Prog1
    replace it with P(T1,...,TN) :- Body, not(PPrime(T1,...,TN)),
  append(Prog1,Prog4,Prog3).
flatten_snt(P,Prog,Prog).
```

Fig. 4. Flattening of a SNT in pseudo Prolog code. *P* and *PPrime* are predicate symbols, *ProgN* are programs. *P* is the predicate symbol *Prog1* was induced for.

Table 1. Meta-rules used during evaluation. Name, well-formed formula, existential quantified variables σ, and universal quantified variables τ are shown.

Name	wff	σ	τ
Const	$P(A, B) \leftarrow$	$\{P, B\}$	$\{A\}$
And1	$P(A) \leftarrow Q(A), R(A)$	$\{P, Q, R\}$	$\{A\}$
Chain	$P(A, B) \leftarrow Q(A, C), R(C, B)$	$\{P, Q, R\}$	$\{A, B, C\}$
Curry	$P(A) \leftarrow Q(A, B)$	$\{P, Q, B\}$	$\{A\}$

$$\text{leapyear}(X) \leftarrow \text{divisible}(X,4), \text{not\_divisible}(X,100).$$
$$\text{leapyear}(X) \leftarrow \text{divisible}(X,400).$$

Fig. 5. Clausal theory to classify leap years using background knowledge B_{ndiv}.

induced in shorter time, with less background knowledge. Afterwards, we will compare both systems on a larger dataset, reporting predictive accuracy and run times.

4.1 Proof of Concept Evaluation

As small proof of concept, we tried to induce the leap year rule from a limited number of examples using Metagol$_{SN}$ and Metagol$_{AI}$. For positive examples, we used the years 4, 20, and 400. Negative examples were the years 2, 100, and 200. The positive examples were either sorted ascending (dataset *poc-asc*) or descending (dataset *poc-desc*), negative examples were always sorted descending.

Meta-rules and Background Knowledge. We provided the meta-rules *And1* and *Curry* (see Table 1) to both systems. We tested the systems with three sets of background knowledge B_{div}, B_{ndiv}, and B_{max}. All three contain the predicate *divisible/2*, while only B_{ndiv} and B_{max} contain *not_divisible/2*. Both predicates were provided as rules. Since the arguments of the predicates are integers, the set of constants C is infinite and thus learning is neither in the MIL setting nor in the SNL setting decidable. In order to have a decidable problem, we limit possible constant choices to a finite number. For *divisible(X, Y)* and *not_divisible(X, Y)* in B_{div} and B_{ndiv}, Y may be any natural number from 1 to X. In B_{max}, Y may be any natural number which exactly divides any positive or negative example. X is naturally constraint by the example years. An overview of the defined variants of background knowledge is given in Table 2.

Parameters. For Metagol$_{SN}$ we varied the maximal allowed false positive fraction with possible values 0.34, 0.5, 0.67, and 0.75. Additionally, we limited the SNT depth to 1, 2, or 3. For both systems learning was cut off after 30 min.

Table 2. Background knowledge defined for leap year domain. *divisible(X, Y)* and *not_divisible(X, Y)* indicate whether these predicates are available in the background knowledge.

	B_{div}	B_{ndiv}	B_{max}
divisible(X, Y)	✓	✓	✓
not_divisible(X, Y)	X	✓	✓
Constraint on Y	$1 \leq Y \leq X$	Y divides any example

> leapyear(A) ← leapyear_1(A), leapyear_2(A).
> leapyear(A) ← divisible(A,16).
> leapyear_1(A) ← divisible(A,4).
> leapyear_2(A) ← not_divisible(A,25).

Fig. 6. Leap year theory induced by Metagol$_{AI}$ for *poc-desc* using B_{max}.

Results. Both Metagol$_{AI}$ and Metagol$_{SN}$ were able to learn the correct theory (in some configurations) as shown in Figs. 6 and 7. Main results for single runs on the *poc-asc* dataset are given in Table 3 and on the *pos-desc* dataset in Table 4. Metagol$_{AI}$ was not able to induce a theory using B_{div}, neither for the *poc-asc* data set nor for *poc-desc*. However, this was to be expected as there is no datalog solution to the learning task with this background knowledge.

Using B_{ndiv} Metagol$_{AI}$ failed on *poc-asc* within short time (0.7 s). This is due to the ordering of the examples and the imposed constraint on the numeric constants. In *poc-asc* the number 4 is the first positive example. Since 25 and 400 are greater than 4, neither *not_divisible(X,25)* nor *divisible(X,400)* can be abduced from this example. Learning fails as no theory can be found which is consistent with the negative examples. For descendent ordering this does not hold. Either *not_divisible(X,25)* and *divisible(X,400)* could be abduced from the first example (400).

However, reordering the data set seems to increase the search space massively. This hypothesis is supported by the observations that Metagol$_{AI}$ timed out on this data set and that Metagol$_{SN}$ timed out or took much longer to induce a theory. Even in failed attempts to induce a theory, both Metagol$_{AI}$ and Metagol$_{SN}$ took longer for *poc-desc* than *poc-asc*. We conclude that Metagol$_{AI}$ and Metagol$_{SN}$ are susceptible to the ordering of examples.

Finally, B_{max} allowed both Metagol systems to induce theories. There are no differences in results between *poc-asc* and *poc-desc*. However, Metagol$_{SN}$ always found a theory with 3 clauses whereas Metagol$_{AI}$ required 4 clauses. Regarding learning time, differences between the systems are negligible.

To induce a theory Metagol$_{SN}$ required a SNT depth of two for B_{div}. And a depth of one was sufficient for B_{ndiv} and B_{max}, but a depth of two produced smaller theories in shorter time for B_{ndiv}. Increasing the depth limit further did

leapyear(A) ← divisible(A,4), not(_leapyear(A)).
_leapyear(A) ← divisible(A,100), not(__leapyear(A)).
__leapyear(A) ← divisible(A,400).

Fig. 7. Leap year theory induced by Metagol$_{SN}$ for *poc-asc* using B_{div}. Maximal allowed false positive fraction was 0.67, SNT depth was limited to 2.

not change performance. A maximal false positive fraction of 67%, or two of the initial negative examples, was required for B_{div} and B_{ndiv}. A higher value did not improve performance further. For B_{max}, a maximal false positive fraction of 34%, or one of the initial negative examples, delivered good results. No improvement with increasing value can be deduced.

Table 3. Results for single runs on *poc-asc* data set. Shown are the maximal allowed false positive fraction (max. FP), the limit on the SNT depth (limit), the number of clauses in the learned theory (#c) where – denotes a failed run, the SNT depth (d), and the used time in seconds (t).

	max. FP	limit	B_{div}			B_{ndiv}			B_{max}		
			#c	d	t	#c	d	t	#c	d	t
Metagol$_{AI}$			–	–	0.4	–	–	0.7	4	0	0.2
Metagol$_{SN}$	0.34	1	–	–	0.5	–	–	1.0	3	1	0.0
	0.50	1	–	–	0.5	–	–	1.0	3	1	0.0
	0.67	1	–	–	1.7	4	1	0.3	3	1	0.0
		2	3	2	0.0	3	2	0.0	3	2	0.0
	0.75	1	–	–	1.7	4	1	0.3	3	1	0.0
		2	3	2	0.0	3	2	0.0	3	2	0.0

4.2   Performance Evaluation

Based on the results of the proof of concept we conducted a larger experiment to study the influence of SNL parameters on performance. Meta-rules are as for the small data sets. To have a fair comparison for both systems, we choose to use only B_{max} in our experiments.

Examples. As examples we use all years from 1582, where leap years following the current rule were introduction with the Gregorian calendar [1], to the current year. Years were separated in leap years and not leap years using the rule from Fig. 5. For the experiments we randomly sampled 20%, 40%, 60%, 80%, or 100% of the positive and negative examples. Metagol$_{AI}$ and Metagol$_{SN}$ were evaluated on the same samples.

Parameters. We varied the maximal allowed false positive fraction with possible values 0.05, 0.10, 0.25, 0.50, 0.75, and 0.95, and the depth limit with possible values 1, 2, or 5. Every parameter combination and $Metagol_{AI}$ were evaluated 10 times, each time with a different sampling. Learning was cut off after 30 min.

Evaluation. We evaluated the systems on theory complexity (number of clauses and SNT depth), learning time, and predictive accuracy. Therefore, we applied the induced theories on the next thousand years (2019–3018).

Results. In general, accuracies are very high (greater than or equal to 97.6%) for all sample sizes and all SNT depth limits (see Fig. 8). However, $Metagol_{AI}$ was not able to learn for sample sizes larger than 60% with the given time limit. $Metagol_{SN}$ was able to learn for all sample sizes when allowing up to 25% false positives and a SNT depth of two or five. For SNT depth one, $Metagol_{SN}$ was able to learn from 80% of the data but not from 100% within the time limit. When training on the complete data set succeeded, $Metagol_{SN}$ has an accuracy of 100%. For both systems runtime increases with sample size (see Fig. 9). In general, $Metagol_{AI}$ has higher run times than $Metagol_{SN}$. For both systems, the number of time-outs increases with sample size. For $Metagol_{SN}$ time-outs increase with maximal allowed false positive fraction.

Table 4. Results for single runs on *poc-desc* data set. Shown are the maximal allowed false positive fraction (max. FP), the limit on the SNT depth (limit), the number of clauses in the learned theory (#c) where – denotes a failed run, the SNT depth (d), and the used time in seconds (t). † denotes that the run did not finish within 30 min.

	max. FP	limit	B_{div}			B_{ndiv}			B_{max}		
			#c	d	t	#c	d	t	#c	d	t
$Metagol_{AI}$			–	–	14.6	–	–	†	4	0	0.1
$Metagol_{SN}$	0.34	1	–	–	17.1	–	–	†	3	1	0.0
	0.5	1	–	–	17.3	–	–	†	3	1	0.0
	0.67	1	–	–	34.0	4	1	25.8	3	1	0.0
		2	3	2	0.0	3	2	0.1	3	2	0.0
	0.75	1	–	–	33.7	4	1	25.8	3	1	0.0
		2	3	2	0.0	3	2	0.1	3	2	0.0

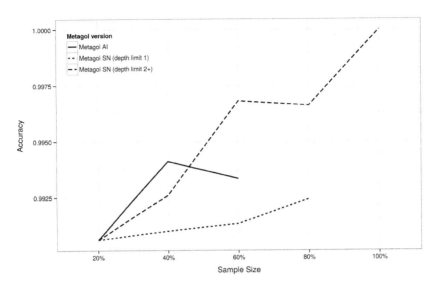

Fig. 8. Average accuracies (standard deviations are similar for all cases and approximately 0.05) for different sample sizes given different SNT depth limits. Results for depth limits 2 and 5 were identical and thus are show in a single line. Metagol$_{SN}$ was run with 0.05 maximal allowed false positives.

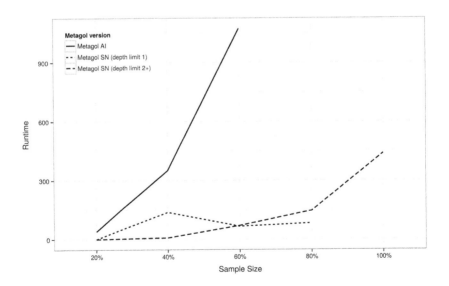

Fig. 9. Average run times for different sample sizes given for different SNT depth limits. Results for depth limits 2 and 5 were identical and thus are show in a single line. Metagol$_{SN}$ was run with 0.05 maximal allowed false positives.

5 Conclusion

We introduced the concept of step-wise narrowed theories to tackle domains which can best be characterized by an over-general rule and cascading exceptions. We could show that the ILP system Metagol which allows predicate invention but cannot deal with negation can be extended to learn such theories. Evaluation has been performed on the leap year domain. As a next step, we plan to compare Metagol$_{SN}$ with other systems, like ATRE and XHAIL, on the leap year and additional domains. For example, we want to investigate rule plus exception concepts in the Michalski train domain [15]. Learning a rule such as, *a train is eastbound if it contains a rectangle in any carriage but not in the first one.* Furthermore, we expect to gain better performances for learning grammars for facial expressions of pain than with a previously explored grammar induction approach [16]. Relaxing the MIL framework allows learning of imperfect theories. This could be exploited in an iterative deepening approach on the false positive limit, producing a stream of improving theories, that is an anytime algorithm.

Acknowledgements. We like to thank Andrew Cropper for valuable discussions on negation in Metagol. This work was funded by the Deutsche Forschungsgemeinschaft (DFG, German Research Foundation) – SCHM 1239/10-1.

References

1. Richards, E.G.: Calendars. In: Urban, S.E., Seidelmann, P.K. (eds.) Explanatory Supplement to the Astronomical Almanac, pp. 585–624 (2013)
2. Quinlan, J.R.: Induction of decision trees. Mach. Learn. **1**, 81–106 (1986)
3. Mitchell, T.M.: Machine Learning. McGraw-Hill, New York (1997)
4. Muggleton, S., Buntine, W.: Machine invention of first-order predicates by inverting resolution. In: Machine Learning Proceeding, pp. 339–352 (1988), https://doi.org/10.1016/B978-0-934613-64-4.50040-2
5. Bain, M., Muggleton, S.: Non-monotonic Learning. In: Machine Intelligence 12 - Towards an Automated Logic of Human Thought, pp. 105–120 (1991)
6. Malerba, D., Esposito, F., Lisi, F.A.: Learning Recursive Theories with ATRE. In: ECAI (European Conference on Artificial Intelligence), pp. 435–439 (1998)
7. Malerba, D.: Learning recursive theories in the normal ILP setting. Fundamenta Informaticae **57**, 39–77 (2003)
8. Ray, O.: Nonmonotonic abductive inductive learning. J. Appl. Logic **7**, 329–340 (2009)
9. Stahl, I.: Predicate Invention in ILP - an Overview. In: Machine Learning: ECML-1993, pp. 313–322 (1993)
10. Muggleton, S.H., Lin, D., Pahlavi, N., Tamaddoni-Nezhad, A.: Meta-interpretive learning: application to grammatical inference. Mach. Learn. **94**, 25–49 (2014)
11. Lin, D., Dechter, E., Ellis, K., Tenenbaum, J., Muggleton, S.H.: Bias reformulation for one-shot function induction. In: ECAI (European Conference on Artificial Intelligence), pp. 525–530 (2014). https://doi.org/10.3233/978-1-61499-419-0-525
12. Cropper, A., Muggleton, S.H.: Learning higher-order logic programs through abstraction and invention. In: IJCAI (International Joint Conference on Artificial Intelligence), pp. 1418–1424 (2016)

13. Muggleton, S.H., Lin, D., Tamaddoni-Nezhad, A.: Meta-interpretive learning of higher-order dyadic datalog: predicate invention revisited. Mach. Learn. **100**, 49–73 (2015)

14. Cropper, A., Muggleton, S.H.: Metagol System (2016). https://github.com/metagol/metagol

15. Larson, J., Michalski, R.S.: Inductive Inference of VL Decision Rules. ACM SIGART Bull., 38–44, June 1977

16. Siebers, M., Schmid, U., Seuß, D., Kunz, M., Lautenbacher, S.: Characterizing facial expressions by grammars of action unit sequences - a first investigation using ABL. Inf. Sci. **329**, 866–875 (2016)

Targeted End-to-End Knowledge Graph Decomposition

Blaž Škrlj[1,2(✉)], Jan Kralj[2], and Nada Lavrač[2,3]

[1] Jožef Stefan International Postgraduate School,
Jamova 39, 1000 Ljubljana, Slovenia
[2] Jožef Stefan Institute, Jamova 39, 1000 Ljubljana, Slovenia
{blaz.skrlj,jan.kralj,nada.lavrac}@ijs.si
[3] University of Nova Gorica, Vipavska 13, 5000 Nova Gorica, Slovenia

Abstract. Knowledge graphs are networks with annotated nodes and edges, representing different relations between the network nodes. Learning from such graphs is becoming increasingly important as numerous real-life systems can be represented as knowledge graphs, where properties of selected types of nodes or edges are learned. This paper presents a fully autonomous approach to targeted knowledge graph decomposition, advancing the state-of-the-art HINMINE network decomposition methodology. In this methodology, weighted edges between the nodes of a selected node type are constructed via different typed triplets, each connecting two nodes of the same type through an intermediary node of a different type. The final product of such a decomposition is a weighted homogeneous network of the selected node type. HINMINE is advanced by reformulating the supervised network decomposition problem as a combinatorial optimization problem, and by solving it by a differential evolution approach. The proposed approach is tested on node classification tasks on two real-life knowledge graphs. The experimental results demonstrate that the proposed end-to-end learning approach is much faster and as accurate as the exhaustive search approach.

Keywords: Knowledge graphs · Network analysis
Supervised machine learning

1 Introduction

Network analysis was established as an independent research discipline in the early eighties [1]. While it initially addressed the analysis of homogeneous information networks, analysis of *heterogeneous information networks* [2] has recently gained a lot of attention. In contrast with standard (homogeneous) information networks, heterogeneous information networks describe heterogeneous types of entities and different types of relations. Examples of heterogeneous networks are e.g., *biological networks* that contain different entity types such as species, genes, Gene Ontology annotations [3], proteins, metabolites, etc. There are diverse

© Springer Nature Switzerland AG 2018
F. Riguzzi et al. (Eds.): ILP 2018, LNAI 11105, pp. 157–171, 2018.
https://doi.org/10.1007/978-3-319-99960-9_10

types of links between such mixed biological entities; for example, genes can belong to species, encode proteins, be annotated by an ontology annotation, and so on.

In this work we focus on *knowledge graphs* [4], i.e. heterogeneous information networks with annotated nodes and annotated (relation-labeled) edges, like in the following examples from a biological knowledge graph:

$$protein_1 \xrightarrow{\text{interactsWith}} protein_2$$

$$protein_1 \xrightarrow{\text{annotatedWith}} function_A$$

$$protein_2 \xrightarrow{\text{annotatedWith}} function_B$$

Some of the common tasks on knowledge graphs [5] include relation extraction, triplet classification, entity recognition as well as entity classification, where the task is to assign correct labels to a specific set of nodes in a knowledge graph. For example, if the nodes are different proteins, one of the possible goals is to classify the proteins based on their function. Take another example, where the nodes are different movies, and the goal is to classify the movies to different genres. The problem arises when different relations between individual movies and other movies, actors or directors are considered (e.g., $actor_1 \xrightarrow{\text{actsIn}} movie_5 \xrightarrow{\text{directedBy}} director_4$).

The problem of node classification can be formally stated as follows. Let $G = (N, E, R, C)$ represent a knowledge graph, where N is a set of nodes (of possibly different types), E a set of edges, R a set of relations on edges and C the set of classes assigned to nodes. The goal is to construct a mapping $\theta : N \rightarrow C$, which assigns the most probable class to a node to be classified.

One of the possible approaches to node classification is through *network decomposition* [6,7], where a knowledge graph is aggregated into a homogeneous network consisting of a single target node type, and the information derived from the graph is encoded in the form of weighted edges of the aggregated homogeneous network. Different down-stream machine learning algorithms can then be applied to the aggregated network to perform node classification [7,8]. One of the remaining open questions is whether homogeneous network construction can be performed in an automated, end-to-end manner. The main contributions of this work include a novel, interpretable end-to-end knowledge graph decomposition approach based on state-of-the-art network decomposition approaches, an improved parallel decomposition algorithm and the inclusion of ground-truth edge information between the target nodes into the network decomposition process.

This paper is structured as follows. The next section provides a brief overview of state-of-the-art approaches to learning from different types of networks. We continue the discussion by describing the optimization procedure used in this work. Finally, the proposed approach is presented along with the results of its experimental evaluation.

2   Background and Related Work

There are different methodologies for the analysis and construction of knowledge graphs, which can be broadly divided into methods that focus on entities (nodes) and those focused to relations (links). This section only addresses methods for node classification that significantly influenced our approach to knowledge graph decomposition. Given that our approach leverages combinatorial optimization, a brief outline of relevant optimization methods is provided as well.

2.1   Background: Network Decomposition

In this section, we first explain the concept of network decomposition and then introduce the HINMINE approach, a recently developed algorithm for network decomposition.

On Network Decomposition. One of the main problems with node embedding approaches is that they do not take into account different types of relations. Further, in most cases only a single node type is supported. To address this task, a graph first needs to be transformed into a suitable input for downstream learning methods, which are typically capable of handling nodes of a single type, such as logistic regression, SVM, random forests etc. In this work we refer to the addressed transformation task as *network decomposition*.

Network decomposition is formally defined as follows. Given a knowledge graph $G = (N, E, R, C)$, the main objective is to construct a mapping $G \to G_H$; where G_H corresponds to a homogeneous network $G_H = (N_H, E_H, W_H)$, where N_H are nodes of a single type (also referred to as the *target* type) and W_H represents a set of weights induced from the relations present in the knowledge graph. Network decomposition is illustrated in Fig. 1.

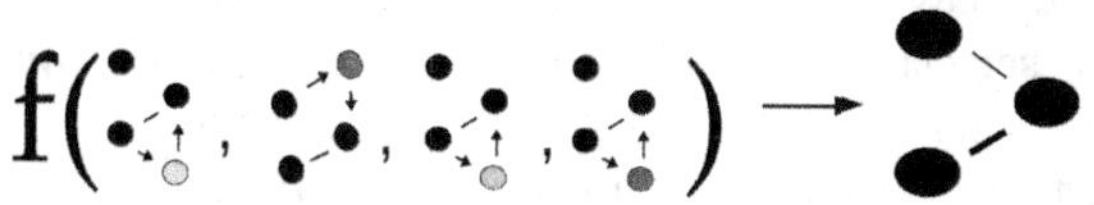

Fig. 1. Schematic representation of network decomposition. Intermediary nodes (yellow, green and purple) are used to weight the edges in the final network, consisting exclusively of target nodes (black). (Color figure online)

The particular class of network decompositions we are interested in is based on node triplet counts. Here, a set of nodes $\{u, m, v\}$ is used to construct a weighted edge between u and v. The node m corresponds to an intermediary node, to which both u and v are connected. A triplet thus corresponds to a directed path of length two ($u \to m \to v$). In this work we build on HINMINE methodology [6], a recently proposed approach for knowledge graph decomposition, which introduces eight different heuristics for triplet enumeration and their transformation to weighted edges in the final homogeneous network.

The HINMINE Approach. The HINMINE approach [6] is a recent development that uses text mining inspired heuristics in network decomposition. A similar approach was taken in DeepWalk [9] showing that text mining inspired approaches can be successfully applied to network analysis. The in-house developed HINMINE methodology proposes eight text mining heuristics, which consider different triplets as different words. The simplest heuristic corresponds to simple term counts, which translates directly to $\{u, v, m\}$ triplet enumeration. Each edge is thus weighted based on the number of manually chosen triplets, the two target nodes under consideration are part of.

More formally, given a heuristic function f, a weight of an edge between the two nodes u and v is computed as

$$w(u, v) = \sum_{\substack{m \in M \\ (u,m) \in E \\ (m,v) \in E}} f(m); \tag{1}$$

where the $f(m)$ represents the weight function and m an intermediary node. Here, M represents the set of intermediary nodes and E the set of a knowledge graph's edges. All weight functions used in this study are summarized in Table 1. The node set B denotes all nodes of the base type. We use the following notations: $f(t, d)$ denotes the number of times a term t appears in the document d and D denotes the corpus (a set of documents). We assume that the documents in the set are labeled, each document belonging to a class c from a set of all classes C. We use the notation $t \in d$ to describe that a term t appears in document d. Where used, the term $P(t)$ is the probability that a randomly selected document contains the term t, and $P(c)$ is the probability that a randomly selected document belongs to class c. We use $|d|$ to denote the length (in words) of a document, and avgdl denotes the average document length in the corpus. Heuristics considered in this work are summarized in Table 1.

One of the main caveats of the current HINMINE implementation is non-automatic triplet selection—the choice of representative triplets is left to a domain expert. Further, the original HINMINE methodology does not address the issue of heuristic selection, even though it was empirically proven that heuristic selection is clearly data-dependent, i.e. different heuristics are optimal for different knowledge graphs [6]. The original contributions of this work are aimed at addressing these issues.

2.2 Related Work on Node Classification

The task of node classification has been previously addressed in the field of complex network analysis. The first group are knowledge graph aggregation approaches, where relational graphs are used as main inputs. For example, the *Trans* family of algorithms [10,11] projects subject-predicate-object triplets to hyperplanes, where entity resolution and similar tasks can be conducted. With the recent success of deep learning-based methods, neural network architectures for triplet embedding construction have also gained considerable attention [12].

Table 1. Term weighing schemes, taken from [6], tested for decomposition of knowledge graphs and their corresponding formulas in text mining.

Scheme	Formula
tf	$f(t,d)$
if-idf	$f(t,d) \cdot \log \left(\dfrac{|D|}{|\{d' \in D : t \in d'\}|} \right)$
chi^2	$f(t,d) \cdot \sum\limits_{c \in C} \dfrac{(P(t \wedge c)P(\neg t \wedge \neg c) - P(t \wedge \neg c)P(\neg t \wedge c))^2}{P(t)P(\neg t)P(c)P(\neg c)}$
ig	$f(t,d) \cdot \sum\limits_{c \in C, c' \in \{c, \neg c\} t' \in \{t, \neg t\}} \left(P(t', c') \cdot \log \dfrac{P(t' \wedge c')}{P(t')P(c')} \right)$
gr	$f(t,d) \cdot \sum\limits_{c \in C} \dfrac{\sum_{c' \in \{c, \neg c\}} \sum_{t' \in \{t, \neg t\}} \left(P(t', c') \cdot \log \frac{P(t' \wedge c')}{P(t')P(c')} \right)}{-\sum_{c' \in \{c, \neg c\}} P(c) \cdot \log P(c)}$
delta-idf	$f(t,d) \cdot \sum\limits_{c \in C} \left(\log \dfrac{|c|}{|\{d' \in D : d' \in c \wedge t \in d'\}|} - \log \dfrac{|\neg c|}{|\{d' \in D : d' \notin c \wedge t \notin d'\}|} \right)$
rf	$f(t,d) \cdot \sum\limits_{c \in C} \log \left(2 + \dfrac{|\{d' \in D : d' \in c \wedge t \in d'\}|}{|\{d' \in D : d' \notin c \wedge t \notin d'\}|} \right)$
bm25	$f(t,d) \cdot \log \left(\dfrac{|D|}{|\{d' \in D : t \in d'\}|} \right) \cdot \dfrac{k+1}{f(t,d) + k \cdot \left(1 - b + b \cdot \frac{|d|}{\text{avgdl}} \right)}$

The second family of classification methods are based on node embeddings, including algorithms SDNE [13], LINE [14], Personalized PageRank-based methods [6,15,16] and similar. They produce a vectorized representation of a graph corresponding to individual nodes, from which θ can be constructed. Embeddings obtained by such methods are commonly used for classification of nodes in homogeneous networks—networks with only a single type of node, or need to be specifically adapted for e.g., hierarchical network structure [17]. In this work we leverage the latter, where node labels are learned from a homogeneous network, obtained from a knowledge graph via network decomposition. Here, a homogeneous network consists of a subset of knowledge graph's nodes, and its edges are derived from the knowledge graph's edges.

2.3   Related Work on Parameter Optimization

Optimization is one of the key components of majority of machine learning, data mining, as well as network analysis algorithms. Given a set of constraints $\mathfrak{C}$, a parameter space ψ and a scoring function $g(x)$, where x corresponds to a n-dimensional solution vector, the optimization objective can be formulated as a maximization (or minimization) problem of the form:

$$R_{opt} = \arg\max_{x \in \psi} \big[g(x) \big];$$

$$\text{subject to } \mathfrak{C}$$

Combinatorial optimization deals with discrete parameter spaces. In a common setting, multiple sets of possible inputs are considered. In this work we leverage the differential evolution algorithm for the proposed optimization task.

Differential Evolution. Differential evolution (DE) [18–20] is an iterative approach, where possible optimal solutions are represented as parts of a larger set of solutions evolving over several generations. Given a nonempty set $X \subseteq \mathbb{R}^n$ and an objective function $f : X \to \mathbb{R}$, the objective of DE is to find such $x^* \in X$, such that $f(x^*) \neq -\infty$ and $f(x^*) \leq f(x)$ holds for all $x \in X$. Parameter vectors are formulated as $x_{i,\mathcal{G}} = \{x_{1,i,\mathcal{G}}, x_{2,i,\mathcal{G}}, \ldots, x_{n,i,\mathcal{G}}\}; i = 1, 2, \ldots, A$. The number of parameter vectors A is called the population size, while $\mathcal{G}$ denotes the current generation of vectors. The set of solutions is evolved via different evolution operators;

1. **Mutation**, defined as a combination of three randomly chosen vectors x_a, x_b, x_c, combined into a new vector $x_{\mathcal{G}+1}$, where $F \in [0, 2]$ is a constant. Formally the mutation is defined as:

$$v_{\mathcal{G}+1} = x_{a,\mathcal{G}} + F(x_{b;\mathcal{G}} + x_{c;\mathcal{G}})$$

2. **Recombination**, where successful solutions from the previous generation are incorporated into current generation. Elements from the solution vector v are incorporated into vector x to form the final vector u, defined as:

$$u_{j,i,\mathcal{G}+1} = \begin{cases} v_{j,i,\mathcal{G}+1}, & \text{for } \text{rand}_{j,i} \leq CR \vee j = I_{rand} \\ x_{j,i,\mathcal{G}} & \text{for } \text{rand}_{j,i} > CR \wedge j \neq I_{rand}; \end{cases}$$

   where $i = 1, 2, \ldots, A$ and $j = 1, 2, \ldots, n$. For all i, j, $\text{rand}_{j,i}$ is a sample of a random variable distributed as $U[0, 1]$, and I_{rand} is a random element of $\{1, 2, \ldots, Q\}$ which ensures that $u_{i,\mathcal{G}+1} \neq x_{i,\mathcal{G}}$. The CR denotes crossover-rate, the probability of a recombination event.

3. **Selection**, where best individuals from current population are used for a new population, meaning that

$$x_{i,\mathcal{G}+1} = \begin{cases} u_{i,\mathcal{G}+1}, & \text{if } f(u_{i,\mathcal{G}+1}) \leq f(x_i, \mathcal{G}) \\ x_{i,\mathcal{G}} & \text{if } f(u_{i,\mathcal{G}+1}) > f(x_i, \mathcal{G}) \end{cases}.$$

Each possible solution in the population must have predetermined lower and upper bounds of possible values. Initial solutions x_0 are initialized randomly, i.e. $\forall s \in x_0; s \sim U[0, 1]$. Differential evolution can be used for optimization of both discrete, as well as continuous objective functions [21]. One of the key parts of each stochastic optimization procedures is solution representation. We discuss solution representation along with the proposed approach in the next section.

3   The Proposed Approach

The proposed approach consists of the following two steps. First, the learning problem and solution are presented. This step is followed by differential evolution of different decomposition heuristics.

We begin by describing some of the improvements to the original HINMINE methodology, which form the basis for the proposed knowledge graph decomposition. As stated in Eq. 1, edges between target nodes are artificially constructed based on different triplet count heuristics, summarized in Table 1. In this work we first address two issues, that arise when real networks are considered: ground-truth edge information and parallelism needed for analysis of larger networks. In this section we first describe the proposed improvements. We then present the problem of finding the optimal network decomposition as an optimization problem. The section concludes with the description of the graph decomposition algorithm.

Current version of the HINMINE methodology enumerates individual triplets iteratively, i.e. one at a time. This process is spatially non-demanding, as triplets are dynamically generated. Building on this idea, we propose the following modification. First, a set of triplets is generated upfront and temporarily stored. Next, decompositions, corresponding to the triplets are computed in parallel. Once computed, the set of decompositions is returned. This modification is controlled by a single parameter—the batch size. The memory consumption increases linearly with respect to the number of triplets used in a single batch.

Ground-Truth Edge Information. Let u and v represent two target nodes, between which an artificial edge is to be constructed. Currently, any prior information on edge information between the two nodes is not taken into account. This means that the current version of the HINMINE methodology works best for target nodes with no ground truth edges. In this work we extend the methodology to include also the set of ground truth edge weights w_g.

$$w(u,v) = \alpha\Big(w_g(u,v)\Big) + \beta\Bigg(\sum_{\substack{m \in M \\ (u,m) \in E \\ (m,v) \in E}} f(u,v,m)\Bigg); \tag{2}$$

where m represents an intermediary node between u and v. The w_g represents ground-truth network weights and f a network decomposition heuristic. We further introduce two parameters, α, β, which are used to weight the contributions of the two different edge types. When α is set to 0, only artificial edges are used—this is the current implementation of the HINMINE methodology. As the focus of this work is learning from aggregated graphs, the final decomposition D_f is normalized to a right-stochastic matrix, where the weight between two nodes is redefined as: $w_{norm}(u,v) = \frac{1}{\sum_{v=1}^{K} w(u,v)} w(u,v)$; where K represents the number of columns in the graph-adjacency matrix. The final graph $G = (N_{norm}, w_{norm})$ can be used for different down-stream learning tasks, such as node and edge classification, as well as clustering. This proposition is one of the first network decomposition schemes, where prior information on edge weights can be taken into account.

Network Decomposition as an Optimization Problem. The main objective of this study can be formulated as follows. Given a permissive set of decomposition heuristics $P(\mathfrak{D})$, a set of operators for combining different heuristics $\mathfrak{G}$ and a set of permissible triplet sets which are used for decomposition $P(\mathfrak{T})$, the objective is to calculate best possible network decomposition $X \in \mathbb{R}^{n \times n}$, computed with decomposition function $\tau : P(\mathfrak{D}) \times \mathfrak{G} \times P(\mathfrak{T}) \to \mathbb{R}^{n \times n}$. The n represents the number of target nodes. Individual decomposition X is evaluated via a scoring function $\rho : \mathbb{R}^{n \times n} \to \mathbb{R}$. The optimization objective function can thus be stated as:

$$X_{opt} = \underset{(d,o,t) \in P(\mathfrak{D}) \times \mathfrak{G} \times P(\mathfrak{T})}{\arg \min} \left[\rho(\tau(d,o,t)) \right].$$

The proposed formulation does not take into account any specific decomposition scoring function ρ as the definition of this function is context-dependent. We continue with descriptions of the parameter space, defined as $P(\mathfrak{D}) \times \mathfrak{G} \times P(\mathfrak{T})$.

The set of all possible triplet sets $\mathfrak{T}$. To construct decompositions of a knowledge graph, we use one or more possible triplets from the set $\mathfrak{T}$ of all possible triplets. We consider all forward relations between a node triplet (u, m, v), e.g., $u \xrightarrow{\text{Directed}} m \xrightarrow{\text{LikedBy}} v$; where u for example corresponds to a person, m to a movie and v to another person. Further, we also consider reverse relations, such as for example $u \xrightarrow{\text{associatedTo}} m \xrightarrow{\text{associatedTo}} v$; which emerge as relevant for biological problems, where for example different functional domains or similar are common to two proteins. The proposed approach supports decomposition based on multiple triplet sets simultaneously. Here, enumerations obtained from individual triplets are summed into a single scalar, used as input for heuristic evaluation. The proposed approach explores the triplet parameter space, defined as $P(\mathfrak{T})$, meaning that the upper bound for the number of triplets considered (exhaustive search) is $2^{|\mathfrak{T}|}$.

Set of decomposition heuristics $\mathfrak{D}$. The proposed approach can leverage all heuristics defined in Table 1. In the approach, we explore the space of all possible heuristics as well as their combination, meaning that the heuristic parameter space is $P(\mathfrak{D})$.

Set of heuristic combination operators. Let $\{h_1, h_2, \ldots, h_k\}$ be a set of matrices, obtained using different decomposition heuristics. We propose four different heuristic combination operators.

1. **Element-wise sum.** Let $\oplus$ denote elementwise matrix summation. Combined aggregated matrix is thus defined as $M = h_1 \oplus \cdots \oplus h_k$, a well defined expression as $\oplus$ represents a commutative and associative operation.
2. **Element-wise product.** Let $\otimes$ denote elementwise product. Combined aggregated matrix is thus defined as $M = h_1 \otimes \cdots \otimes h_k$.

3. **Normalized element-wise sum.** Let $\oplus$ denote elementwise summation, and $\max(A)$ denote the largest element of the matrix A. Combined aggregated matrix is thus defined as $M = \frac{1}{\max(h_1 \oplus \cdots \oplus h_k)}(h_1 \oplus \cdots \oplus h_k)$. As $\oplus$ represents a commutative operation, this operator can be generalized to arbitrary sets of heuristics without loss of generality.

4. **Normalized element-wise product.** Let $\otimes$ denote elementwise product, and $\max(A)$ denote the largest element of the matrix A. Combined aggregated matrix is thus defined as $M = \frac{1}{\max(h_1 \otimes \cdots \otimes h_k)}(h_1 \otimes \cdots \otimes h_k)$. This operator can also be generalized to arbitrary sets of heuristics.

In this work we consider whole decomposition space, i.e. $P(\mathfrak{D}) \times \mathfrak{S} \times P(\mathfrak{T})$.

Solution Representation and Graph Decomposition Algorithm. Having defined the parameter search space, we discuss in this section the representation of individual solutions, evaluated with DE. Let $v \in \mathbb{R}^c; c = |\mathfrak{D}| + |\mathfrak{T}| + |\mathfrak{S}| + 2$ be a random vector with components $v_i \sim U([0,1])$ represent a one-dimensional input vector corresponding to the set of heuristics, operators and triplets used to obtain a decomposition. Each heuristic, operator as well as triplet correspond to an element in $\mathbb{R}^c$. A *solution* vector s is defined via an indicator function $\mathbb{I}$, where each element is defined as $\mathbb{I}(v_i \geq 0.5)$. The first $|P(\mathfrak{D})|$ components of the resulting vector determine the decomposition heuristics, used for the decomposition, the second $|P(\mathfrak{T})|$ determine the triplets and the third $|\mathfrak{S}|$ components determines the heuristic combination operator used. The final 2 components of the vector correspond to parameters α and β from Eq. 2.

As each field in the vector corresponds to either a triplet or a heuristic, once the indicator function is applied, a solution can be uniquely defined. The first non-zero value in the operator vector denotes the operator used for combining possible solutions. Hence, we consider only a single type of operator for each individual solution. The proposed approach can be compactly summarized as follows.

1. First, a set of decomposition triplets and heuristics is selected.
2. Next, a set of solution combination operators, described in the previous section is selected.
3. Iterative evolution consists of the following three steps. Mutation, followed by recombination and selection. Selected solutions represent potential optima, and are used in the next generation (iteration). Evolution is run for a predefined number of generations.

As this work is focused on the general approach for finding the near-optimal network decomposition, we discuss an example using a task-specific evaluation function in the next section.

4 Experimental Setting

We test the proposed approach on the following datasets.

The IMDB Dataset. The main classification task related to this dataset corresponds to classification of individual movie's genres, based on actors, directors and movies [6]. Here, 300 nodes are labeled, whereas the whole network consists of 6,387 nodes and 14,714 edges. An example triplet yielding a valid decomposition for this dataset is: $Actor \xrightarrow{\text{actsIn}} Movie \xrightarrow{\text{directedBy}} Director$. This network does not contain any ground-truth edge information, and thus the α parameter is not relevant for this problem. The DE was parameterized with 15 generations of size 10. The CR rate was set to 0.4, mutation rate to 0.05 and the selection strategy *best1bin*, the default option in [22]. The same parameterization is used for the epigenetics dataset.

The Epigenetics Dataset. An example from the biological domain used is the recently introduced epigenetics knowledge graph [23], where proteins, genes and other biological entities are connected with different relations. Further, different protein-protein interactions are annotated with ground-truth edge weights corresponding to reliability of interactions. We annotate each protein in the network with the corresponding GO terms, associated with their functions, which is achieved as follows. Functional annotations are obtained from the Intact database [24]. We sort annotations by frequency and select 100 of the most common terms, which correspond to 100 classes being predicted. The α parameter was selected directly from the interval between 0 and 1. The classification goal for this dataset is thus protein function prediction. The network consists of 2,204 nodes and 2,772 edges, 456 nodes are target nodes for which the classification is $Protein \xrightarrow{\text{contains}} Domain \xrightarrow{\text{contains}} Protein$.

Performance Evaluation. We evaluate the performance as follows. If possible, we compute scores for all possible combinations of triplets, heuristics and operators. Once computed, a global parameter landscape is obtained, which can be used to directly assess the algorithm's performance. Further, we use randomized grid search as the baseline approach.[1] In this work we evaluate an aggregated network's quality by computing a classification performance metric in a process of 10-fold cross validation. The node label classification approach is the same as used in the original HINMINE methodology. The aggregated network is used to construct a set of personalized page-rank vectors (PPR), which represent the feature matrix F. Label matrix T corresponds to individual labels, assigned to distinct nodes and consists of $N \cdot |C|$ cells, where N is the number of all nodes and C the set of all classes.[2] The tuple (F, T) is used as input for one-vs-many

---

[1] The machine used for evaluation was an of-the-shelf Lenovo $y510p$ laptop with an i7 Intel processor (8 cores) and 4 GB of RAM.

[2] The feature matrix is not memory efficient, as it uses $\mathcal{O}(N^2)$ space, yet optimization of this part of the procedure is out of the scope of this study.

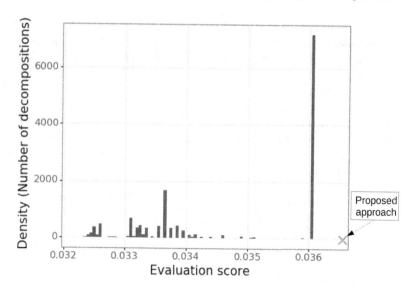

Fig. 2. Score distribution over all parameter space for the IMDB network decomposition problem. The red line denotes the optimal solution found by the proposed approach. (Color figure online)

logistic regression classifier. In this work we use the macro F_1 measure for evaluation of individual solutions. The macro F_1 score averages individual, pairwise F_1 scores, defined as : precision $= \frac{tp}{tp+fp}$;, recall $= \frac{tp}{tp+fn}$, $F_1 = 2 \cdot \frac{\text{precision} \cdot \text{recall}}{\text{precision} + \text{recall}}$; over all classes, where fp denotes false positives, tp true positives and fn false negatives. The C represents the set of target classes. The total score thus equals

$$\text{macro}F_1 = \frac{1}{|C|} \sum_{i \in C} F_{1(i)}.$$

We leave extensive computational evaluation of different DE parameterizations for further work.

5   Results and Discussion

For the IMDB network we compute all possible decompositions and visualize the solution obtained by the proposed as the red line in Fig. 2.

We observe, that the proposed approach found the global maximum—here corresponding to the rightmost combination of decompositions. The final decomposition was obtained by combining the following heuristics: ig and gr. The following triplets were used: $Movie \xrightarrow{\text{features}} Person \xrightarrow{\text{actsIn}} Movie$, $Movie \xrightarrow{\text{directedBy}} Person \xrightarrow{\text{directed}} Movie$, $Movie \xrightarrow{\text{features}} Person \xrightarrow{\text{directed}} Movie$. The combination operator used was element-wise product.

As computing all decompositions for the epigenetics problem is not computationally feasible, we compare the result obtained with the average decomposition performance obtained by sampling the decomposition distribution. The mean performance for this approach estimates to 0.0284, whereas the mean performance using 10000 different decomposition samples estimates to 0.0253. The samples were selected by randomly permuting the solution vectors with values between 0 and 1. Further, in this case the obtained decomposition is not optimal, as the best sampled decomposition scored with 0.0293. The decomposition returned by the proposed approach consisted of the following heuristics: `ig`, `gr` and `bm25`. The triplets:

$$Protein \xrightarrow{\text{contains}} Domain \xrightarrow{\text{contains}} Protein$$

$$Protein \xrightarrow{\text{interactsWith}} Protein \xrightarrow{\text{subsumes}} Protein$$

$$Protein \xrightarrow{\text{belongsTo}} Family \xrightarrow{\text{belongsTo}} Protein$$

$$Protein \xrightarrow{\text{isRelatedTo}} Phenotype \xrightarrow{\text{isRelatedTo}} Protein$$

$$Protein \xrightarrow{\text{interactsWith}} Protein \xrightarrow{\text{interactsWith}} Protein$$

were found as the combination used to obtain the best decomposition. The combination operator used for decomposition aggregation was elementwise product. The results from both experiments averaged over five runs with different stochastic seeds are summarized in Table 2.

Table 2. Empirical result summary. The F1 corresponds to macro-F1 score. The bold numbers denote the global optimum, identified for the IMDB dataset. Min and Max F1 scores denote minimum and maximum network decomposition performance.

Dataset	Min F1	Max F1	Mean F1	Proposed approach	DE	Exhaustive search
IMDB	0.0315	**0.0372**	0.0346	**0.0372**	50 min	≈ 22 h
Epigenetics	0.0211	0.0296	0.0243	0.0284	6 h	> 1 day

The two experiments indicate that the proposed approach can provide the currently not known solution to proper knowledge graph decomposition and aggregation for node label classification. The approach in both cases outperforms the mean baseline, where for the IMDB dataset it performs the same as the best possible decomposition, where for the epigenetics dataset it performs worse compared to the best decompositions out of 10000 random samples. To understand the limitations of the proposed approach, different stochastic optimization procedures could be tested, yet such extensive experimental evaluation is left for further work.

The decomposition triplets, found as crucial for the epigenetics dataset are biologically relevant, supported by the following observations. Protein domains have been previously associated and recognized as key features for function prediction [25]. Latent interaction partners are often used for constructing protein-protein interaction prediction tools, i.e. two proteins often interact if they both interact with a third partner [26]. Phenotypes are highly correlated with protein function [27]. Protein families are also relevant for function prediction, as they can correspond directly to protein binding sites and similar functional domains [28–30].

The proposed method performs significantly faster compared to exhaustive search. For the IMDB dataset, the global optimum was found more than twenty times faster. A similar pattern was observed for the Epigenetics dataset, yet the number of possible combinations was too exhaustive and was evaluated via sampling.

6   Conclusions

In this work we present a novel end-to-end stochastic-optimization-based approach for network decomposition and subsequent aggregation. This work builds on current state-of-the-art HINMINE methodology, which does not provide a fully automated procedure for obtaining dataset-specific decompositions. We demonstrate the use of the proposed method on two real life knowledge graphs, where in one there is also ground-truth edge classification information available. The proposed method performs better than average decomposition, which indicates that the proposed stochastic optimization in the form of differential evolution could provide a feasible approach for automated knowledge graph-based learning.

As the proposed approach automatically identifies the relations that are relevant for node classification, we can interpret the final result in terms of novel, meaningful relations, previously not considered as important for the given knowledge graph for the given classification task. The biological interpretations indicate one of the possible uses of final decomposition triplets. Apart from obtaining a better predictive model, the final result is interpretable and can be linked to existing knowledge. Further, the final set of triplets uncovers the novel candidate relations. As the set of relations differs from task-to-task, the triplets could potentially offer qualitative explanation for key relations relevant to black-box models, such as deep neural networks.

Further work includes extensive experimental evaluation on more types of knowledge graphs, as well as the investigation of different optimization routines, for example Bayesian optimization, which has proven invaluable for automated machine learning. Further, we will investigate how the spatially intensive homogeneous networks could be reduced during the learning process.

References

1. Burt, R., Minor, M.: Applied Network Analysis: A Methodological Introduction. Sage Publications, Beverly Hills (1983)
2. Sun, Y., Han, J.: Mining Heterogeneous Information Networks: Principles and Methodologies. Morgan & Claypool Publishers, San Rafael (2012)
3. Consortium: Gene Ontology: Tool for the unification of biology. The gene ontology consortium. Nat. Genet. **25**(1), 25–29 (2000)
4. Ehrlinger, L., Wöß, W.: Towards a definition of knowledge graphs. In: SEMANTiCS (Posters, Demos, SuCCESS) (2016)
5. Nickel, M., Murphy, K., Tresp, V., Gabrilovich, E.: A review of relational machine learning for knowledge graphs. Proc. IEEE **104**(1), 11–33 (2016)
6. Kralj, J., Robnik-Šikonja, M., Lavrač, N.: HINMINE: heterogeneous information network mining with information retrieval heuristics. J. Intell. Inf. Syst., 1–33 (2017)
7. Sen, P., Namata, G., Bilgic, M., Getoor, L., Galligher, B., Eliassi-Rad, T.: Collective classification in network data. AI Mag. **29**(3), 93 (2008)
8. de Sousa, C.A.R., Rezende, S.O., Batista, G.E.A.P.A.: Influence of graph construction on semi-supervised learning. In: Blockeel, H., Kersting, K., Nijssen, S., Železný, F. (eds.) ECML PKDD 2013. LNCS (LNAI), vol. 8190, pp. 160–175. Springer, Heidelberg (2013). https://doi.org/10.1007/978-3-642-40994-3_11
9. Perozzi, B., Al-Rfou, R., Skiena, S.: Deepwalk: Online learning of social representations. In: Proceedings of the 20th ACM SIGKDD International Conference on Knowledge Discovery and Data Mining, pp. 701–710. ACM (2014)
10. Wang, Q., Mao, Z., Wang, B., Guo, L.: Knowledge graph embedding: a survey of approaches and applications. IEEE Trans. Knowl. Data Eng. **29**(12), 2724–2743 (2017)
11. Wang, Z., Zhang, J., Feng, J., Chen, Z.: Knowledge graph embedding by translating on hyperplanes. In: Proceedings of AAAI, vol. 14, pp. 1112–1119 (2014)
12. Cai, H., Zheng, V.W., Chang, K.: A comprehensive survey of graph embedding: problems, techniques and applications. IEEE Trans. Knowl. Data Eng. (2018)
13. Wang, D., Cui, P., Zhu, W.: Structural deep network embedding. In: Proceedings of the 22nd ACM SIGKDD International Conference on Knowledge Discovery and Data Mining, pp. 1225–1234. ACM (2016)
14. Tang, J., Qu, M., Wang, M., Zhang, M., Yan, J., Mei, Q.: Line: Large-scale information network embedding. In: Proceedings of the 24th International Conference on World Wide Web, International World Wide Web Conferences Steering Committee, pp. 1067–1077 (2015)
15. Grčar, M., Trdin, N., Lavrač, N.: A methodology for mining document-enriched heterogeneous information networks. Comput. J. **56**(3), 321–335 (2013)
16. Kralj, J., Valmarska, A., Robnik-Šikonja, M., Lavrač, N.: Mining text enriched heterogeneous citation networks. In: Cao, T., et al. (eds.) PAKDD 2015. LNCS (LNAI), vol. 9077, pp. 672–683. Springer, Cham (2015). https://doi.org/10.1007/978-3-319-18038-0_52
17. Žitnik, M., Leskovec, J.: Predicting multicellular function through multi-layer tissue networks. Bioinformatics **33**(14), i190–i198 (2017)
18. Fleetwood, K.: An introduction to differential evolution. In: Proceedings of Mathematics and Statistics of Complex Systems (MASCOS) One Day Symposium, 26th November, Brisbane, Australia, pp. 785–791 (2004)

19. Price, K., Storn, R.M., Lampinen, J.A.: Differential Evolution: A Practical Approach to Global Optimization. Springer, Heidelberg (2006). https://doi.org/10.1007/3-540-31306-0
20. Das, S., Mullick, S.S., Suganthan, P.N.: Recent advances in differential evolution-an updated survey. Swarm Evol. Comput. **27**, 1–30 (2016)
21. Das, S., Suganthan, P.N.: Differential evolution: a survey of the state-of-the-art. IEEE Trans. Evol. Comput. **15**(1), 4–31 (2011)
22. Jones, E., Oliphant, T., Peterson, P.: SciPy: Open Source Scientific Tools for Python (2014)
23. Škrlj, B., Kralj, J., Vavpetič, A., Lavrač, N.: Community-based semantic subgroup discovery. In: Appice, A., Loglisci, C., Manco, G., Masciari, E., Ras, Z.W. (eds.) NFMCP 2017. LNCS (LNAI), vol. 10785, pp. 182–196. Springer, Cham (2018). https://doi.org/10.1007/978-3-319-78680-3_13
24. Orchard, S., et al.: The MIntAct project-IntAct as a common curation platform for 11 molecular interaction databases. Nucleic Acids Res. **42**(Database issue), pp. D358–D363 (2014)
25. Marchler-Bauer, A., et al.: CDD: NCBI's conserved domain database. Nucleic Acids Res. **43**(D1), D222–D226 (2014)
26. Szklarczyk, D., et al.: String v10: Protein-protein interaction networks, integrated over the tree of life. Nucleic Acids Res. **43**(D1), D447–D452 (2014)
27. Kelley, L.A., Mezulis, S., Yates, C.M., Wass, M.N., Sternberg, M.J.: The Phyre2 web portal for protein modeling, prediction and analysis. Nat. Protoc. **10**(6), 845 (2015)
28. Finn, R.D., et al.: Interpro in 2017beyond protein family and domain annotations. Nucleic Acids Res. **45**(D1), D190–D199 (2016)
29. Lee, J., Konc, J., Janežič, D., Brooks, B.R.: Global organization of a binding site network gives insight into evolution and structure-function relationships of proteins. Sci. Rep. **7**(1), 11652 (2017)
30. Škrlj, B., Kunej, T., Konc, J.: Insights from ion binding site network analysis into evolution and functions of proteins. Mol. Inform. (2018)

Correction to: How Much Can Experimental Cost Be Reduced in Active Learning of Agent Strategies?

Céline Hocquette and Stephen Muggleton

Correction to:
Chapter "How Much Can Experimental Cost Be Reduced in Active Learning of Agent Strategies?" in: F. Riguzzi et al. (Eds.): *Inductive Logic Programming*, LNAI 11105, https://doi.org/10.1007/978-3-319-99960-9_3

Due to an internal error during the production process, the wrong affiliation of an author was entered in the originally published article. This was corrected.

The updated online version of this chapter can be found at
https://doi.org/10.1007/978-3-319-99960-9_3

F. Riguzzi et al. (Eds.): ILP 2018, LNAI 11105, p. E1, 2018.
https://doi.org/10.1007/978-3-319-99960-9_11

Author Index

Cropper, Andrew 1

Dash, Tirtharaj 22

Folschette, Maxime 118

Hocquette, Céline 38
Horrocks, Ian 54

Inoue, Katsumi 118

Kalayc, Elem Güzel 54
Kharlamov, Evgeny 54
King, Ross D. 22
Kralj, Jan 157

Lavrač, Nada 157
Legras, Swann 72

Magnin, Morgan 118
Mehdi, Gulnar 54
Muggleton, Stephen 38

Nickles, Matthias 88
Nutt, Werner 54

Orhobor, Oghenejokpeme I. 22

Rabold, Johannes 105
Ribeiro, Tony 118
Ringsquandl, Martin 54
Roshchin, Mikhail 54
Rouveirol, Céline 72
Roux, Olivier 118
Runkler, Thomas 54

Savković, Ognjen 54
Schmid, Ute 105, 141
Siebers, Michael 105, 141
Škrlj, Blaž 157
Srinivasan, Ashwin 22

Tourret, Sophie 1

Ventos, Véronique 72
Vig, Lovekesh 22

Xiao, Guohui 54

Printed in the United States
By Bookmasters